"*We Are the Baby-Sitters Club* is a complicated paean to Ann M. Martin's serial magnum opus, grappling with its loose ends and blind spots through the passionate insight of grown-up fans; it's a varied volume of deeply personal literary criticism that takes tween girls' lives and culture seriously—finally!"

—Johanna Fateman, founding member of Le Tigre

"From brains and bodies to dating and dieting, and from race and representation to the cool, cute, and near queer, this pathbreaking book sheds light on readers' active reception and critical reflections of the pop culture phenoms of their generation. An outstanding work that expertly and insightfully places girls and girlhoods at the center of analysis!"

—Miriam Forman-Brunell, author of *Babysitter: An American History*

"One of my happiest moments of 2020 was binge-watching Netflix's *The Baby-sitters Club* with my seven-year-old niece—it was the first time we ever watched something we were equally invested in. I'm excited to keep the BSC vibes going with this fun anthology, featuring work from Myriam Gurba, Kristen Arnett, and others."

—*LitHub*

"*We Are the Baby-Sitters Club* made me cry, laugh, and appreciate now more than ever the heart and soul of the BSC. Every contribution feels personal and unafraid to challenge—with love—this well-read series. Ann M. Martin teaches kids a unique lesson in emotional literacy that we now get to enjoy—fully grown—in the works within *We Are the Baby-Sitters Club*. If the Baby-Sitters Club was in your life in any way, this anthology is a must-read!"

—Katy Farina, bestselling artist of the Baby-Sitters Little Sister series

"An explorative collection of essays that sends you right back to those nostalgic moments of childhood."

—Shannon Wright, cocreator of indie bestseller *Twins*

WE ARE THE BABY-SITTERS CLUB

ESSAYS AND ARTWORK FROM GROWN-UP READERS

EDITED BY

MARISA CRAWFORD AND MEGAN MILKS

CHICAGO
REVIEW
PRESS

Published by Chicago Review Press Incorporated
814 North Franklin Street
Chicago, Illinois 60610
ISBN 978-1-64160-490-1

"Could the Baby-Sitters Club Have Been More Gay?" by Frankie Thomas previously appeared in the *Paris Review*.

"I Want to Be a Claudia but I Know I'm a Stacey" by Marisa Crawford previously appeared in *Weird Sister*.

Library of Congress Cataloging-in-Publication Data
Names: Crawford, Marisa, editor. | Milks, Megan editor.
Title: We are the Baby-Sitters Club : essays and artwork from grown-up
   readers / edited by Marisa Crawford and Megan Milks.
Description: Chicago, Illinois : Chicago Review Press, [2021] | Summary:
   "Ann M. Martin's Baby-Sitters Club series featured a complex cast of
   characters and touched on an impressive range of issues that were
   underrepresented at the time: divorce, adoption, childhood illness,
   class division, and racism. In We Are the Baby-Sitters Club, writers and
   a few visual artists from the original BSC generation will reflect on
   the enduring legacy of Ann M. Martin's beloved series, thirty-five years
   later-celebrating the BSC's profound cultural influence"— Provided by
   publisher.
Identifiers: LCCN 2021007884 (print) | LCCN 2021007885 (ebook) | ISBN
   9781641604901 (trade paperback) | ISBN 9781641604918 (pdf) | ISBN
   9781641604925 (mobi) | ISBN 9781641604932 (epub)
Subjects: LCSH: Martin, Ann M., 1955—Appreciation. | Martin, Ann M.,
   1955- Baby-sitters Club.
Classification: LCC PS3563.A72322 W44 2021 (print) | LCC PS3563.A72322
   (ebook) | DDC 813/.54—dc23
LC record available at https://lccn.loc.gov/2021007884
LC ebook record available at https://lccn.loc.gov/2021007885

Cover design: Rebecca Lown
Interior design: Jonathan Hahn

Printed in the United States of America

5 4 3 2 1

✩ CONTENTS ✿

BE BOSSY: ENTREPRENEURSHIP AND THE BUSINESS OF BABYSITTING

GREAT IDEAS: THE WORLD BEYOND STONEYBROOK

FOREWORD

Mara Wilson

*W*hen I was six, I tried to start a babysitters club.

It didn't last too long. I think I came up with the idea to start one on a Thursday, and I'd moved on by Monday even though my family was encouraging and all promised they would join. (One of my brothers responded in a very Sam Thomas–like way: "You guys don't actually SIT on babies, do you?") It was absolutely inspired by the books, although I was still a little too young to have actually read them, and definitely too young to be a babysitter. But I was well-versed in the Little Sister series. I'd seen the TV show, and I knew one thing: the Baby-Sitters Club was incredibly cool. *Dibbly* cool.

When I started reading the books at age nine—I got my first few copies, appropriately, as hand-me-downs from a cool older girl—I was not disappointed. Kristy, Mary Anne, Stacey, Claudia, Dawn, Jessi, and Mallory were the ultimate cool older girls. They had unbelievable style, a nice amount of responsibility, spending money, sometimes even boyfriends. Best of all, they didn't let that go to their heads. They were loyal friends who always made up after fights and were still nice to younger kids. They were everything I wanted to be.

I did what probably every other kid who ever read the series did and tried to figure out who I was most like. I figured I was a Kristy/Mary Anne hybrid: a loud, occasionally bossy tomboy who had big ideas but sometimes struggled with "decorum," but also the sensitive, cat-loving daughter of a loving but overprotective widower father. (There was more than a bit of Mallory in me, too: I had a lot of siblings, dreamed of being a writer, and also eventually left home to go to an arts boarding school.) My favorite characters, though, were Claudia, Stacey, and Jessi, who were nothing like me. Their lives were more interesting, and they were good at all the things I secretly wished I could be good at—fashion, art, math, dance.

I don't know if I ever talked about the books with my friends. My preteen years were a confusing time for me, with shifting friend groups, grief over my mother's death from breast cancer, and trying to live two lives as a normal kid and as a "child star." I think I feared my tomboy friends would think I was "too girly" for loving the Baby-Sitters Club, and my bookish friends would think the books were "too babyish." They wouldn't have understood how much the books had *helped* me. Mary Anne's struggles with her father were very familiar. Jessi felt grown up in dance classes, just as I did on film sets, but she and I quickly turned back into children as soon as we got home with our parents (and Aunt Cecelia!). I finally understood why my grandfather, a diabetic, needed to test his blood sugar and got tired so easily, thanks to Stacey. My three older brothers were A students while I struggled to turn in my homework on time, much like Claudia. Ann M. Martin's California Diaries, an extension of the original series focusing on Dawn and her friends, had one of the most realistic depictions of parental loss I've ever read. The girls from the Baby-Sitters Club understood me when I felt like no one else did.

If I didn't talk about the books with my childhood friends, I made up for it as an adult. The Baby-Sitters Club, it turns out, is something that nearly everyone in my generation knows, and many of us loved. In my early twenties, I stayed up late with my roommate Jessie (a Claudia/Stacey) and talked about Claudia and her many outfits, laughing about her insistence to Kristy that "sheep are IN" while Kristy's snowman sweater was out. Fellow California girls and I have talked at length about Dawn, and how we wished our California lives had been more like her hip surfer-girl life. (Her best friend from Palo City, the pessimistic, ironically named Sunny Winslow, was much more my speed.) I've lost count of how many times I've had the "was Kristy actually a lesbian?" conversation with fellow LGBTQers. When I watched the new Netflix adaptation, I cried at the scenes between Mary Anne and her father—and I was not surprised to find out many of my thirtysomething friends had also watched the series, and also cried. There's a feeling of community among us, those who grew up with these girls.

And it's exactly what I felt reading *We Are the Baby-Sitters Club.*

I smiled when Megan Milks described themself as a fellow "Kristy/Mary Anne dyad," and felt a pang of recognition when Kristen Arnett wrote about having crushes on girls who looked like Claudia and Stacey. I marveled at how many of us felt like Mary Annes or Mallorys, but wanted to be more like the cooler characters—especially Claudia! Sue Ding, creator of the documentary *The Claudia Kishi Club*, wrote about Claudia's lasting hold on us. For many Asian American girls coming of age in the 1980s and '90s, she explains, Claudia was the first Asian American character they could relate to, or even the first Asian American they saw in American pop culture at all. Yodassa Williams writes of Jessi as a "personal hero" of hers, a character she could relate to as a Black girl growing up in a suburb not unlike Stoneybrook.

That's not to say that the books were perfect. The constant referral to Claudia's "almond-shaped eyes" comes off as fetishizing, and while there's a lot of talk of Jessi's "cocoa-brown skin," Jamie Broadnax points out that the illustrations always depict Jessi as a light-skinned Black girl. For all their junk food binges, all of the girls in the BSC are described as thin, which Jennifer Epperson resented as a young girl who was described as "big." Haley Moss writes that while *Kristy and the Secret of Susan*, in which Kristy babysits a child with autism, does get many things right about autism, it still centers on Kristy's and Susan's family's well-being and preferences rather than Susan's. What if we had been able to learn more about what Susan wanted, and her experience of the world, Moss writes, rather than seeing her autism as a burden to her family?

I had some similar issues with the books, both as a child and as an adult. While I remember being thrilled that the newest member of the BSC, Abby, was Jewish like me, I always felt that her supposedly "punning in Yiddish" was a little stereotypical. And why did Dawn only seem to have white friends in California when half of my Californian friends were Latinx? Claudia not being able to go to school for two months after breaking her leg was horrific to me and made the books feel a bit dated: in the late '90s my middle school had ramps and a wheelchair lift, and my hometown was nowhere near as wealthy as Stoneybrook.

But I think that we can acknowledge the series' shortcomings while still appreciating them. What has lasted is the feeling of positive femininity in these books, and the love all the girls had for each other. We deeply appreciated the books' values: friendship, talking out problems, sharing, and caring for others. Gabrielle Moss, author of the wonderful book about middle-grade and YA fiction *Paperback Crush*, suggests that one of the most important things the

Baby-Sitters Club books did was make these values seem trendy and cool. *Dibbly* cool, even!

Maybe the truth is that we weren't the Baby-Sitters Club, but we all wanted to be. And, in a way, we all are part of a club now.

INTRODUCTION

WE ARE THE BABY-SITTERS CLUB

Marisa Crawford and Megan Milks

In 1986, the first-ever meeting of the Baby-Sitters Club was called to order in a messy Stoneybrook, Connecticut, bedroom strewn with Ring Dings, scrunchies, a landline phone, and hollowed-out books stuffed with licorice and Milk Duds. Kristy, Claudia, Stacey, and Mary Anne launched the club that birthed an entire generation of loyal—dare we say obsessive?—readers.

From The Baby-Sitters Club #1: *Kristy's Great Idea* to #131: *The Fire at Mary Anne's House*, Ann M. Martin's wildly popular book series lasted thirteen years: the age of its five core characters—who remained forever frozen in eighth grade—and a remarkably long life for a children's series. It spawned several spinoffs, including the BSC Mysteries and Baby-Sitters Little Sister, not to mention a TV show, a feature film, and a very riveting board game. The series featured more than three hundred titles and generated close to two hundred million printed copies—copies that millions of readers like us devoured with near-religious fervor in the 1980s and '90s. We snatched up each new title at our schools' Scholastic book fairs and libraries, savoring every new adventure, and crafted our outfits, our handwriting, and our personalities to mirror our favorite characters—or quietly formed secret crushes on them.

Thirty-five years later, we're all grown up. But we've never stopped thinking about the BSC—and we're far from alone. While we couldn't join the Baby-Sitters Club, as much as we may have wanted to at the time, we've become proud members of a different club: a whole generation of adults who grew up under the well-appointed care of these seven extremely reliable babysitters and were impacted by the series in so many ways. Whether it's talking with our friends about how they use the new graphic novels to teach their kids about blended families, or (still) aspiring to Claudia's iconic style, it's become clear to us that the BSC has remained an influential presence in many of our lives. As we've watched various homages unfolding over the past decade or so—from Kim Hutt Mayhew's blog cataloging the books' sartorial style, *What Claudia Wore*, to a whole slew of comics and podcasts, and now a Netflix BSC adaptation—we wanted to carve out a space to give this series the celebration and consideration it deserves. After all, media aimed at young girls is so often dismissed as frivolous. But, as Maria Sachiko Cecire of the Data-Sitters Club writes about the BSC books, "In giving our attention to texts that meant so much to so many readers as they charted their various ways toward adulthood, we recognize that these books, these structures, and these readers are as important to our world as financial models, canonical literature, and scientific breakthroughs."

The essays and artwork in this book take a closer look at how Ann M. Martin's series shaped our ideas about gender politics, friendship, family, fashion, and beyond. They celebrate parts of the series that were, in many ways, ahead of their time: a stereotype-defying Asian American girl who loved art and fashion (Claudia); an African American girl confronting racism within a mostly white community (Jessi); a preteen living with diabetes (Stacey); a gender-nonconforming tomboy, who, if written today, many believe would have been overtly queer (Kristy); an assortment of diverse family structures; and a pre-#Girlboss model of young women as serious, successful entrepreneurs who put their business first, even before they'd entered high school.

The pieces collected here approach the BSC series in all its complexities, including its gaps and shortcomings, particularly around race, disability, and queerness. Our contributors explore, for example, why Jessi was so often singled out for and defined by her Blackness, what it means that illnesses and disabilities, like Stacey's diabetes, were often called "secrets," and how queerness in the series and its spinoffs was always coded, never overt. And we put on our metaphorical directors' visors to ponder what it means that the business-savvy

BSC members were also nurturing caregivers, never straying too far from acceptable roles for young women even as they expanded on them.

Throughout, we reflect on the models of lasting friendship the series has given us. For many of us—at least as kids—this kind of friendship may have been more aspirational than realistic. As adults, we're still taking cues from the BSC and continuing to form new clubs and communities around it: whether it's Sue Ding's *The Claudia Kishi Club*, a film about Asian American artists inspired by Claudia; or Jack Shepherd's encyclopedic *The Baby-Sitters Club Club* podcast; or a group of academics known as The Data-Sitters Club, who delve into the language patterns in the books; or the vibrant BSC fan fiction community. Working collaboratively as editors on this collection over countless coffee shop brainstorms, email threads, and phone calls that may or may not have taken place over a landline, we are pleased to add this book to the list.

For us and so many of our contributors, we couldn't possibly write about the Baby-Sitters Club without also writing about ourselves—the kids we were when we first read the series, and the adults we've grown into. We are all the legacy of these books, which taught us to see young people's lives as serious business. We are the aspirations born out of looking for ourselves reflected in these stories, and not always finding them. We're the products of reading and dreaming about creative collaborations, joyful friendships, and where the two combine. We are the Baby-Sitters Club.

Say Hello to Your Friends

Girl Groups and Friendship Culture

Fun with Role-Play

Kristen Arnett

It took months to get your mother to allow you to read them. Those books about babysitters; a series that all your friends at school have already been reading for well over a year. Your family usually only lets you read Baptist Bookstore offerings: Janette Oke novels about widowers who find wholesome Christian love with schoolteachers, a series called the Mandie Collection that features a blonde-haired, blue-eyed girl who solves mysteries with the help of prayer and claims to be one-sixteenth Native American. These books are so boring that you want to scream.

You argue that the Baby-Sitters Club books are wholesome, too—what's more wholesome than babysitting children?—but your mother only relents after another mother at church says they're actually okay. That they're not Christian, but they don't have any KISSING in them. Nothing sexual. Your mom reads the entire first book of the series before handing it over to you. It is something you'll always remember: how you stared at her reading it, praying she would let you in on the fun.

Once you're finally allowed, you read the Baby-Sitters Club books religiously. You love them better than anything else in your life. All your friends love them, too, even your church friends. They all start out the exact same way: a description of the club itself, a listing of the different members, and then a point-by-point account of an actual meeting. It should be boring to read the same thing over and over again, but it's decidedly not. In fact, you delight in the repetition. It reminds you that at the heart of it, they're kids, but they want to be taken seriously. Ann M. Martin does take these girls seriously, but most grown-ups never do. Especially your parents.

The books are organized in numerical order. You try to read them that way, but your parents don't buy you books (only those ones from the Baptist Bookstore that they still supply you with every Christmas and birthday). You can only ever get the Baby-Sitters Club books from the library, and you delight in the few occasions when someone's just returned a bundle of books you haven't gotten to touch yet. The elusive number three. Any books about Mary Anne, who likes to read and is a dork but is still sweet and smart and cute, which appeals to you. Later in life, when you become a librarian, you'll realize this is what you were trying to create for yourself. Order out of chaos. Your parents are never on time for anything and they're always behind on bills, constantly on the phone with collections, and they have three kids even though they can barely afford anything for you, the oldest. They never tell you the truth or trust you with any important information. To be a librarian means to hold all the knowledge and turn that chaos into shareable wisdom. It doesn't hurt that one of the librarians at your branch looks just like Mary Anne.

You take the books home in a big brown Publix bag and spend hours sorting them into piles, organizing them both numerically and into the order you'd most like to read them. You don't want to save all the worst ones for last. For instance, when it comes to Mary Anne's boyfriend, you could care less. He's soft-spoken and sweet, but he takes up too much space. Time that could be spent on other stories. You're much more interested in how she fights with her stepsister, Dawn, and how they share a room together. What that would look like: to share a room with a beautiful blonde. All you've got as a roommate is your very annoying sister. She's eight years younger than you and sleeps in a crib.

After reading the books, you want to live inside them. You think about them constantly. You imagine the world they live in—the place, sure, Stoneybrook, but mostly you wonder about the things you didn't get to read between the pages. What happens after the book shuts?

Do the friends go on living their lives? What happens in their families? Are there stories there—maybe even more interesting, darker ones—places where the girls might act differently than they would through the lens of the author? You like to imagine them dealing with a mother who slaps them when they ask about sex, like your own mother did the first time you brought up the idea of kissing.

There are stories you start telling yourself. First, in your head. About all the babysitters. You get so bored in church—your family goes there at least four days a week—and the services are unbearable. Instead of listening to the same sermon you feel like you could recite in your sleep, you imagine what all the girls would be doing right at that moment. Sometimes you imagine yourself there with them, but you're never really yourself. The girl you conjure in your mind is taller, more daring. She's good at tennis, which is a sport you've never played but sounds so fancy and you love the outfits that those women wear. Everyone in these fantasies babysits, but it's about more than that. There are sleepovers. Notes you pass each other during class. Hanging out in Claudia's bedroom after school where you all raid her junk food and eat candy and chips, share sips of soda when you pass the bottle back and forth. You imagine the lips of the other girls touching that same place on the bottle where yours had been. This makes you feel important; it makes your chest fill with heat. You squirm there in your seat in the middle of the sanctuary. You think about the girls some more, anyway, even though you know Jesus is listening.

You want to write the stories down, so you do. Or, you try. It's hard when your handwriting is so bad and you don't have things like journals or even pens that work very well. Your parents don't want you to use any of your school paper for activities that don't include homework because they don't have the money to buy more paper right now. That's what your mother tells you, anyway. Regardless, it's hard to shift the narratives from your brain— those beautiful fun afternoons in Claudia's bedroom—onto the page in a way that does justice to how those stories make you feel. It's easy to get frustrated with yourself when you can't write it down the way you want it to look, to sound. You wonder if there are other ways to make these stories happen. And then you remember the Barbies.

Your favorite part of Barbies is the role-playing. The fantasy. The out-of-body lived experience. It is also a form of control. You have so little of that in your life. You're not allowed to choose how you dress, who your friends are outside of church, or even how to style your own hair. It's a relief and a pleasure to force those dolls to do whatever you want. To make them act out anything you wish. Role-play with the dolls allows you to exit your body. The dolls are an extension of your fingers, your hands, your arms. Your entire self.

And by role-play you mean that you love to call your Barbie any name other than the one she's born with. She's never Barbie. She's Delilah. She's Sidney. Once she's even your own name—Kristen—but prettier and cooler and with much better hair than you could ever hope to grow. Barbie is wish fulfillment. She likes playing pretend almost more than you do. As an adult, you still role-play, but oftentimes it's with the women you date. You can be who they need, you think. You can role-play as anything: smart, charming, a good listener.

But when you're young, you don't understand why role-play feels important. You just know that it's good. And you want to role-play with your Barbies as those babysitters. Even if you can't yet write those stories down the way you want, you can act them out any way you wish through the dolls. The first thing you do is designate characters. After you do this, there is no going back. The dolls will never be Delilah or Sidney or Kristen ever again. They'll remain the babysitters until you play with them for the final time, putting them away forever in their vinyl box.

Mary Anne is your newest Barbie with the dark blonde hair, even though Mary Anne isn't blonde. You braid her hair into pigtails and dress her in a romper with a big lace collared shirt underneath so she can look appropriately modest. Dawn is a beach Barbie who comes in a very tiny bikini and has a clip-on strip of hair that turns bright fuchsia in the sun. Claudia is Barbie's friend Kira, who is so beautiful you spend almost all your time after you receive her staring directly at her face. Stacey is not technically a Barbie. You've been given another doll that was popular at the time called "Maxie"—a line of dolls that have different noses and eyes and mouths, features that are supposed to be more "natural" looking; dolls with slightly smaller tits and slightly larger waists (but let's face it, they all still have tiny waists), and she seems much more sophisticated to you, which is what you think of Stacey, since she grew up in New York and you've only ever seen that city on TV and in movies. New York City feels like a whole other country.

Kristy is Skipper, obviously. Short. Flat-footed. Underdeveloped. She wears a baseball cap that you snatched from a friend who had a McDonald's uniform for her Barbies. It looks funny on her head, all that hair stuffed underneath the brim. Kristy feels the most familiar to you, and that's why she's the least interesting. You don't want to be yourself, ever. You want to escape. Kristy is bossy and never likes boys. Kristy argues with everyone and gets dirty and doesn't know how to dress right. Kristy barely brushes her hair and neither do you, though you like looking at all the girls who do—girls like Stacey and Claudia. You wish you were a Stacey, but you know you're a Kristy. And there is something so embarrassing about that fact—something you won't recognize until you're much older and realize it's because Kristy is a little queer and so are you.

But before that happens, there are scenes to act out. Roles to play. The girls take phone calls, plan babysitting gigs. But they also do a lot of other things. Stuff that never, ever happens in the books. Those are the stories you're most interested in—that stuff that happens in your own head that Ann M. Martin never writes about. They talk about breasts, for instance. Trade clothes and do fashion shows. Wear each other's bras and underwear. The babysitters all own lingerie for some reason. They order pizza and they talk about maybe drinking beers (but they never actually do, even though for some reason one of your off-brand Barbie kitchen sets comes with some wine glasses and a fake bottle of Cabernet). They gossip about each other. They say mean things about their parents. They get in fights. Sometimes the fights are physical. They slap each other, pull hair. They scream and kick. But they hug after, even though it's so hard to make the Barbies want to bend their bodies in that way. And occasionally they kiss, even though you have never done that with any of your friends, though you've sometimes thought about doing it.

You make Kristy get her period. That's one of the plotlines to a story you make up yourself, one of the first ones you write that you actually like and sounds the way the narrative actually goes in your head, because it's something you and your church friends discuss constantly and you think the babysitters should too. Period. Blood. Tampons. Pads. The fact that maybe only one of you has gotten your period, but not the others, and you're all waiting for it eagerly and simultaneously dreading the day it arrives. You wonder why the babysitters never talk about menstruation.

Using a red Sharpie, you draw a patch of blood in Kristy's underwear. She discovers that she's bled through them and onto her pants, staining Claudia's bedspread. It's the middle of a meeting and all the girls are upset with Kristy for ruining Claudia's nice things. They yell at her and she cries. It's cathartic to watch Kristy have to deal with all of that. You get used to making her the brunt of jokes. The babysitters make her take off her dirty clothes in the middle of the room and she stands there naked as they all stare. You realize you're staring, too, and you hurriedly dress her again. The other babysitters all apologize to Kristy for yelling at her. Kristy forgives them immediately. She is dry-eyed, of course, because Skipper never actually cries. Her eyes are big and blue and always staring openly. You cry all the time. You cry when you get your period at your friend's house and she calls you disgusting for asking for a tampon.

The stories you make up in your head become more elaborate. The babysitters all take turns being mean to each other. Mostly they're just mean to Kristy. There is always someone who is getting called out, yelled at, made to feel bad about themselves. It gives you a good feeling when they do this. You like making one of them get into trouble. Part of it is because girls make fun of you all the time, and this gives you the opportunity to be mean to someone else. The other part you like is all the making up they do afterward. They are sorry, they are always so, so, so sorry, and there is always forgiveness. There is nothing that one of the babysitters can ever do that will make the other ones stop loving them. They are like a family in that way, you think. Except the reason forgiveness feels so important to you is because you know there are certain secret things about yourself that your family wouldn't forgive. You can forgive, though. And you do, over and over again.

Kristy likes Mary Anne, but Mary Anne loves Dawn. Kristy wants to hang out with Stacey and Claudia, but they're doing a fashion show and everyone knows Kristy can't dress right. You punish Kristy over and over again for things she can't help. The way she sits. The way she looks. The way her voice sounds. Kristy decides to try out for the school musical and everyone laughs her off the stage because she can't sing very well. You treat her with such derision that even you begin apologizing to her.

Sorry, you say, petting her shiny hair, and of course she forgives you. You can't ever manage to forgive yourself, but all the babysitters love you. They remain true friends, even when other real life friends abandon you. Later in life, you will wonder about how you treated the dolls and, when you're writing fiction and other stories, think back about the repeated narrative of role-play. How you had to make the dolls hurt in order to make yourself feel better. How you wanted them to be the babysitters even though the original ones, the ones from the books, would never dream of acting this way. The babysitters became the dolls became an extension of yourself. You miss them sometimes, after you're too old to read those books and play with the dolls anymore. You try to take them out of their cases, secretly, but they don't speak to you the same way they used to when you were young. You miss them, you think. You miss that little family. The one you created yourself with the help of a book series and a ratty assortment of Barbies. The ones that acted ugly, but loved each other anyway. Loved hard, regardless.

Thirteen Things a Middle-Aged Man Can Learn from the Baby-Sitters Club

Jack Shepherd

'm a Mary Anne. I like to read and I'm shy. Wait, no, that's not quite right. I'm a Kristy, because I am a control freak; a big-but-not-entirely-thought-out-ideas guy; an optimist. I think, with all deference to your extremely interesting approach to this particular problem, that you should do it my way. Actually, I'm a Mallory. Confident. Practical. Would probably be much better off in a boarding school for the terminally earnest somewhere in rural Massachusetts. OK, no. I am none of these things. Or all of them? Hard to say, but what I definitely am is a forty-one-year-old man who has read every single BSC book, every Mystery, every Super Special, all of the California Diaries, and somewhere north of seventy Little Sister books. Today, as it happens, I am embarking on the first installment of the Friends Forever series: *Everything Changes*. I hope, very much, that everything doesn't change.

In fact, I have come to rely on the comforting, hopeful presence of these girls in the background of my life. Trapped in amber. Fated to perennially repeat the eighth grade, year after year after year with different iterations (this time, Logan and Mary Anne don't dance at the Halloween Hop; this time, we see a gentler side of Alan Gray; this time, Jessi pursues her ballet dreams in New York) but somehow still accumulating weight and sadness that couldn't possibly be contained in a single year: Mimi always dies. Stacey always leaves. Patrick Thomas never, ever learns. The BSC, to me, is not a series for young readers about friendship and babysitting: it is an epic cycle; a mythological world full of triumph, tragedy, and magic. It begins with the hope and promise of a Great Idea, and ends, inevitably, in *fire*. BSC #131: *The Fire at Mary Anne's House*, to be specific. Everyone's mostly OK, but the house is never the same.

Of course, this may be the sort of slightly off-kilter viewpoint you get when you read all of these books in your middle age. It's not how they're supposed to be read. It's not even how I originally read them. I first read the Baby-Sitters Club series when I moved (suddenly) to the United States from England as a nine-year-old in 1988. My best friend was my cousin, and she had her copies (along with the Sweet Valley High books) lined up in order on a little bookshelf in her bedroom. There was an appeal, even then, in the sense of a world contained inside those books, an appeal that was even stronger for me because it was a world that belonged to girls and to Americans, two things I had profound difficulty understanding at the time. At the time, I relished the books because they were an invitation at a moment in my life when I felt like an unwelcome guest.

Thirty years later, I still hadn't shaken the BSC loose from my consciousness, and from that unfinished business, *The Baby-Sitters Club Club* was born. My "Great Idea" was a joke: alongside a friend who had never even heard of the BSC, we would read and discuss, for a podcast, every BSC book in order until we got tired of it. The entire substance of the joke was basically, "Why would two grown men do this?" I still think that's a pretty funny premise for a joke, but after more than four years of reading and discussing a BSC book every single week, it's pretty clearly more than a joke (and anyone who's spent time with these books knows how foolish people look who try to dismiss them as superficial). Like the babysitters themselves, we have built a world for ourselves through these books that cannot possibly be contained inside the events of one year in Stoneybrook, Connecticut. Meaning has accumulated. Everything (to be just a little bit melodramatic about this) has changed.

And these are some of the things I've learned along the way.

1. THE SAT WILL ONE DAY BECOME THE SITTER

"Luckily," says Mary Anne, in BSC #4: *Mary Anne Saves the Day*, "Kristy dresses more like me than like Claudia and Stacey. It's nice to have someone to feel babyish with." These are the words of one of literature's most iconic babysitters as she embarks on a storied sitting career in which she will "save the day" dozens if not hundreds of times. Mary Anne exists in the great babysitting tradition of Bithiah, the pharaoh's daughter who found baby Moses in a basket; Faustulus, the humble shepherd who babysat Romulus and Remus until they were ready to found Rome; and Mary Poppins (British nanny, umbrella), and yet she exists in this moment at the intersection between "sat" and "sitter," longing at once to "feel babyish" with her friend and to take on the heavy mantle of responsibility that all great sitters must bear.

It is this tension that drives Mary Anne, and it exists in all of us. When we are sat, we long to sit, and when we sit, we long to be sat. The sat will inevitably become the sitter, and the sitter contains the sat within herself. Or as Wordsworth has it, "The Child is father of the Man." As a middle-aged man who reads a frankly shocking number of books for tweens every year, this tension is something I think about a lot.

2. NOT EVERY IDEA IS A GREAT IDEA . . .

The temptation to have a Baby Parade can be a strong one. You will be sitting in your armchair reading a book or idly watching sports when the idea to assemble the town's babies onto a large float that you have built yourself with the grudging support of your friends and colleagues will lodge itself in your brain, and you will feel a compulsion to act.

> "I was sure that my friends would be excited about the baby parade, too. Maybe Jessi would want to enter Squirt! And there are lots of other babies whom we sit for. This could be a great activity for the whole club!"
> —BSC #45: *Kristy and the Baby Parade*

But the distance between your fantasy about how such a project might turn out and the final product can stretch further and further as your daydream meets reality. For instance, when I started writing this item on the list, I thought there was going to be a lot more to it.

3. . . . SO YOU HAVE TO LEARN TO RECOGNIZE A GREAT IDEA WHEN YOU SEE ONE

But the Baby Parade Fallacy™ has an inverse, and you ignore it at your peril. The older you get and the more failed Baby Parades you have in your past, the stronger the impulse becomes to find fault with your own ideas. To envision a disappointed audience rejecting your finished product before you've even put pen to paper (or baby to float, or whatever).

Any writer knows these twin demons—the one who builds up impossible expectations of success so high that you're afraid to start, and the other who mocks and belittles whatever spark you have until it goes out. They work together. And the only way to defeat them is to embrace your inner Kristy. Because one admittedly catastrophic Baby Parade is a tiny price to pay for Kristy's Krushers, Kid Kits, the Baby-Sitters Club notebook, and yes, the BSC itself, without which none of us would even be here. Kristin Amanda Thomas is a powerful reminder always to err on the side of doing something.

4. IF YOU DON'T KNOW, MAYBE YOU DON'T WANT TO

The most profound question Ann M. Martin ever asked was this:

"Kristy + Bart = ?"

Even saying it out loud feels like a paradox: I like to pronounce the question mark as a questioning sound—a *"hmmm?"* with a rising intonation; other readers like to just say "question mark" or "what" in its place. But there is no right or wrong way to speak the riddle and, as with any great *kōan*, the meaning resides in the search for an answer, not in the answer itself.

And so while Martin chooses not to solve her own equation in BSC #95: *Kristy + Bart = ?*, it is a novel full of wisdom, and it has taught me to listen more carefully to the quiet voice in the back of my mind that says to me (during meetings always, and parties sometimes, and, for three whole years, at least once every day I walked into the office), "I don't want to do this anymore." Sometimes it's good to listen to that voice. Usually the worst case scenario is just that it's a little bit weird between you and Bart for a while.

5. IF YOU CAN, QUIT YOUR DUMB JOB TO SPEND MORE TIME WITH YOUR FAMILY

This is essentially a corollary to Item #4 above, but I learned this one from Watson and not Kristy. Ann M. Martin had to give Watson a heart attack to teach him this lesson (BSC #81: *Kristy and Mr. Mom*) and my personal route to a similar place has been . . . complicated . . . but my job was dumb and my family is great, so it really should have been a no-brainer. Nobody even knows what Watson does anyway. It's not important.

6. YOU CAN BE SOMEONE ELSE SOMEWHERE ELSE

This is controversial, but I don't believe that Mallory Pike really became who she was meant to be until she left the Baby-Sitters Club (technically she's still an honorary member, but we all know that's a meaningless distinction to keep Kristy from losing her mind) and went to boarding school in Massachusetts (BSC #126: *The All-New Mallory Pike*). And the Dawn of California Diaries is almost unrecognizable compared with Dawn in Stoneybrook, where she wore her California past like a disguise, or protective gear, rather than letting it grow with her into the person she was becoming.

The Baby-Sitters Club is a series about *place* as much as it is about anything else. Stoneybrook is safe, for the most part, but it's also static. Time does not pass in the normal way in Stoneybrook. Yet outside its boundaries, you can become something else. New York Stacey and New York Jessi are the promise that Stoneybrook holds in abeyance, as are California Dawn and Boarding School Mallory.

Having left my own small town, and indeed my country, at a fairly young age, I know that a place can define you by its absence in you just as much as your presence in it, and so I sympathize with Dawn and Stacey, whose presence in Stoneybrook is almost fully defined by their desire to leave it and return to their homes. But it is ultimately (and surprisingly) Mallory who escapes to a place of her own, somewhere entirely new where she can embrace a new identity rather than inhabiting an old one. There's a power in that.

7. WE WILL NEVER KNOW WHAT HAPPENED ON JUNE 10

In BSC #32: *Kristy and the Secret of Susan*, Kristy's autistic babysitting charge, Susan Felder, has the gift of being able to tell you the day of the week that corresponds with any date in history:

> Zach consulted his paper. . . . "Okay, June tenth, nineteen sixty-two."
>
> "Sunday," said Susan in her monotone voice.

Previously, in the author's note (what I like to call the "Happy Reading" section) for BSC #29: *Mallory and the Mystery Diary*, Ann M. Martin offers this encomium to diary-keeping:

I have never been a diary or journal keeper, but when I was young—in fact, starting on the day I was born—my mother kept a diary for me. I love looking back through the diary to find out all sorts of things—what my first day of school was like, when I (finally) learned how to ride a two-wheeler, or simply what I did on June 10, 1958. I'm so glad my mother kept a diary for me, but I wish I had kept one for myself, too.

In Little Sister #76: *Karen's Magic Garden*, also a novel about the secrets we keep in diaries, Karen Brewer finds a diary that refers to an event that will occur five days after June 5:

Diana squinted and turned the diary this way and that. Finally she read out loud:
    "June fifth, nineteen-oh-two
    "Dear Diary,
    "Toby and I have come to Lobster Cove to see my family. I cannot believe that in only five days I will be Toby's bride."
    "Bride!" I shrieked.
    Diana's eyes were big. "She was only nineteen."

Why does the date June 10 recur so many times in Ann M. Martin's Baby-Sitters Club series? And why am I so obsessed with finding it? I don't know the answer to either of those questions, though I should probably worry more about the second question than the first one. This isn't, like, a life lesson or anything. I just think it's cool to think about.

8. DON'T BE THE TRIP-MAN

The Trip-Man is the man Dawn's mother, Sharon, dates before she seals the deal with Mary Anne's father, Richard Spier. In BSC #9: *The Ghost at Dawn's House,* Dawn describes him thus:

"Mr. Gwynne's name is Trip," was all I could answer. "*Trip*. Can you believe it?"

Jeff laughed. "Oh, yeah. Man, that is so cool," he said sarcastically.

"I bet he wears pink socks and alligator shirts and his friends call him, like, the Trip-Man or something."

"I bet he plays golf," said Jeff, with a snort of laughter.

"I bet his idea of an amusing afternoon is balancing his checkbook. And," I added, "I bet he has real short hair, wears wire-rim glasses, and has gray eyes, but wears contacts to make them look blue."

I think about the Trip-Man a lot, which is another weird thing about reading these books as a grown-up—you pay way more attention than anyone intended to the lives of the adults, who would be your peers and colleagues if you lived in Stoneybrook. When Trip actually shows up, he's nothing like what Dawn and Jeff have pictured, but he's not much like anything else either. The Trip-Man is an empty vessel, a blank canvas where Dawn can freely paint her golf-playing, checkbook-balancing caricature. There is nothing intrinsically wrong with the Trip-Man except that he has allowed himself to become a ghost, and Dawn's house is already haunted.

9. DON'T BE TRAVIS

Travis is the "Older Boy" in BSC #37: *Dawn and the Older Boy*. He wears all denim and shades and likes to talk about his car. His self-worth is tied up in his high school accomplishments. Travis will be a ghost, too.

10. KNOW WHERE YOU ARE ON THE BOYS QUADRANT

Kristy's Boys Quadrant (from BSC #20: *Kristy and the Walking Disaster*) can help you avoid the vulgar excesses of a Travis as well as the exhausting blandness of a Trip-Man. It is simple, effective, and true. Kristy's view is that there are four kinds of boys:

JERKS	SNOBBY JERKS
SNOBS	NON-JERK / NON-SNOBS

As a man, I have found that the best way to use the Boys Quadrant is not to endlessly ruminate on which corner defines me but instead to think about which corner I'm in *at the moment*. It can be very grounding.

11. DON'T GET TOO STRESSED ABOUT YOUR TITLE

Look, Claudia is smart, she's creative, she's an incredibly talented artist and a damn good babysitter. I'd hire her (or work for her) in a second. But the fact is that the only reason she's vice president is that she has a phone in her room. The title is meaningless. I've spent a large portion of my career trying to impress vice presidents who have the phone in their room but not any of the other things, if you catch my drift. And I've spent a smaller but not insignificant portion of my career worrying about my own title. Looking back, I wish I hadn't done either of those things. Claudia's a true artist who sat the hell out of any kid who came her way, and those are things that matter.

12. WE HAVE TO LET PEOPLE LEAVE

Good-bye Stacey, Good-bye. Farewell, Dawn. Mallory leaves too, but her good-bye book is called *Mary Anne in the Middle*, which is typical Mallory erasure. And each departure creates a rift; reveals a faultline in the club and the friendship that exists among its members. I used to have trouble letting people leave, too, because I saw it as a negative referendum on me, a negation of our shared project.

The paradox of the BSC is that for as much as it is about the unbreakable bonds that exist between friends, it's also about the fear that comes along with anything good enough to be afraid of losing. The ghost at Dawn's house is a premonition of that loss (I know I said it was the Trip-Man earlier, but that was nonsense), and the fire at Mary Anne's house (same house. They became sisters. This is basic stuff.) is its messy, tumultuous, tragic, inevitable arrival. Everything changes . . .

13. MAKE SOMETHING WITH YOUR FRIENDS

. . . but the Baby-Sitters Club is forever. Kristy shouldn't have been quite so worried. Here I am more than thirty years after I first picked up a BSC book, poring through the archives to see if I missed a moment where Ann M. Martin says something cryptic about the tenth day of June. And in the process I've made something with a friend. He hadn't even heard of these books when we started reading them together more than four years ago, but last year he named his new baby after a BSC ghostwriter.

And so how on Earth did we get from there to here? From a goofy joke of a "Great Idea" to a big, beautiful (and I can't emphasize this enough, *extremely silly*) thing we've made together out of well over two hundred Baby-Sitters Club (and Baby-Sitters Club–adjacent) novels? Well, in retrospect it's because we're both Kristys: we had the idea and then showed up every week at the same time for nearly half a decade because we figured out that a Baby Parade isn't going to organize itself. Hmmm, no, that's not quite right. It's because we're Claudias: we let the creative demands of our project guide us past our insecurities. If Claudia can pull off dressing as *the sun* (BSC #71: *Claudia and the Perfect Boy*: "You'd be amazed by the colors that go together. Take pink and gold. You might not think to wear pink socks with gold stretch pants, and then add a gold turtleneck under a pink sweater. But that's what I did yesterday, and then I added blue jewelry. It was great! I looked like a human sunset."), then surely we can have the courage to put our thing out into the world.

No, that's definitely not it. We're Mallory and Jessi: in it for the babysitting, sure, but really just thrilled to have an excuse to spend more time together. OK, hear me out—we're Shannon and Logan: pulled unexpectedly into the club's powerful orbit by the centripetal force created by the boundless energy of its core members. Or maybe we're all of these things and none of them, and the enduring lesson of the Baby-Sitters Club (even for a middle-aged man) is not about who you are or who you want to be, but who you figure those things out with.

No Boys Allowed:
On Girl Groups, Boyfriends,
and Kristy's Great Anxiety

Megan Milks

"I wonder what Mary Anne and Logan are doing right now," says Kristy to Dawn in the Baby-Sitters Club #10: *Logan Likes Mary Anne!* In a first for their shy friend, Mary Anne is on a date: out at the Cineplex with handsome newcomer Logan Bruno. This has led to another first, which is that Kristy and Dawn are hanging out *by themselves* (if we ignore the ambient chatter of Kristy's stepsiblings). On any other Friday it would have been Mary Anne (Kristy's BFF since birth) sleeping over, but now that Mary Anne is ahem, *with boy*, Kristy's invited Dawn. This is a big deal. Sparked by the new-friend jealousy so many of us experienced as preteens, Kristy has for several books treated Dawn with stubborn aloofness, punishment for her growing closeness with Mary Anne. Dawn jumps at Kristy's change of heart. "Talk about ecstatic," says Mary Anne, narrating in absentia, of her second best friend's reaction to her first best friend's invitation. Facing each other on the living room couch, the two girls envision their mutual best friend's evening. "The movie's probably just beginning," says Dawn. "The theater's all dark . . ." Kristy continues. "Maybe they're holding hands . . ." Dawn says. "I wonder if they'll, you know, kiss."

The two girls are drawing their faces more closely, excitedly, together. Maybe they can feel the soft sighs of one another's breath on their cheeks. I wonder if they'll, you know . . .

"Ew!" Kristy recoils, disrupting the moment, and any queer potential to be found in their vicarious scene.

Oh, Kristy. Still so reliably immature. Still so painfully kiddish. But in another first, Kristy takes a long pause here. It's as though, confronted by her own childishness as her "Ew!" resounds through her head, she wishes she could take it back. She tries again. "Maybe they will," she offers, this time resigned, no longer protesting. If Mary Anne is as serious about Logan as she seems, Kristy understands, she'll have to take her friend's feelings seriously—which doesn't lessen the anxiety they provoke. Kristy sighs. "You know," she goes on, "I was always the brave one and Mary Anne was always the scaredy-cat. Now everything's reversed. And suddenly she's . . . I don't know . . . ahead of me, and I've been left behind."

It's a moment of unusual candor for Kristy (perhaps aided by the soft intimacy of sprawling on the couch with Dawn). But what is it that loud, bossy, opinionated Kristy is so scared of? Is it . . . boys? Or is it compulsory (hetero) sexuality? Is her "reversed scaredy-cat" position one of immaturity or of resistance? And what, in the framework presented here, do "ahead" and "behind" really mean?

Though in this scene Kristy is comparing herself against Mary Anne, historically she and Mary Anne have stuck together on Team Behind. Let us not forget that the Baby-Sitters Club was spawned *not only* as a solution to the problem of Kristy's mother being unable to find a last-minute sitter for David Michael, as recounted fondly in the origin story trotted out in each book. It was also devised as a deliberate strategy to bind Kristy's friends together as they drifted apart, specifically as she and Mary Anne were being left behind by Claudia, who, Kristy notices in book #1, is "growing up faster than us." Her evidence: Claudia has started wearing a bra—"and the way she talks, you'd think boys had just been invented." Kristy's fit of greatness works: the BSC keeps her friends together, and trapped in middle school . . . forever. But throughout the original series' 131 books, the anxiety of uneven maturation—who will grow up the fastest, and who will be left behind?—flares up again and again. And while it agitates various members at various times, it most often attaches itself to Kristy.

✳   ✳   ✳

As a young BSC reader, I didn't have awareness of or language for my own incipient queerness or transness—but I related to Kristy's anxieties deeply.

Who am I? I'm Megan Milks. I'm thirty-eight and I'm a white queer nonbinary transmasculine writer and teacher from Chester, Virginia—but I haven't lived there in two decades. I've moved all over the country and wherever I've gone, I've brought the Baby-Sitters Club with me. Right now, I live in Brooklyn, and my BSCs are in two stacks to the left of my laptop.

As a girl and as a reader of the series, my identifications flashed across the Mary Anne/Kristy dyad. I was bookish and shy like Mary Anne, when I wasn't brash and bossy like Kristy (let me explain: I'm a Gemini). Like both of them, I was uninterested in boys—until Mary Anne changed, and Kristy and I didn't.

Growing up means a lot of things for the BSC members. It means learning how to stand up for yourself and be independent (a frequent Mary Anne arc). It means being accountable to your responsibilities when you'd rather be painting or reading Nancy Drew novels (Claudia). It means honoring your body's needs (Stacey). Cultivating sensitivity and patience (Kristy). Facing loss and uncertainty, and learning how to seek support from—and provide support for—family and friends (all of the BSC members).

It also means getting a boyfriend, at least according to the path of normative maturation that the girls frequently invoke. Oddly or not, the character who invokes it most often is childish, gender-nonconforming Kristy, even as she consistently challenges it.

That Mary Anne is the first in the group to start a serious relationship was a shocker. She's the shyest, the quietest, the youngest. Okay, sure, we were prepared by #8: *Boy-Crazy Stacey*, when Mary Anne goes off to Sea City with Stacey and meets a boy named Alex. Sparks fly. Fast forward two books and we're watching open-mouthed as Mary Anne falls in luv (Stacey's word) at first sight. "I nearly spit out a mouthful of milk," she reports about her first vision of dreamboat Logan, new to Stoneybrook from Louisville. "I was in love with him." After a short flirtation consisting mostly of Mary Anne being tied of tongue whenever *he* is around, Logan asks her to the upcoming dance. She accepts. Soon they're officially an item.

When book #10 came out in 1988, I was seven years old. I don't remember how old I was when I actually read it—probably eight or nine—but I remember experiencing the same searing betrayal that I felt when tomboy Jo in *Little Women* accepted Professor Bhaer's marriage proposal. No! How could she? Where many readers have protested this plot point on the grounds that Jo should have accepted Laurie's proposal instead, I felt strongly that Jo should have stayed single. That story really went off the rails, I thought, wrinkling my nose and pretending it away. She was supposed to stay with her sisters. (This, in fact, was Louisa May Alcott's initial inclination.)

I had favored the BSC books precisely because they didn't emphasize crushes and boys the way their competing franchise the Sweet Valley Twins/ High books did. Now Mary Anne had gone the way of Jo, *falling for* (which does suggest being fooled, as in *a gag*) this suspicious *new* boy with the voice like dark brown syrup, otherwise known as black treacle (I remember having to look up *molasses*).

But Mary Anne doesn't just get the guy. The writers make her confront, in his company, the gleaming force that is her personal kryptonite: Too Much Attention. Shortly after the dance, Stacey plans an ill-conceived surprise party for Mary Anne's birthday. Showing up for what she thinks is a harmless back-to-school party, Mary Anne flees the scene at the first sign of birthday cake. When no one comes after her or even bothers calling, she's sure her friends (and Logan) are done with her, fed up with her oversensitive babyishness for once and for all. The next morning, friendless and bereft, she asks her father if she can get a cat. He agrees.

Who does Mary Anne call to share this breaking news? Stacey, who generously planned a *distant* (if I may casually drop the BSC's word for "cool"), albeit misguided, party in Mary Anne's honor? Claudia, who helped Mary Anne put together a killer outfit for the dance? Dawn, her second best friend, who gets very few pages in this book? No, it must be her first best friend Kristy, who herself is feeling friendless and bereft, now that she's living in a new neighborhood surrounded by unfriendly snobs.

Ehhh. Wrong answer. The boy Logan gets not just first phone call *but also* the high honor of accompanying Mary Anne to pick out the gray, tiger-striped kitten whose loss will provide the central crisis of #25: *Mary Anne and the Search for Tigger.*

Yes, Kristy. It's happened. You have been left behind.

Well, not totally. In fact, not much at all: Mary Anne and Kristy will remain close throughout the series, even as their relationship shifts to make room for many other intimacies. Still, Kristy's anxiety is real, and it's an intimately (if not strictly) queer one.

In BSC #10, it's triggered twice. First by Mary Anne's new relationship, and then by Stacey's party. At the school dance, Kristy went stag, in jeans, had a great time. Leave it to sophisticated Stacey to *require* her friends to bring dates. "I really wish Stacey hadn't decided on a boy/girl party," Kristy tells Dawn back on the couch. "Even if I could think of a boy I wanted to go with, I wouldn't know how to ask him." Dawn shares none of Kristy's anxiety, swiftly shifting the topic to her crush on Bruce Schermerhorn. For lack of a better option, Kristy winds up asking Alan Gray who is "a pest but . . . at least I'd know what to expect from him." He delivers, walking around with M&Ms on his eyes all night.

✴ ✴ ✴

Logan is the first of many boys whose pull imperils the survival of the Greatest Girl Group of All Time. Most often it's Kristy who pushes them out, or at least throws unsubtle shade in her friends' directions. Here's Kristy to Mary Anne after Mary Anne has ditched her to hang out with Logan in #60: *Mary Anne's Makeover*: "I mean, there are *some* people who give up their girlfriends for the sake of their boyfriends." This, yes, is deserved, and just one example of escalating us vs. them friction in the club. The crisis finds its breaking point in #83: *Stacey vs. the BSC*, when Stacey at last succumbs to her aforementioned boy-craziness, flagrantly missing meetings because of the boy Robert. What does Kristy do? She fires her. Stacey is *out*.

Always in these cases, I was with Kristy. One must defend the girl group at all costs. It was clear to me that the girl group was the last bastion, a sacred shelter from which one could ward away the horrifying inevitability of growing up and into a world ruled by gender inequality, gendered divisions, and straight sex. I'll say it with you, Kristy: Ew.

In the interest of binding my own friends to me, I formed a few BSC-inspired groups. First it was Sticker Club, which consisted of my best friend Kate and I meeting at each other's houses with overstuffed binders of stickers to cannily negotiate trades: How about two fuzzy Scottie dog stickers for one of your Lisa Frank panda bears? Nnnope. Two fuzzy Scottie dogs and this shiny rainbow? Nnnope. Two fuzzy Scottie dogs, this shiny rainbow, and a purple Lisa Frank heart? Mmmaybe.

Sticker Club collapsed when two new girls moved across the street from Kate's house. The new girls preferred spending their days at the pool in the company of boys. Pale, chunky, susceptible to both vicious sunburn and fatphobic taunts, I garnered no joy from spending any time at the pool. So I lured some school friends into forming a new club. This one was called Book Club. We would exchange our books and read them, recording our impressions in a club notebook. Like Kristy, I was club president, the big boss. But my idea lacked Greatness: we could have just gone to the library. Book Club faded away.

When I was old enough to babysit, I considered forming a new club, the obvious club: a babysitters club. But unlike my heroes, I was no Super Sitter. Anyway, the BSC books were seen as too kiddish then: no one I knew still read them. Except me.

✳ ✳ ✳

"Do any boys like you?" I remember my mother asking me on the car ride home from school when I was in third or fourth grade. "No," I said, matter-of-fact. "It'd be better if I were a boy. Lots of girls would like me."

But then, I wouldn't have been part of the club.

Even as a girl, my membership proved temporary. As my girl groups dissolved and my friends turned their passions to boys (among other pursuits), I felt more and more like Logan: the associate member. So much that I felt like a voyeur even *reading* books aimed at girls—presumably straight (and cis) girls. Though I would have never admitted it out loud, I was no longer sure that meant me.

By the time #95: *Kristy + Bart = ?* came out in March 1996, I was in high school, and I, too, had left Kristy behind. At fifteen, I was officially too old for the BSC, these middle school friends, though I could have learned more from them still.

Case in point: In #95, Kristy comes close to becoming her buddy Bart Taylor's girlfriend. The possibility incites confusion and uncertainty—especially after a movie date where she feels ambivalent about his attempts to kiss her. "Boys are so goony," she remarks, comparing his fingers on her shoulder to "a bunch of mini-bananas." But she does genuinely enjoy him, a state she describes as "advanced LIKE" in comparison to Mary Anne and Logan's "deep LUV." Kristy doesn't know what to do: hence the titular question mark.

She turns to Mary Anne for advice. "That's a tough one," her friend says. "You and Bart had such a great friendship. Can you just go back to the way it was?"

"But he wants it to be more," Kristy replies. "Maybe it *should* be more. I mean, we're not little kids. Do you think I'm being babyish?"

"It doesn't sound like you're ready for Bart to be your boyfriend," Mary Anne observes sensibly.

"But I'm thirteen!" (Indeed, she's been thirteen for eight years.)

Mary Anne reminds her first BFF that she, Mary Anne, took her first steps many months after Kristy did. Her point: "People don't do everything at the same rate."

Mary Anne's counsel helps Kristy understand—and justify—her position. "Look, I'm not ready to be what you want me to be," she tells Bart over the phone. "I always thought of us as just buds. . . . Different people mature at different rates," she concludes. Yes, the implication here is that eventually Kristy *will* be ready to be what he wants her to be; eventually she *will* mature that way. But for now, at least, Kristy continues to defy the path of normative maturation she is so hell-bent on worrying about.

I did not. And I suspect that if I had read this book in 1996, the spring of my first year in high school, I would have dismissed any insights it had to offer. By this point, I didn't *want* to be Kristy. Kristy the tomboy, probable dyke, whom I loved, loved, loved, but no longer knew how to like. I was embarrassed for her, her drippy jeans and sweatshirts. Her juvenile sense of humor. Her refusal to conform to the expectations of conventional femininity.

I wanted to conform, desperately. Gone were my *ews* and my failed clubs. If participating in girl culture meant manufacturing Gigantic Crushes on Boys, I would supply them. That's what I wanted: girls. I don't mean that in a predatory, objectifying way. I mean that I loved being part of girl groups—until I hit some nebulous point where things shifted, and girl culture became suddenly alienating and incomprehensible. I no longer belonged. Now it seems clear that I wasn't at ease as a straight girl, or in that gender, or that body. Instead of acknowledging these frightening feelings—or my confusion about them—I did my best to perform the role of *the most* conventional straight girl I could concoct. Which meant, in what I see now was a remarkably distorted worldview, absorbing as gospel *Seventeen* magazine's tips for hair, makeup, and life, which included dieting. By my junior year I had dropped fifty pounds and developed a serious eating disorder.

For better or worse and despite my best efforts, I did not perform this imaginary straight girl very well. Under my new, form-fitting clothes and suppressed personality, I was still Kristy, in full blown panic whenever occasions like dances came up, especially as it became an immaturity to go in groups of friends. For my senior prom, I took my new friend Anthony, both of us way gay, though we didn't know it. We were confused. I thought I might be in love with him but could not for the life of me envision us touching mouths. In trying to imagine such a scene, my attitude was not "ew," exactly; more like "?" Did I bother talking to him—to anyone—about my feelings, as Kristy did? Nope. I decided the issue was my weight: I needed to lose more. Five pounds? Ten? Only then could I be the kind of girl who could become intimate with a boy. I never did get there. I just kept losing.

⁂

For a long time after I started taking T, I thought I might change my name. "Logan" was a top candidate. Though I resented Logan for taking Mary Anne away from Kristy, I also felt some kinship with him. Like me, Logan is patient, sensitive, fun, with that sleepy southern drawl. (Myself, I'm from Virginia.) Like me, Logan doesn't find his masculinity threatened by performing feminized labor such as babysitting. (Myself, I'm a teacher. And, well, it's not labor but . . . I sometimes practice yoga while listening to Fiona Apple.) Unlike me, Logan seems totally comfortable with himself, all the time. Of all the characters in the series he may be my most aspirational.

After all these years, I'm finally doing right by Kristy: holding fast to friendship and refusing normative paths of maturation that privilege the romantic couple as goal. My new girl group is a gender-diverse queer/trans/feminist book club in Brooklyn. I started the club three years ago with my friend Liza, who moved away last year for a job—we miss her. The core members are me, Ez, Max, and Sonya, with a few associate members who pop in when they can. Do we do anything besides talk about books? Sure, lots. We eat snacks, drink beer, attend Dyke March, Drag March, and the occasional movie. Sometimes we just like to gossip and fool around. This new book club meets monthly. We're very organized. I should know. I'm in charge.

COULD
MARY ANNE
SAVE THE
SOUL?

by
JEANNE THORNTON
APRIL–JULY 2020

THE **SCHOLASTIC BOOK FAIR** WAS BETTER THAN GOING TO THE BOOKSTORE BECAUSE THE BOOKS WOULD COME TO YOUR CLASSROOM. THAT WAY YOUR FRIENDS COULD SEE THEM AND KNOW WHAT KIND OF PERSON YOU WERE.

AT PREVIOUS BOOK FAIRS, I'D FOUND HAPPINESS IN A CERTAIN SET OF CLASSICS—

—AND NOW HERE WAS ANOTHER BOOK THAT SEEMED TO FIT THE BILL!

IT SEEMED LIKE ALL THE BOOKS I ENJOYED: SENSITIVE CHARACTERS STANDING IN RELATION TO ONE ANOTHER.

BUT THERE WAS A DIFFERENCE BETWEEN THIS BOOK AND THOSE BOOKS.

SO WHAT BOOKS DID YOU GET?

OH! HERE'S ONE I'M REALLY EXCITED ABOUT—

...A DIFFERENCE I'D FAILED TO PERCEIVE.

THAT'S A **GIRL BOOK**

ARE YOU A **GIRL**

NO! NO! I DIDN'T KNOW! IT WAS A **MISTAKE**—

I CAN'T READ THESE BOOKS NOW WITHOUT REGRET. WHAT WOULD IT HAVE BEEN LIKE TO HAVE THESE RELATIONAL MODELS OF FRIENDSHIP?

I CERTAINLY REMEMBER LOVING AND RESPONDING TO OTHER BOOKS WITH FRIENDSHIPS IN THEM. (OFTEN RETROACTIVELY QUEER FRIENDSHIPS.)

WE'RE THROUGH WITH YOU CONTROLLING US, JUPITER JONES!

HOW QUAINT

FIRST INVESTIGATOR

(THE THREE INVESTIGATORS SERIES)

BUT THOSE FRIENDSHIPS, ALTHOUGH THEY COULD BE FRUSTRATING—

DON'T WORRY, FERGIE—IT'S JUST THE PROFESSOR IN HIS WORRY CLOSET—

bang PUNCH AAAAAAA SLAM NO NO NO

FROM JOHN BELLAIRS' THE TROLLEY TO YESTERDAY

—WERE NOT THE MAIN ATTRACTION, ANY MORE THAN KIRK/SPOCK/BONES IS THE MAIN ATTRACTION OF STAR TREK.

RUN, PETE! THE WICKED SPIRIT IS EMERGING FROM THE CHIAVO GLASS!

SCENE OF CHILDHOOD HORROR*

FROM "SECRET OF THE HAUNTED MIRROR," M.V. CAREY

THE BABYSITTER'S CLUB FACED PHANTOM CALLERS AND MYSTERIES AND TROUBLES, SURE. BUT THE IMPORTANT CHALLENGE WAS TO KEEP THE SOCIETY FROM CRACKING UNDER THE WEIGHT OF INDIVIDUAL NEEDS.

I DON'T CARE HOW TOUGH AND SPECIAL YOU THINK YOU ARE BECAUSE OF YOUR DUMB DIABETES!

DON'T CALL STACEY'S DIABETES DUMB!!

THE MODEL OF FRIENDSHIP I DIDN'T REALIZE I DIDN'T HAVE — THAT I'VE SPENT YEARS SINCE COMING OUT AND GAINING NEW POWERS OF EMOTIONAL HONESTY WANTING AND SOMETIMES WORKING TO BUILD — IS AT THE CENTER OF THESE BOOKS.

ONE DAY, CLAUDIA, YOU AND YOUR SISTER WILL BE FRIENDS.

CLAUDIA'S GRANDMOTHER

I HESITATE TO TALK ABOUT MALE SOCIALIZATION.

IT IS A TERM MORE USED AGAINST US THAN FOR US: A REASON WE SHOULD STOP TALKING, A KIND OF ORIGINAL SIN.

TRANSSEXUAL BABYSITTERS CLUB! SOMEONE WHO RECEIVED MALE SOCIALIZATION SPEAKING!

JEANNE DON'T FUCK THIS UP FOR THE REST OF US

BUT IT'S THIS TERM THAT SWIMS IN MY MIND WHEN I INVESTIGATE MY FEELINGS ABOUT THE BSC UNIVERSE.

SPECIFICALLY, WHEN I'M READING THE BOOKS FOR THIS STORY, I'M ASKING MYSELF WHY I NEVER PUT IN THE TIME TO LEARN TO BE A GOOD FRIEND.

I MEAN... NO ONE ACTUALLY HAD FRIENDS LIKE THIS?

(M. MILKS REASSURES ME)

MY MEMORIES OF MALE SOCIALIZATION DON'T INVOLVE BUILDING FRIENDSHIPS
AND TRUSTS, BUT FINDING A PREDETERMINED PLACE.

AS A KID, I DIDN'T SEE ANY REASONS TO FOLLOW THE CODE OF FRIENDSHIP ON OFFER TO ME. I LIKED MAKING LITTLE ART PROJECTS AND PRETENDING MY FRIENDS AND I OWNED A DONUT STORE. I DIDN'T WANT TO COMPETE. I WANTED US ALL NOT TO LIVE IN REALITY TOGETHER.

I FOUND ANOTHER DINOSAUR BONE!

I FOUND TWO!

pile of stones

THE CODE ON OFFER DIDN'T SEEM AS BAD TO THE FRIENDS I'D HAD. IT WAS AROUND THE TIME I MADE MY TERRIBLE BABY-SITTERS CLUB ERROR THAT MY FRIENDS STOPPED WORKING ON LITTLE ART PROJECTS AND FAKE COMICS COMPANIES WITH ME.

ONE DAY MY FATHER AND I WERE AT THE MOVIE STORE, AND ALL MY FRIENDS CAME IN TOGETHER AND PRETENDED NOT TO SEE ME. WAS THIS BECAUSE I WAS REALLY A GIRL? WAS MY PERSONALITY JUST BAD IN SOME OTHER WAY THAT IT IS STILL BAD??

OLD

ANIMATION & CULT

HOT AND NEW

WILD

Y'ALL, LET'S RENT A HORROR MOVIE TONIGHT!

NIRVANA

RANMA 1/2... I WONDER IF THAT'S A SAFE MOVIE TO RENT, NOT A GIRL MOVIE...

I'D GOTTEN RID OF THE BABYSITTERS CLUB BOOK, BUT NOT EVEN THAT ACT OF FAWNING SUBMISSION WON THEIR TRUST.

AND HE PRETENDS TO HEAL ME.

Getting Over Claudia
and Calories

Jennifer Epperson

It's 1993 and I am nine years old. I am about to put myself on my first diet.

I have three best friends, and we all sit in the front rows of desks in our third grade classroom. Each of us has black pigtails of varying lengths, brown skin of varying shades. We are all smart, among the smartest in our classroom. We are all bubbly and full of nine-year-old joy.

We are Black, we are active in multiple sports, and we are perfectly made. But upon closer inspection, one of us doesn't quite match the others. At least, that's what it feels like to me.

My best friends are strong and thin. I am strong and bigger. I'm just shy of being "robust," as my dad might say, since he doesn't believe in calling people fat.

In addition to this suspected salient difference, each of us has our individual style. I love short sets, and my favorite is red shorts with white polka dots, and a shirt with white and cerulean stripes and a big flower pot on top. I like the saturated colors and the softness of the short set. Its clashing patterns would probably garner approval from Claudia, the trendiest, most outrageously styled member of the Baby-Sitters Club.

Here's Claudia comparing herself with decidedly less fashionable Kristy in BSC #12: *Claudia and the New Girl*: "I was wearing a very short pink cotton dress, white tights, and black ballet slippers. I had swept all my hair way over to one side," she explains. "Only one ear showed, and in it I had put my big palm tree earring. (Kristy was not wearing any jewelry.)" She goes on to describe the rest of the Baby-Sitters Club members on a scale of who dresses interestingly and who doesn't. Of course, in Claudia's eyes, no one dresses with as much interest as she does.

Claudia is also characterized by her other love: junk food. Her devotion to junk food is immediately relevant to my newfound understanding that I'm bigger than my friends. Baby-Sitters Club meetings invariably involve Claudia retrieving junk food from some nook or cranny. "I found a bag of Doritos in my stash of junk food and passed it around," Claudia says in *Claudia and the New Girl*. Or it's Gummi Bears from a pencil case, or licorice sticks from under her mattress (BSC #1: *Kristy's Great Idea*). Life Savers hidden in a shoebox (BSC #3: *The Truth About Stacey*). Ring Dings at the bottom of the pajama bag (BSC #4: *Mary Anne Saves the Day*). "You can't pick up a pillow without finding a Hershey bar underneath it," says Dawn in Mystery #2: *Beware, Dawn!*

Along with nearly every description of Claudia's junk food adoration, a detail that gets repeated in book after book, is a note assuring us that she "never seems to gain an ounce, or to get so much as the hint of a pimple" (BSC #4). It's this omission of body consequence that my little girl mind latches onto. The omission of fretting about gained cavities or sugar hyperness (a popular parental concern in the 1990s) or, most glaringly, of any concern about weight gain. By omission, I assume that everyone in the Baby-Sitters Club has a body mass index deemed appropriate, that everyone is generally pretty and right-sized.

My brain acts like a color-by-numbers illustration in which society gets a number and pop culture like the Baby-Sitters Club books gets a color, and together they gradually fill in the spaces to complete my mind's idea of what the world expects of me. I'm expected to be the same size as my friends, who seem to possess Claudia's ability to eat whatever they want without any physical consequence. So I'm expected to be able to eat whatever I want without consequence, too.

Claudia becomes the embodiment of these unofficial standards laid before me. She is one of those girls who can eat anything they want and never have to worry about fitting into their clothes. I am very familiar with these girls.

Despite her penchant for Fruit by the Foot, Shameika, my bestest of best friends, looks effortlessly perfect in her form-fitting Guess jeans. Even though there is no trace of meanness between us, I can't help but notice the subtle differences in how people react to her. I'm not yet old enough to watch Uncle Jesse and Aunt Becky kiss on *Full House*, but I'm already noticing other girls want to be Shameika and—most important to my increasing boy craziness— boys want to be with her. (As Stacey says of the boy craziness she shares with Claudia, "All boys are pretty interesting.")

I start mentally grouping girls into two groups: who gets a second glance and who doesn't. Shameika is smart, hilarious, and beautiful, just like I know myself to be. At nine, I am not able to articulate the real feeling that, as a Black girl, my existence is already hard. I *must* sit at the front of the class. I *must* enunciate. I *must* project my voice to make sure white gatekeepers to something like the American Dream can hear me. And now this, an internal battle about food and weight. I lament that I will have to work even harder still for a shot at the normal body, as predefined by society.

So, Shameika gets second glances from boys. I know she's smaller than I am, but if I can just fit into those Guess jeans, then it will mean I'm small enough.

It's a quiet, muggy Friday night in Houston. Mom and I are shopping at Marshall Fields at the Galleria, which is the location with the best candy store, conveniently located next to the kids' department.

While Mom surveys racks of potential church dresses, I set off on my own quest for a pair of Guess jeans. I appreciate that, in the BSC universe, Claudia's eclectic style exists on one end of the fashion spectrum and Stacey's conformity on the other end, but I don't care where Guess jeans are positioned on this spectrum. Aesthetically, Guess jeans are fine enough. I am only invested in the perceived social currency that's awarded to those who can fit into them.

I thumb through the sizes and, eyeballing the miniature waistlines, I pick the biggest size. I add these to the armful of clothes that Mom has found and make my way to the dressing room. Mom says we should choose quality over quantity, look for sales, but splurge on things we really want. If I can fit into these jeans, they certainly qualify as a thing I really want. I want to know that I fit into these jeans, that I'm worthy of a second glance. That I too can eat Dunkaroos and Funyuns, Doritos and Gummi Bears, and still fit into the Guess jeans of my choosing.

I slide the latch to lock my dressing room and set the pile of clothes on the chair. Mom sits in the chair in the modeling area with the three giant mirrors. I dutifully model all the clothes she picked out first.

"I just have one more pair of jeans to try," I tell her. Her eyebrow furrows up.

I skip back to the fitting room and pick up the prized Guess jeans, give the slender waistline another glance over, then bravely begin the process of putting them on. I tug on the pants to budge them past my calves, careful not to let out any audible sign of struggle. Internally, I know if they're this hard to pull up over my calves, we'll be at a loss once they meet my thunder thighs. But they go up, albeit with barely any space to spare. I am silently pleading with the waistline to join and snap over my belly when Mom tells me to come on. "Let's see them," she says.

"I'm . . . almost . . . ready," I say with each tug of mercy.

"Just come on so we can go," she says, patience wearing thin.

I walk out still holding the waistline, my belly poking out like it has been holding back its laughter the whole time.

"Uh-oh," Mom says, "Too much ham for the sack!"

I can't help but release my belly from its sucked-in position and laugh myself. "Mom!"

"What brand are these?" She turns me around and sees the Guess brand.

"Hmph," she says with the suspicion of a cop who is sure there are drugs in someone's car. "We don't need to do all that for jeans."

I am relieved to get them off, but I am defeated.

While Mom pays for my non-Guess items, I ask to go buy some candy. It's customary after shopping. During the walk over to the candy shop, I am newly aware of my thighs rubbing together ever so slightly. I'll be well into my thirties before I realize that because of my narrow, athletic build—barring malnutrition—my thighs are anatomically guaranteed to rub together for the rest of my life.

I place my fingers into the bag, feeling the smooth, hard coating that houses the most delicious blend of sweet-and-sour gooey delight, and I think of Claudia again, how she is always reaching into some hiding place full of salty, sugary snacks. Every nonchalant retrieval of a sugary treat sans ramification feels like a taunting indictment, an unsolicited spotlight on how effortlessly seemingly everyone around me gets to exist with food. Maybe not everyone: We hear plenty about Stacey's diabetes and Dawn's refusals of Claudia's junk food. In her first turn as narrator, Dawn describes her lunch of tofu, dried apple slices, and grapefruit to Kristy, punctuating it with an authoritative, "It's very healthy" (BSC #5: *Dawn and the Impossible Three*). The books always framed Dawn's *very healthy* food preferences as evidence of her laid-back California roots, but I could feel—and relate to—her restriction with each read.

Reaching into my bag of candies, I stop mid-grab. It occurs to me that Claudia, Shameika, and all the other Claudias and Shameikas of the world can eat these same candies and still fit into Guess jeans.

It is all so unfair. Shameika and Claudia get to live, blissfully, in a world where their pants size is the right size, a world without dieting or extra awareness of the food they eat. I want in. I want to be small enough to know that I can wear Guess jeans. So with a somber chewing of my last red sweet-and-sour ball, I go on my first diet.

Because it's the '90s, the decade known for fat-free everything, I don't think anyone suspects that I am on a diet, especially since its key tenet is consuming copious amounts of SnackWell's cookies.

No one has ever called me fat, but my grandmother certainly offers unsolicited commentary. "Oh, she's getting so big!" She says this whenever I hop into her kitchen to see what the adults are talking about. Her body language suggests that it's simply a remark on the fact that I'm growing up. I am on the taller end for my age, and I probably tick up an inch each visit to her house outside of Baton Rouge. She's usually sitting there with a tomato or a piece of fresh okra or some other vegetable she helps herself to. She cuts a piece with this knife that looks like it's a Civil War relic and puts the vegetable sliver in her mouth.

The sound of her teeth crunching it is all that I hear. Her eyes are sawdust brown and they pierce holes into the souls of whatever or whoever she's looking at. She's looking at me, briskly, from my Keds to my short set that's just a hair snug around my belly to my pigtails. "Mmmhmm," she says as she thinks and crunches like Black grandmothers do. "She's getting big."

I never lost any noticeable weight on my SnackWell's diet. I gave up my Guess jeans obsession pretty quickly, and I had plenty of other things like violin and art contests to fill my elementary school mind. My pediatrician also helped to put my mind at ease. During a regular checkup, I asked her why my friends could eat all they wanted while staying small. A tall, striking white woman who looked like she could have been an athletic model, she knelt down to get to my eye level and gently reached for my wrist.

"Look at your wrist next to mine," she said. "I am much older than you and taller than you, but our wrists are just about the same size," she continued. "Your bones are just bigger and stronger than your friends. You are perfect and healthy and don't need to worry."

I was hoping she'd give me the secret to thinness, but this reassurance would do for now. Lurking just behind the curtains of my mind's mainstage was a pesky suspicion that my body and food issues would not resolve themselves anytime soon.

By the time I make it through high school, I've updated my best friend roster to include Sofia, a petite Colombian Puerto Rican who will never grow past the five foot mark. We share a devotion to Little Debbie Oatmeal Cream Pies, but only one of us notices that Little Debbie Oatmeal Cream Pies come in a box of twelve that rarely lasts a school week. Only one of us notices that she has to shop in the larger sizes in the juniors department.

Sofia makes me think about Claudia in a new way. While it's notable that Claudia is never concerned about any health or physical side effects from hidden snacks, so much of her identity is wrapped up in what she eats. As Stacey says: "Claudia is a junk-food addict (although she won't admit it)" (BSC #3: *The Truth About Stacey*). I still resent Claudia's ability to sidestep noteworthy weight gain, but I also don't want food to have so much power over me, whether it's nutritious food or not.

Sofia doesn't avoid Little Debbie Cream Pies like Dawn probably would, and she doesn't subsist on them like Claudia probably would. I want food to be food—something that is nourishing and something that brings me joy. That's how it feels when Sofia and I casually share laughs, gossip, and Little Debbies. I don't want food, on either end of the health spectrum, to become my identity. This is a tall order for a teenager who has already spent years with on-again, off-again diets.

As I get older, my love of long-distance running becomes a major part of my identity. As unsatisfied as I am about my bigger body's place in the world, I continue to be in awe of it. My full, strong body runs miles and miles on guided neighborhood runs with my soccer teammates. I see them in front of me (always in front of me) with their gym shorts staying in place as they run. I see this while picking mine out from riding up my inner thighs every fifty feet. But still, I run and I love every minute of it. By the time I get to college, I do my best to mute the taunting cacophony of Claudias in the back of my mind. I feel like I am getting old, or that I won't be young forever. This one body is the only body I've got.

Today, in my mid-thirties, I've grown too exhausted with adulthood to keep up with that old desire to look a certain way. Plus, my participation medals from dozens of half marathons and a full marathon keep me company. My polka-dot short set aesthetic has manifested itself into a creative career as a writer and product designer. Sensible, soft jeans from Old Navy are my jeans of choice. I am strong and grateful for every inch of my body.

Every so often, I'll get wooed into some new ~~dieting~~ "lifestyle" trend or thirty-day fitness challenge. When I do get lassoed into these get-thin-quick schemes, I usually quit upon catching a passing glance of my strong body in the mirror. Usually fellow Houstonian Megan Thee Stallion is playing in the background, an audible reminder that a big, thicc body is a body to be loved like every other body. While we were married, my then-husband regularly praised my ham hocks, adopting my family's moniker for powerful thighs. His belief in my thighs will sustain me for the rest of my days.

I have heavily leaned into being the woman that I am—a sarcastic, opinionated, foul-mouthed woman who knows that this society still prizes thinness, but that thinness no longer has to be my own prize. I consider this a great personal victory. I no longer harbor resentment for Claudia's sugar-fueled, consequence-less diet. As an adult, I frequently cross paths with women like Claudia who can eat whatever they want. With time, I've accepted that I too can eat whatever I want. I don't need Dawn's restrictive diet nor Claudia's junk food addiction. I can eat what my body wants, and in return, my body will fit the jeans it needs.

Fashion Statements

Personal Style in the BSC

WHAT THE BSC WORE (AND WHAT IT MEANT)

Kim Hutt Mayhew

There's something about the outfits in the Baby-Sitters Club. And it's not just Claudia's decadent concoctions. The members of the BSC use clothes as armor, as costume, as adolescent exploration of self in a way that still feels very real thirty-five years later. The club's style choices stuck with us—ask any millennial bookworm to describe the babysitters, and you'll probably get a pretty complete sartorial picture, from their baseball caps (Kristy) to their wire-rimmed glasses (Mallory) to their double-pierced ears (Dawn).

When I first revisited the series in the mid-aughts, I was a wayward twentysomething browsing thrift store bookshelves. Every book I opened felt like coming home, and the outfit descriptions were especially familiar. Which makes sense, considering the amount of time I'd spent poring over them as a child. Those outfits unleashed an incredibly strong sense of nostalgia, maybe even more so than the plots. Reading a good outfit description put me right back in my childhood bedroom, imagining how cool the babysitters must've looked in their high-top sneakers.

I wanted to share that feeling of side-ponytail-induced time travel, so I started a blog to catalog the outfits of the most iconic dresser of the series,

Claudia Kishi. Claudia's style is so bombastic and maximalist that an outfit description could easily take up half a page. While *What Claudia Wore*'s original focus was limited to the zany creations of the club's vice president, it soon grew to include the rest of the club. As it turns out, fashion served the sitters in a multitude of ways. Style lessons and fashion journeys were as much of a constant in the books as babysitting adventures.

KRISTY THOMAS INVENTS THE CONCEPT OF UNIFORM DRESSING

And we didn't even appreciate her innovation. While a personal-style uniform is now widely accepted (think Elizabeth Warren's jewel-toned cardigans and blazers over black shirts and pants, Emmanuelle Alt's luxe tops belted into impeccably tailored pants, or Ariana Grande's oversized sweatshirts and thigh-high boots), Kristy's choice to embrace wardrobe monotony is bemoaned by both readers and her fellow babysitters. All those chapter 2 outfit descriptions—when the narrator even bothered to walk you through Kristy's outfit—were pretty much the same: that time-tested combination of a turtleneck, jeans, running shoes, and maybe a baseball cap. As a character trait, it's shorthand for Kristy's pragmatism and tomboy nature. And sometimes, in less generous retellings, her immaturity. We delighted in the paragraph-long walkthroughs of Claudia's and Stacey's style creations, and our eyes glazed over reading yet another Kristy sweater-and-jeans combo.

But today, with the concept of uniform dressing heralded as smart, minimalist, and effective, we can look at Kristy's closet with a new eye. Advocates of the personal style uniform (from entrepreneurs like Richard Branson to minimalist writers like Joshua Becker) point to it as a productivity enhancer, and who is more productive than Kristin Amanda Thomas? Concepting businesses (the BSC), products (Kid Kits), and line extensions (mini-camp). Undergoing a long daily commute (from the upper class neighborhood to Stoneybrook Middle School via bus, while her friends have the luxury of walking or biking). Even, for a short while, running for public office (eighth grade president) before recognizing her bandwidth limitations and stepping back. Adherents to uniform dressing say it reduces decision fatigue. As CEO of the BSC, Kristy is certainly more susceptible to decision fatigue than your average eighth grader. How's she gonna have time for all those great ideas if she's distracted by a closet full of options?

DRESS FOR SUCCESS LIKE KRISTY, BSC PRESIDENT

- Sneakers mean you're ready for anything, from a babysitting crisis to an impromptu Krushers practice. Consider a snazzy pair of blue Velcro PONYs if you're feeling wild.
- Wardrobe diversity is for fools. All you need are enough T-shirts, turtlenecks, and sweaters to make it to laundry day.
- Cuff. Those. Jeans.

CLAUDIA KISHI IS HER OWN BEST CANVAS

For vice president Claudia Kishi, a closet full of options isn't just fashion, it's freedom. For someone who feels like an outsider within her own family, getting dressed is as much an act of rebellion as it is self-expression. Claudia is a character of contradictions: at once one of the coolest girls in Stoneybrook Middle School, and also an outcast who's never had a best friend until stylish Stacey McGill moves to town. She's a dedicated artist who is devoted to honing her craft, and also an absentminded student who can barely bring herself to pay attention in class. She's so grandly experimental with clothes that she'd likely be ostracized for it in most middle school settings, but her absolute joy in getting dressed makes her able to pull off anything, as her fellow club members assure us. Even bungee-cord belts.

Claudia's outfits are bold and celebratory, showcasing her artistic spirit. But there are times when they backfire, activating her insecurity about her place in a conservative family of bankers and librarians. It happens in book #33: *Claudia and the Great Search*, when Claudia attends an academic award ceremony for her genius sister, Janine.

"Janine was wearing one of her usual plain outfits," she narrates, "a long pleated plaid skirt, a white shirt with a round collar, stockings, and blue heels . . . I on the other hand was dressed in one of my usual wild outfits—a very short black skirt, an oversized white shirt with bright pink and turquoise poodles printed on it, flat turquoise shoes with ankle straps, and a ton of jewelry, including dangly poodle earrings. . . . People kept looking at Janine and then looking at me. I could just tell they were all thinking, I can't believe you're sisters. Then they would ignore me and congratulate Janine. I could not wait to leave that auditorium."

Now, probably most of us would feel a little self-conscious in a poodle-print shirt and matching canine earrings. But this is an aberration for Claudia, who typically takes her family's bemusement in stride, brushing off comments like "interesting outfit, honey" with a breezy "thanks!" Because Claudia doesn't dress for the outside world. When she's lying in bed concocting her next complicated outfit, she's not doing it for adolescent approval or to catch the eye of a boy she likes. It's a way to turn her body into her own canvas, an eternally morphing art project. And with the next day's masterpiece identified, she can reach under her mattress for one final Mounds bar and drift off into peaceful, self-actualized sleep.

DRESS FOR SUCCESS LIKE CLAUDIA, BSC VICE PRESIDENT

- There are no limits, there are no rules. Go to the outer fringes of fashion, and then keep pushing. Neon? Velour? Clashing patterns? Comically oversized menswear? Yes. All of it. Preferably at the same time.
- Your goal is to look like you're competing in one of those unconventional materials challenges on Project Runway.
- Always wear three earrings. Never match them.

THE SLOW STYLE EVOLUTION OF MARY ANNE SPIER

If Claudia's style is the most memorable, club secretary Mary Anne Spier's might be the most controversial. Her transformation starts with letting her hair down (literally) in book #4 and culminates in the friendship-disrupting short haircut and floral-print leggings of #60: *Mary Anne's Makeover*. While her new look isn't scandalous in and of itself, it triggers a lot of insecurity and hurt feelings. Mary Anne is seen as so reliable and predictable that the minor surprise of a mall makeover sends shock waves through the club. Who knew a little eyeliner could be such a crime?

Mary Anne's slow coming into herself makes sense for the shyest, most sensitive member of the club. Her family is small, hobbled by the trauma of her mom's death. In her first book of the series, she tells us that her uptight, conservative father asks God to watch over her mother at every meal. It's a heavy weight to live under, especially as an only child. And Richard is a clueless father, dictating a little girl room (she still has a framed image of Humpty Dumpty on her wall at age twelve) and a school-uniform style of dress, all pleated skirts and braids and Peter Pan collars.

It's her adventures in babysitting that inspire the courage to change. After a harrowing trip to the emergency room with a four-year-old running a 104 degree fever, Mary Anne's dad realizes she's growing up. And after her ordeal, not to mention a nearly club-ending fight, Mary Anne has the courage to remind him that she's almost a teenager now. She gets permission to update her room, to relax her style a little bit, and even to baby-sit until 10 PM on Fridays and Saturdays. She's still conflict-averse, quick to cry, and more comfortable within a crowd than in front of it. But throughout the series, she learns to stand up for herself and listen to her own instincts more than the opinions of others.

And then comes that makeover. Inspired by a model in a magazine, Mary Anne decides to get a super short haircut. Stuffy Richard even takes her to the mall to get it. Everyone at school is surprised but complimentary about Mary Anne's transformation (despite the fact that, as most of the book covers depict, it is basically a mushroom cap of hair) except her best friends. Middle school ostracization is a norm, of course, but it's shocking for it to happen between this set of friends. The Baby-sitters Club is so wholesome, so pure in their love and support of each other, that real moments of strife between members are series-defining events (Ann M. Martin upped the ante in #100 with the high drama of a temporary club disbandment). And it's almost as painful for the reader as it is for gentle Mary Anne to see her best friends turn their backs on her. They come back together in the end, though, because of course they do. But it's not the only time fashion becomes a point of friction between the club members.

DRESS FOR SUCCESS LIKE MARY ANNE, BSC SECRETARY

- You really like florals and might occasionally be described as fussy.
- You're willing to mix it up with a fun print though, like, say, landmarks from famous cities.
- You're probably at Anthropologie right now.

STACEY MCGILL IS MORE CHIC THAN YOU

Ask anyone to describe club treasurer Stacey McGill and they'll say the same thing: she's sophisticated. She's from New York City. And maybe, if she's passed them notes in the halls of Stoneybrook Middle School, they'll add that she dots her i's with hearts. Stacey's city girl cool is her most defining quality. It's consistently showcased in the way Martin and the ghostwriters dress her and position her against the rest of the club members. She starts off the series a little more wild and wacky (early books mention items like fingerless gloves and sparkly dinosaur pins on her beret) but settles into chic and sophisticated over time. It's the late 1980s and '90s, remember, and so this is signified with blazers, luxe fabrics, wool slacks, the color turquoise.

These big city vibes follow her to her new life in suburban Connecticut. Her mom works as a fashion buyer. Her dad maintains an apartment in the city where her sophistication education can continue. She's totally at home in Bloomingdale's. While she deeply appreciates her friendships with her fellow babysitters, it's this cosmopolitan cool that can create rifts between them. We see this in #18: *Stacey's Mistake*, when Stacey invites the club to New York City for a weekend. From the second they get off the train, Stacey finds herself feeling self-conscious about their visit—among other faux pas, Kristy is wearing a baseball cap with a collie on it, and Mary Anne has her nose in a giant map of the city before accidentally shoplifting from the Bloomingdale's makeup counter.

The worst fashion crimes occur at a party Stacey planned to introduce her small-town friends to her big-city ones. Despite her attempts to manage

DRESS FOR SUCCESS LIKE STACEY, BSC TREASURER

- Think city girl effortlessness, but more Manhattan professional than Brooklyn trendsetter.
- Lots of black, lots of scarves, lots of wool, lots of wide-legged pants. Diamond jewelry, like you've always deserved.
- Like all smart commuters, be prepared with a variety of supportive yet fashionable transit shoes. You can carry your statement shoes in a luxe leather shopper.

their looks, Kristy wears a white turtleneck with a red-and-blue heart print and Mary Anne "looked like she'd walked right out of the pages of *Little House on the Prairie*" in a ruffly white blouse, a long paisley skirt, and little brown boots. While Stacey eventually gets over her humiliation and the club relaxes into their visit (enough for Stacey to even invite them back for a longer stay in Super Special #6: *New York, New York!*), the feeling that she's a little bit elevated from them never really goes away, and Stacey's style serves as a constant reminder of it.

DAWN SCHAFER AND THE LEGACY OF CALIFORNIA CASUAL

Close your eyes and picture another Stoneybrook transplant, West Coast native and BSC alternate officer Dawn Schafer. Corn silk–blonde hair, loose-fitting clothes . . . Dawn Schafer had a generally undone (but not sloppy) aesthetic that Ann M. Martin called "California Casual." This turn of phrase came to represent Dawn as a whole—Dawn the ecologist, Dawn the vegetarian in a world of meat-eaters, Dawn the individual who got her ears double-pierced and wore earrings shaped like oranges to pay tribute to her home state.

Now picture Dawn today. She's pretty easy to translate to modern times. She might be a Madewell model, the brand that defines itself by its tomgirl vibes and affinity for denim-on-denim. She might be a VSCO girl, in her oversized T-shirts and beachy accessories (puka-shell necklaces and Pura Vida bracelets could be the modernized version of orange-shaped earrings, right?), toting a reusable water bottle as an outward-facing sign of her low-waste lifestyle. You can easily place Dawn in 2021 not because of the specifics of her wardrobe but because of what it represented. Dawn is the cool girl. Not the trendy girl, like Claudia and Stacey, but the self-assured girl, the one who is always herself. She's an individual without relying on flashy statement pieces to communicate this.

This is reinforced in #50: *Dawn's Big Date*—aka the makeover that failed. Feeling insecure at the prospect of meeting Logan's cousin Lewis, she's convinced she needs a new image. Heavily applied navy blue eyeliner, hot pink lipstick, hair gel, black textured stockings and a rolled-up skirt—it just might be Dawn's take on 1985's *Desperately Seeking Susan*. The look, along with the teen magazine flirting tips she tries out, lands with a splat. In the end, Dawn and Lewis agree to reintroduce themselves, which Dawn does sans hair gel, in faded blue jeans and a UCLA sweatshirt. (She also makes him a tabouli salad, 'cause if Dawn's gonna Dawn she's gonna Dawn all the way.) Ultimately, the lesson here is similar to the one Mallory learns in Super Special #5: *California Girls*: authenticity matters.

DRESS FOR SUCCESS LIKE DAWN, BSC ALTERNATE OFFICER

- Soft, casual, throw-on-and-go clothes—but make it sustainable. Basically any brand that has a give-back component is gonna be your go-to. You're planting trees. You're saving water. You're buying one, giving one.
- You've probably got a wide variety of Birkenstocks, from sandals to clogs and back again.
- Denim-on-denim never goes out of style, and sometimes a hearty salad can be your best accessory.

MALLORY PIKE AND THE INTOXICATING PROMISE OF A MAKEOVER

Junior officer Mallory Pike was always the babysitter most susceptible to the power and promise of a makeover. As one of the two youngest members of the club, she's often comparing herself to the endlessly glam Claudia and Stacey, or cool-girl prototype Dawn. Looking back to my own thirteen-year-old self, I have to imagine at least some of these girls were still in their awkward stages. But to Mallory, they were goddesses. Thank God she wasn't acquainted with the Wakefield twins.

Mallory wore glasses. She had braces. Her hair was reddish-brown and curly, in an era before the Curly Girl Method helped women embrace their ringlets. As the oldest kid in an eight-child family, she was in the unenviable position of most mature, while still not being mature *enough*—for pierced ears, for cool clothes, for contacts. And when she finally gets to be a member of what she sees as the cool kids (imagine your dorky eleven-year-old self accepted by a group of girls two years older and seemingly the best of friends?), they put her through her paces to prove herself. For Mallory, even after club initiation ends, every club meeting serves as a reminder of her inferior looks.

Mallory's second book, #21: *Mallory and the Trouble with Twins*, is a treasure trove of makeover fantasizing and realization—not just for Mallory but also for the titular twins, Marilyn and Carolyn Arnold, who are unhappy with their matching outfits and lack of recognition as individuals, and therefore need to go to the mall. A late '80s fantasy shopping montage ensues, complete with a moon-and-stars sweatshirt, a pink denim skirt, headbands, and yellow push-down socks. The twins' journey to self-expression inspires Mallory, who convinces her parents to let her get a haircut and pierced ears. It's a grown-up milestone to Mallory, as it probably was to many of us—getting her ears pierced means having more in common with her eighth grade heroes.

Things don't go as well the second time Mallory attempts an image makeover, during a club trip to California. (Superfluous to the makeover, reminder that this trip was funded by the Connecticut State Lottery because these girls are nothing if not lucky.) Inspired by a trip to the Max Factor museum and images of sun-kissed California girls, Mallory blows all her trip money on expensive makeup and blonde hair dye. ("Oh my lord," is all Claudia can say post-blonde transformation.) It's only after a casting director tells her that her looks aren't quite right that Mal comes back to her senses, and when Kristy tells her she's "trying to look like someone she isn't," Mallory finally snaps out of her California dreams. The club is supportive in her retransformation, helping her pick out a shade of red dye that looks closest to her natural color and celebrating the return of the Mallory they know and love.

Now, the image of an eleven-year-old with a blonde dye job and stage makeup is patently ridiculous, or at least it was in a pre-Kardashian era. Would Mallory's blonde experiment have petered out on its own without the club's disapproval? Most likely. But here the club's resistance to change comes from love, not fear. When Mary Anne changed her style, it shook her friends' sense

DRESS FOR SUCCESS LIKE MALLORY, BSC JUNIOR OFFICER

- Round or horn-rimmed glasses are your signature look.
- You've always wanted to wear miniskirts like your cooler friends—why not now?
- Celebrate the dichotomy within yourself—wear the loafers, sure, but also treat yourself to the extremely cool pink shoes with green trim your mom never wanted you to have.

of who she was and what their friendship meant (until they realized that nothing had changed besides ten or so inches of hair). But Mallory's California makeover is the manifestation of all her adolescent insecurity, and here the club lovingly helps her regain her true self—curly red hair and all.

JESSI RAMSEY TEACHES US TO DRESS FOR THE JOB WE WANT

Junior officer Jessi Ramsey has the least explored personal style of all the club members. Jessi's identity revolves around her love for ballet, and that love tends to drive most of her plotlines. She's more than just a dancer, of course, but in comparison to the rest of the club members she—and her relationship to clothes—seems underdeveloped. As millennials grew up from these books and gained a more mature lens, it has become clear to us how clunky (if well-intentioned) the series' handling of race was. Giving Jessi a makeover journey or style evolution wouldn't solve for that—but its absence, when it's key to so many other stories of self-expression within the series, is worth noting.

And so, Jessi's fashion story is entwined with her identity as a dancer. Book #16: *Jessi's Secret Language*, begins with Jessi waking up at 5:29, before her alarm can ring a minute later. Immediately, we get it—she is an extraordinarily disciplined eleven-year-old, foregoing sleep to dress in her leotard and warm-up clothes and practice ballet in her makeshift basement studio. Jessi is the BSC's embodiment of the fashion (slash professional) rule *dress for the job you want*. Like Kristy, Jessi is dressing for the future. She showcases her passion in her outfits—keeping her hair in severe ballerina buns, wearing leotards as shirts. She's often running to babysitting jobs or club meetings from dance classes, and so this is a pragmatic decision as much as it is a style one.

DRESS FOR SUCCESS LIKE JESSI, BSC JUNIOR OFFICER

- Athleta. Alo Yoga. Capezio. It's athleisure time, baby, spandex it up.
- Leg warmers are a little too on-the-nose. Try stocking up on ballerina wrap cardigans in soft, feminine knits.
- You're gonna need some scrunchies for those ballerina buns.

But it also serves as a constant reminder to Jessi (and everyone around her) of where her priorities are. She is a dancer, she wants to be a professional dancer, and she carries that with her in dress as much as in her proper posture or natural turnout. You have to imagine that a kid so focused and disciplined at age eleven would end up going places.

✳ ✳ ✳

It's always fun to envision what might have become of these beloved childhood characters as they grew up. Would Stacey, with her head for numbers and enduring love for the Big Apple, wind up on Wall Street? Would Claudia's penchant for pattern-mixing make her the free-spirited darling of a *Project Runway* season? Would Dawn open her own co-op? (Yes, and the employee aprons are recycled lightwash denim.) But the enduring magic of this series is partly due to the way it freezes time for us—and for the sitters, who had endless eighth grade winter vacations and spring breaks—while showcasing its passing at the same time. I've gone from a seven-year-old reading about the coolest group of best friends I could ever look up to, to a thirty-something who now feels downright maternal toward these kids. What a journey, even if I never managed to pull off those double-layer slouch socks.

While the outfits themselves might be dated (though certain elements have come back around again thanks to the cyclical nature of fashion), the lessons are timeless. Growth and change are part of life, but authenticity is way more important than looking cool. Normal middle school jealousies arise but are always resolved, because ultimately the bond the babysitters share is bigger than any fashion differences or makeover misfires. In the end, everyone winds up back in Claudia's room, laughing and sharing stories and pillowcase snacks—whether they're wearing ballet flats or sweatpants. Where else could you possibly want to be on a Monday, Wednesday, or Friday at 5:30?

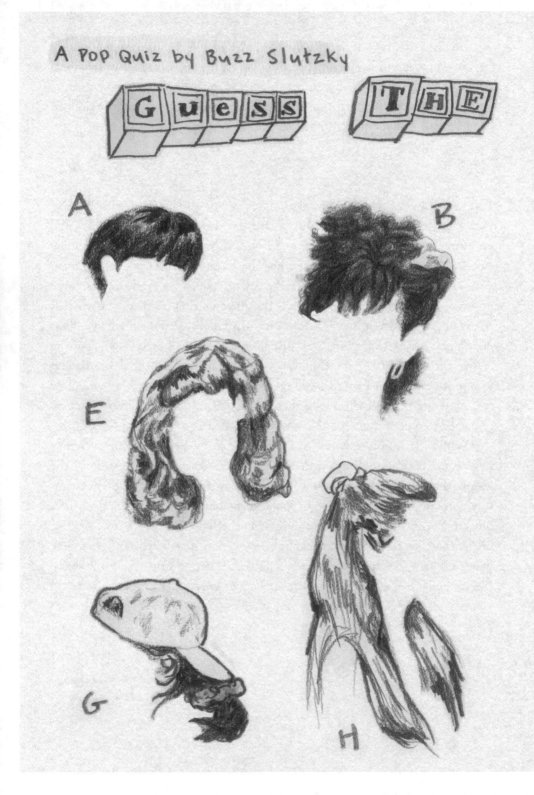

BABYSITTER

(OR AT LEAST THEIR HAIR)

J   LOGAN

I   CLAUDIA

H   DAWN

G   KRISTY

F   MARY ANNE

E   MALLORY

D   STACEY

C   MARY ANNE

B   JESSI

A   MARY ANNE

I Want to Be a Claudia But I Know I'm a Stacey

Marisa Crawford

'm eight years old and in my mom's car. We're driving home at night, and I'm reading *Claudia and Mean Janine* in the backseat in a beam of light from the car behind me, my new trick for reading in the dark. I'm wedged between my two sisters. My mom and stepdad are fighting in the front. I'm channeling Claudia's visionary artistic sensibility with my outfit choice: a white T-shirt covered in puff paint, lace-trimmed floral leggings, a scrunchie made out of rainbow tinsel. All I want is for the world to see me as a Claudia, to see myself that way. But inside, listening to my stepdad insult my mom, straining to focus and lift my arms higher to keep my book in the headlights, I have this sinking feeling that I'm more like Stacey.

Claudia and Stacey are two sides of the same coin. Two gals who share a love of fashion, babysitting, and boys. I felt a kinship with both of them growing up, but what drew me to Claudia was her outrageousness, her sure-footed confidence in a vision of the world that made little sense to anybody else—least of all her family—but made perfect sense to her. Her outfits were each relentlessly her own, as was her trio of forbidden interests: candy, art, Nancy Drew. Claudia didn't just eat candy; she ate candy that she kept stashed in a hollow book. She taught so many of us, through her Dickinson-esque riddle of a bedroom, that a *hollow book* was even a thing; an option for those of us who needed it. She was a version of Nancy Drew herself, stealthily hiding away the things she needed to nourish her. She had solved the mystery of how to be who you just *know* you're meant to be, even when your family—or the world—can't see it or refuses to.

It's hard to picture Claudia as a grown-up, because the very essence of who she is feels impossible to tame, to fit into the bogus requirements of the adult universe. I wanted to be the kind of person who carves out time not just for practical, quotidian items like babysitting and pizza parties and teatime with Mimi, but also for the artistry of putting together outfits that help you to make sense of the world, and feel confident that you belong in it. And honestly what even was the point of being alive in a world that wasn't filled with lavender pants and neon green sunglasses, sour straws unearthed from underneath pillows, and books about girls uncovering the secret of the old clock, or who's making those phantom phone calls? I couldn't articulate this artistic impulse as a young reader, but I could feel it, thanks to Claudia. Who wants to live in a world that's sad and boring, flavorless and gray?

Stacey on the other hand is already a mini grown-up at age thirteen. Instead of hours spent perfecting outfits modeled after Mrs. Frizzle and/or The Sea, Stacey spends her time managing chronic illness, traveling to and from New York to visit her dad—a three-and-a-half to four-hour round trip every other weekend adds up—and making sure her outfits align with the fashion bible that is the Bloomingdale's catalog. She's naturally good at math—the of-this-world logic for which Claudia, and so many artists, seem to not have any patience. She moves to Stoneybrook, only to move back to New York, only to come back to Stoneybrook all within the course of a year (although, to be fair, a lot happens in eighth grade for all of the babysitters). Stacey is constantly adjusting to what the world throws at her, like some cruel game of dodgeball. But adhering to the strict rules of fashion, arithmetic, and diabetes management keeps her grounded and safe.

As a kid, I moved from New York to Connecticut too; I too was a child of divorce and department stores. Like Stacey, I rode the Metro North train to and from different family members and different parts of myself. All the while I yearned for Claudia's fashion confidence, and for whatever it was that made her see herself as an artist. "I decided that my theme for the day would be The Sea," Claudia tells us in BSC #40: *Claudia and the Middle School Mystery*, perfecting her look with a sand-dollar barrette and seashell-stickered jellies. "Was it too much? I shook my head. I looked great. I looked like someone who didn't care about what grade she got on a dumb old math test." Claudia, supported by the stable home base of her bedroom, where her very own phone line rings just for her, seemed to always meet her struggles with school and with her family from a place filled with possibility and glitter; to rise above the rest of the pathetically grounded world like a beautiful phoenix in purple fringe cowboy boots.

Inspired by Claudia, I wore my dance school ballet slippers to school one day, riding a fashion high. I thought it looked cool—like, wow who's *that* girl she's really *different*! But when my friends eyed my shoes in utter confusion, I realized that I couldn't take it. I felt self-conscious; I wasn't as bold as Claudia after all. I went to the nurse's office and insisted that I had a terrible stomachache and should be sent home. It wasn't a stretch—I regularly went to the nurse's office with bad stomachaches anyway. I can see now as an adult that they probably had more to do with the stress I was experiencing at home than the gooey chocolate chip cookies I ate in the cafeteria. I seemed to always end up lying on a pea-green cot that totally clashed with my outfit. Looking like Claudia, feeling like Stacey.

After moving to Connecticut at age eight, I hoped I would find, befriend, and join the BSC because I hadn't yet learned that *fiction* means *make believe*. Instead, I listened to my mom and stepdad fight late into the night, or I ran downstairs and watched from the corner. Like Stacey I was caught between my parents, but I positioned myself firmly on my mom's team. My anxiety manifested itself in constant worrying about Chucky, the killer doll from *Child's Play*, which I've still never seen but learned about at my older sister's slumber party. If Chucky could kill people, who's to say the dolls in my closet couldn't do the same? If the dark-haired man with a mustache on *America's Most Wanted* kidnapped girls and put them in boxes, maybe my stepdad—or even my real dad—(they both happened to have iconic '80s mustaches) was secretly a kidnapper too. I threw all my dolls in the back of my closet. I read books late into the night, trying to train my brain to not be afraid. *Mary Anne and the Search for Tigger* was vetoed for its illusion to possible cat-napping. *Dawn on the Coast* was fine. *Stacey's Emergency* was my favorite; it was cathartic to see Stacey navigate her parents' constant fighting and reach her breaking point. I liked how she secretly ate candy bars because she was mad at her mom and dad. It felt like self-harming, which soon became a way for me to cope with my problems, too.

✱ ✱ ✱

Flash forward ten years. I'm a sophomore in college. The 9/11 attacks just happened, and I'm worried about my dad, a firefighter and World Trade Center first responder, and about the state of the world. My grades drop, and I fail several of my finals. Instead of thinking about any of that though, my roommate and I get wasted every weekend on Bacardi and Cool Lemon Nestea from the soda machine. We spend most nights fawning over a group of boys who ignore us as we sit on their dorm room beds and watch them play video games. I change the background on my computer to a repeating image of *Boy-Crazy Stacey*, a joke between me and my roommate.

It's easy for me to imagine Stacey growing up, going away to college, planning her future career. She's already a master in compartmentalizing her feelings in order to function—a skill that comes in handy when navigating jobs, adult relationships, and the general hell of capitalism—even if she sometimes ends up hurting herself in the process. In *Stacey's Emergency*, Stacey's blood sugar numbers are off and she's feeling sicker and sicker, but she doesn't want to tell her parents because they're already so stressed out post-divorce, and they put her in the middle of their fights anyway. In spite of her diabetes symptoms worsening, she sneaks homemade fudge from her babysitting job, and steals Ring Dings from Claudia's room. She tells us, "I was sick and tired of being sick and tired. Nobody else I knew had to stick to a diet like mine." But on the outside, she tries to sound perky, "rather than dead tired," on the phone with her dad. She dots her i's with hearts. Shows up with Kid Kit in hand. Chases cute lifeguards on the Jersey Shore.

We all remember Stacey's infamous Metro North scene—the one where she gets so thirsty while wielding a heavy suitcase on the way to see her dad that she goes into the train bathroom repeatedly to drink directly from the dirty sink. The pressure to be a good daughter, a great babysitter, a perfect girl, lands Stacey in the emergency room. She's bending over backward to make other people happy—everyone except herself.

✳   ✳   ✳

After graduating college, I live in Massachusetts where I work at a jewelry stand at a mall. My life feels utterly directionless except for the one thing that truly matters: boys. I'm dating a Marxist grad student who thinks it's okay to be mean to me because love is a function of capitalism, or some such complicated rationalization that for some reason I retrain my brain to pretend is normal. I hide my real feelings in a hollow book. Every day at work I polish the silver hoop earrings that line the counter, and rearrange the gemstone pendants in the glass display case. At night I get ready to go out, trying on a black dress, turquoise fishnets, and peacock feather earrings in front of a full-length mirror. Like Claudia taught me, the perfect outfit can remind you just how little your math test, or your ridiculous day job, or your condescending boyfriend, matters in the grand scheme of what an awesome and enlightened person you are. Even though my boyfriend mocks my friends and me for going out dancing, and tells me he's staying home to work, he always shows up at the bar late at night. And even after we break up, I always go home with him. His bedsheets covered with glitter from my new dress. Maybe even for Claudia, the perfect outfit only gets you so far.

Later that year, I move to California to start an MFA program. My (brilliant, female, gorgeously dressed) professor calls my long beaded earrings "ambitious," and she says the same thing about my poems. On the one hand, I'm incredibly lonely in a new city, leaving everyone I love behind as they waved to me like Stacey on the cover of *Good-bye Stacey, Good-bye*. On the other, I feel like I'm finally feeding my inner Claudia the steady diet of art, girl detective stories, and sour-patch gummies that she needs.

When I head home for Christmas, I'm Stacey again, planning trips to the mall for last-minute shopping, telling my family about my new job writing catalog copy, but not my poetry, passing the baked ziti. I'm Stacey shuttling from my mom's house in Connecticut to New York to see my dad, pulling an old comforter out of the guest room closet for extra warmth. I'm Claudia when I'm scribbling in my journal until the sun comes up, listening to cassette tapes that I fish out from a drawer of old junk. I'm Stacey when I take a job at a marketing agency in New York, Claudia when I write poems in the Notes app on my phone. Walking around on my lunch break, staring into store windows on Fifth Avenue.

If Claudia is art and freedom and unrestrained creativity, Stacey is the need for a steady paycheck. I'm Claudia when I'm staying up late to perfect my outfit for work the next day, or to fine-tune a poem; Stacey as I slowly accept that there are a finite number of hours in the day, and sleep, and exercise, and eating well are also important. So I soothe my inner Stacey with my inner Claudia. I let myself be Claudia because I know Stacey will keep me safe. I let myself be Stacey because I know Claudia will keep me feeling alive. As a kid, I read the BSC books looking for my deepest fears and hopes reflected back at me, and I found them: I need both of them. The girl I always wanted to be, and the girl I always knew I was.

Scripts of Girlhood: Handwriting and the Baby-sitters Club

Kelly Blewett

I wrote two diary entries on April 17, 1993, and the two don't look the same.

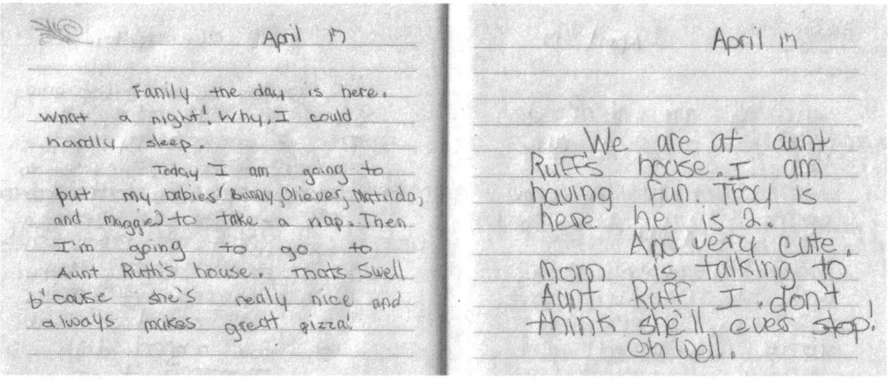

April 17

Family the day is here.
What a night! Why, I could
hardly sleep.
    Today I am going to
put my babies (bunny Pliever, Matilda,
and maggie) to take a nap. Then
I'm going to go to
Aunt Ruth's house. Thats Swell
b'cause she's really nice and
always makes great pizza!

April 17

    We are at aunt
Ruffs house. I am
having fun. Troy is
here he is 2.
    And very cute.
mom   is talking to
Aunt Ruff I don't
think she'll ever stop!
Oh Well.

FIG. 1: THE AUTHOR'S CHILDHOOD DIARY

While the left-side entry features tighter, smaller print that is slightly leaning to the left, the right-side entry displays larger, rounder letters that are standing straight up. Evidently experimentation with penmanship character-ized my private writing practices as a girl. But where did my models for exper-imentation come from? Part of the answer may be found in a sketch that I made of a book I happened to be reading at the time, a series book from the Baby-Sitters Club titled *Baby-sitters at Shadow Lake* (1992).

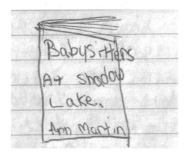

FIG. 2: DRAWING OF SUPER SPECIAL #8: *BABY-SITTERS AT SHADOW LAKE*.

I wonder whether my ten-year-old self would have readily acknowledged how much her own writing was copied from that of the characters in the book she was reading:

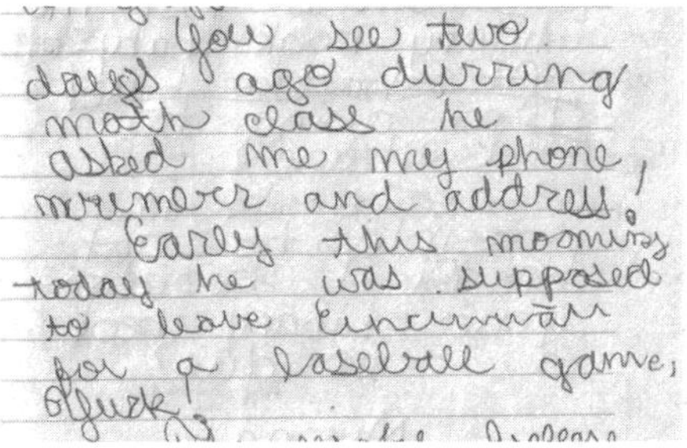

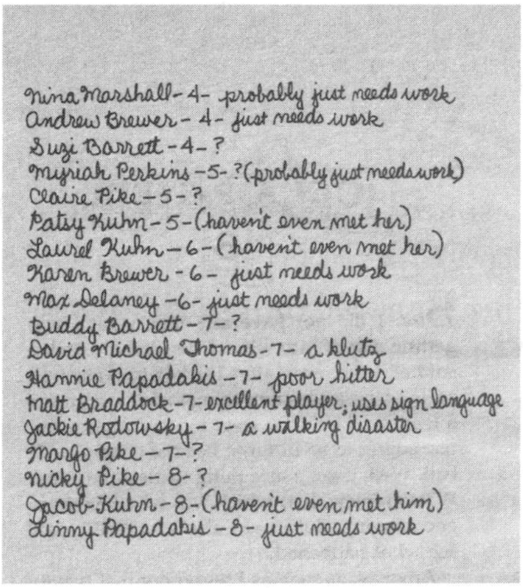

FIG 3: MY HANDWRITING (LEFT); THE HAND-WRITING OF "KRISTY" (RIGHT) FROM BSC #20, PRODUCED BY HOLLIE TOMMASINO.

The lettering styles of BSC protagonists Kristy, Mary Anne, and Stacey, like those of all of the series' characters, were developed by one graphic designer in the art department of Scholastic, Hollie Tommasino.* A look back at the

---

* Tommasino has been underrepresented in public histories of the BSC, such as Margot Becker's *Ann M. Martin: The Story of the Author of* The Baby-Sitters Club (see page 139, which refers to the many people who worked on the series but names only two editors).

history of handwriting in America shows that the handwriting of Kristy and Mary Anne each had an identifiable historical precedent—and how fundamental differences between Kristy and Mary Anne are reinforced through their handwriting. Stacey's script, on the other hand, is not so traditional. Tommasino invented Stacey's penmanship after remembering how the cool kids wrote in Queens, New York, as she was growing up. Maybe that's one reason that so many readers, like my friend Amanda, remember imitating Stacey's handwriting. "I definitely was influenced by Stacey's writing," Amanda told me. "I used to try and make my handwriting more fun and bubbly and even tried to use the hearts to dot my lowercase *I*. I used to wish I could be more girly and fun if I worked on my penmanship."

Handwriting is socially learned and culturally transmitted. And we readers of the BSC were the ones who received the message. In imitating the scripts we admired, we were using them to make sense of our own burgeoning identities. Reading as a child wasn't just to pass the time or enjoy the plot. It was to figure out who we wanted to be.

✷ ✷ ✷

It was Ann M. Martin's idea to include the samples of characters' handwriting in the book. "I wanted the handwriting included in the books in order to bring the idea of the BSC notebook more fully to life, and thus make the club itself seem more real," she explained to me in a 2015 message. Tommasino created scripts for each of the babysitters, which were approved by the publishing team, and then generated script for each series book by hand from 1986 through 1996. In a 2018 interview with the *Los Angeles Review of Books*, she remembered her process for developing each script:

> The editors gave us a description of each of the characters in the series. They told us their general personalities, their likes and dislikes, their strengths and weaknesses. Once I had a picture in my mind of each babysitter, I created a handwriting style that I felt would reflect them. The process felt very intuitive and fun. It came pretty naturally, probably because I loved handwriting and had different styles of my own penmanship anyway.

The handwriting samples usually appeared in the club notebook, which recalls the genre of friendship notebooks that were popular in the '70s and '80s.

In BSC #10, Mary Anne describes the club notebook as "a diary in which we write up every job we go on." Entries from the club notebook rarely continued for more than a single page. The shift from the handwriting to computer-generated font was often flagged in a transitional phrase, such as "It started from the moment she entered the door. . ." Beyond just introducing the chapter, though, the handwriting served a much more important function: it was a visual performance of the identity of the babysitter who was writing.

Like the babysitter's ages, food preferences, or favorite colors, their handwriting styles remained frozen in time from 1986 through 2000 (new reissues have modified the script slightly). The handwriting narrowed what one scholar calls the proximity between the protagonist and the reader, something that children's literature scholar Sara Day notes is crucial to the developing narrative intimacy between them. In a typeset chapter book for middle grade readers, the handwriting jumps out as a visual feature that disrupts the neat and orderly lines of computer-generated font and provides a second, more visceral source of information about the character that young readers crave. Perhaps more so in the past than now, kids were attuned to differences in lettering styles, and what those differences might mean. Tommasino certainly did. She explained:

> As a little girl, I was always writing letters and cards to friends. And I paid attention to the mail. My family got lots of letters, and I could tell just by the handwriting whom it was from. I was very aware of the different personalities the writing styles expressed. I loved what you might call the art of handwriting. I would imitate my mother's handwriting, which was very swishy-swashy and graceful, and my best friend's handwriting, which was more bubbly and bold. . . . Some handwritings I admired and some I didn't, but they all reflected personality—confident, bold, quick, sad, or shy.

Of course, the "personalities" of the scripts were not simply informed by someone's unique interpretation of the twenty-six letters of the alphabet, but also on longstanding traditions.

Handwriting historians show that penmanship has often worked to code both individuality and conformity. One 1855 article reads: "A man's penmanship is an unfailing index of his character, moral and mental, and a criterion by which to judge his peculiarities of taste and sentiment." Handwriting has often been understood as representative of a person's character and identity. Graphologists even believed they could determine someone's inner psychological state through the movement of their hands, a "science" which has since been debunked but whose assumptions about identity and penmanship continue to resonate.

We can see traces of these ideas in the BSC books, where the words the characters use to describe their babysitting adventures are not nearly so important as the way the script *appears*. And achieving a pleasing appearance was not only about using the right tools, but also about embodying the right motion. In an interview, Tommasino recalled using rapidograph pens and markers. But the tools were not, as Tommasino said, "as important as controlling how my hand styled the letters. The fluidity of the movement of my hand was what mattered most." Tommasino held her pen a certain way, pressed down on the paper at varying intensities, drew curly loops and tiny hearts, big swashes and squished-up misspellings. Tommasino was aware of the impact of different penmanship choices and what she needed to do with her pen to achieve particular outcomes—and so were readers.

One reader named HL remembers, "I wrote my 'a's and 'e's like Stacey McGill until my fifth grade teacher told me to cut it out. I obliged him for that year but reverted back in sixth grade. I naturally stopped before middle school, which, maybe not coincidentally, is the same time I stopped reading BSC books." Seeking to imitate the character Stacey McGill, HL shaped particular letters accordingly, and thus imaginatively participated in the BSC world.

When readers made decisions about their handwriting, they may have aimed to deliberately convey their affiliation—however temporary—with a character, like HL and my friend Amanda describe. Or, like me, they might have been oblivious to the influences the books had on their penmanship. Either way, the production team of the Baby-Sitter's Club capitalized on existing ideas about penmanship to link characters' identities purposefully to handwriting style, thus lending each character a handwriting that readers could easily imitate, closing the space between the fictional narrator and the adolescent reader. Some of these handwriting styles were more traditional than others.

TRADITIONAL SCRIPTS: MARY ANNE AND KRISTY

The BSC series is built on the longstanding best-friendship of Kristy and Mary Anne. BSC #1, narrated by the club founder and president Kristy Thomas, describes the Kristy/Mary Anne friendship in this way:

Mary Anne is my best friend. We live next door to each other. We even look a little alike. We're both small for our age and we both have brown hair that falls past our shoulders. But that's where the similarity ends, because I can't keep my mouth shut, and Mary Anne is very quiet and very shy.

The original foursome of the BSC was made up of two dyads: Mary Anne and Kristy; and Claudia and Stacey. Compared to Stacey and Claudia, Kristy and Mary Anne are less sophisticated (less interested in markers of teenage femininity, such as nail polish, makeup, and trendy clothes), more intimate (they've lived across the street from each other their entire lives and Mary Anne refers to her as "like a sister" [BSC #4]), and more opposite (with Kristy being characterized as more masculine and aggressive and Mary Anne and more feminine and passive). They are something like the dyad of Jo and Beth in *Little Women.* Claudia, another character, describes Kristy and Mary Anne in BSC #2:

Even though Kristy and Mary Anne are in seventh grade, just like Stacey and I are, they can be very childish. . . . Mary Anne still dresses up her stuffed animals. And they even *look* younger than we do. . . . And both of them wear kind of little girl clothes—kilts and plain blouses and stuff like that.

These differences—and similarities—between Kristy and Mary Anne also show up in the characters' handwriting.

Mary Anne, the club secretary, is described as organized, neat, and almost painfully shy. Because her mother died when she was a baby, Mary Anne is raised exclusively by her father, whom critic Joseph Noshpitz referred to as "infantilizing." Mary Anne is sensitive, a good listener, and a girl who doesn't like being the center of attention. She's also the only member of the club to have a boyfriend. With these qualities in mind, it seems unsurprising that Tommasino created a very traditional, almost Spencerian script to be associated with Mary Anne.

Elena Schilder, a former reader of the BSC, has written that she perceived Mary Anne's writing to be "old fashioned and feminine," two traits associated with Spencerian script. This script, as the writer Kitty Burns Florey indicates, was popular from "before the Civil War to the end of the Victorian era," and it

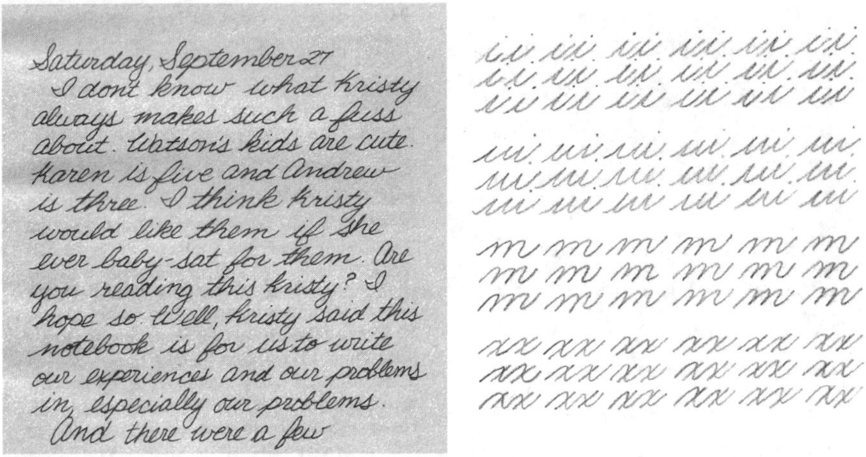

FIG. 4: "MARY ANNE'S" PENMANSHIP FROM BSC #1 (LEFT) AND A SAMPLE OF SPENCERIAN SCRIPT (RIGHT, COURTESY KING KAISER)

was associated with good manners. As Florey says, surely this was the "script of a lady." Although Mary Anne's penmanship is not a perfect replica of Spencerian script, it does more closely resemble the cursive that the babysitters would have learned in school.

Handwriting historian Tamara Thornton saw Spencerian penmanship differently than Florey, writing that she perceived people who performed excellent Spencerian script to be invested in "conformity and ordinariness," their "imitation of penmanship models" suggesting a lack of originality. Mary Anne's passivity as a character—someone overrun by her father and already under the care of a boyfriend—resonates with Thornton's take. Mary Anne's loyalty to her father and her boyfriend can be read as conformity to patriarchal values.

If Mary Anne's traditional girlish script was inspired in part by Spencerian lettering, then Kristy's handwriting seems inspired more by a different script, one known as the Palmer method. Kristy is described as a natural leader, bossy, loud, and active. While Mary Anne is knitting and dressing up her stuffed animals, Kristy wants to earn money, establishes BSC club rules, and coaches a children's softball team. Take for example the scene that starts BSC #3: "'As president of the Baby-sitters Club,' said Kristy Thomas, 'I hereby move that we figure out what to do when Mrs. Newton goes to the hospital to have her baby.'" Unsurprisingly, Mary Anne instantly seconds the motion. Stacey, the narrator of this installment, notes a few pages later that Kristy is "sort of a tomboy."

Kristy's handwriting is visually similar to New American Cursive, a spinoff handwriting model that responded to the work of Palmer, who created a new script for American merchants in the 1860s. Palmer believed that Spencerian script was too ornate to be used by working people. Thornton summarized how he sought to disrupt the Spencerian script by offering a form that was less fussy:

> What [Palmer] described as copybook writing is very pretty, but, he added, that's all. With its ornate forms, which often required extensive lifting of the pen and meticulous shading, which entailed the reworking of letters, copybook script was more akin to painting than to writing.

The Palmer style, in contrast, sought utility—what Palmer called "real, live, usable, legible, and salable penmanship." The style is often described as "muscular." Palmer wanted to enable people to write efficiently using the muscles of their body. Palmer wrote, "If the movement is right, and its application right, the letter will take care of itself and good letters must be the result."

Kristy's penmanship aligns with Palmer's style, which historian Joe Coffey claims "hardly changed over a hundred years," and which Palmer created because he believed that working Americans needed a more movement-oriented script than Spencerian models provided. This history of the script also aligns to Kristy's aggressive, action-oriented personality. It is no mistake that Elena Schilder perceives Kristy's handwriting as "tight, controlled, cheerful cursive of a young athlete."

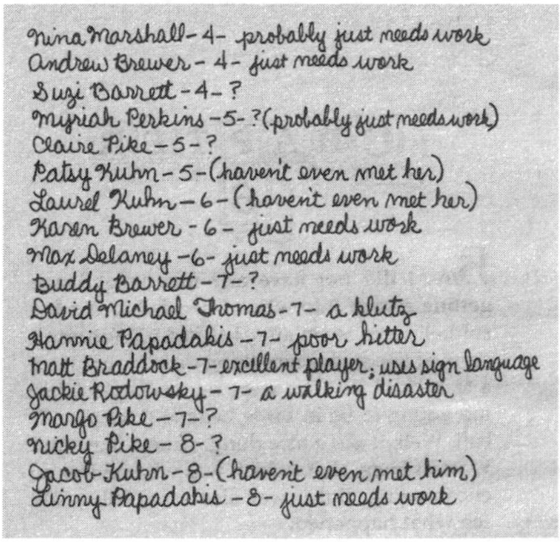
Nina Marshall - 4 - probably just needs work
Andrew Brewer - 4 - just needs work
Suzi Barrett - 4 - ?
Myriah Perkins - 5 - ? (probably just needs work)
Claire Pike - 5 - ?
Patsy Kuhn - 5 - (haven't even met her)
Laurel Kuhn - 6 - (haven't even met her)
Karen Brewer - 6 - just needs work
Max Delaney - 6 - just needs work
Buddy Barrett - 7 - ?
David Michael Thomas - 7 - a klutz
Hannie Papadakis - 7 - poor hitter
Matt Braddock - 7 - excellent player; uses sign language
Jackie Rodowsky - 7 - a walking disaster
Margo Pike - 7 - ?
Nicky Pike - 8 - ?
Jacob Kuhn - 8 - (haven't even met him)
Linny Papadakis - 8 - just needs work

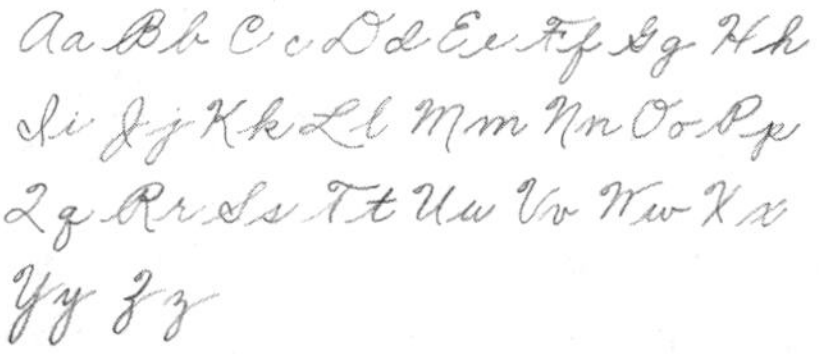

Fig 5: Kristy's handwriting (left) and a sample of Palmer script (above, courtesy King Kaiser)

Spencerian and Palmer scripts offer variations of gender performance that highlight the differences between Mary Anne, a rule-abiding good girl, and Kristy, an entrepreneurial tomboy. In her foundational book *Gender Trouble,* Judith Butler theorizes gender as produced through the repeated stylization of the body and its movements. What we see here is that gender is also coded through something as simple as the way a young person chooses to write a capital *S*. While technically both the Spencerian and the New American cursive feature the same symbol, the Spencerian *S* is what Tommasino would call more "swashy" and loopy, while the Palmer *S* is less so, designed more for functionality than style. Such handwriting choices offered a stage for gendered performance. When readers like me imitated these scripts, we were also performing tomboyishness and femininity.

If Mary Anne and Kristy are foundational and relatable characters whose handwriting is modeled on longstanding styles, other BSC characters—Stacey and Claudia—seem less easily mapped onto historical precedents. They are also positioned as the kind of characters the other characters hope to become. As Mary Anne said in the fourth installment in the series:

> Stacey is glamorous. . . . She's very sophisticated, and is even allowed to have her hair permed, so that she has this fabulous-looking shaggy blonde mane, and she wears the neatest clothes . . . I'd give anything to be like Stacey. . . . Stacey often creates a sensation. So does Claudia. . . . She's pretty glamorous herself.

While Mary Anne and Kristy's scripts seem to be variations of traditional styles, Stacey's script seems to offer something more exciting and unique.

AN INNOVATIVE SCRIPT: STACEY

Stacey is presented as a New York girl who has everything: cute clothes, blonde hair, blue eyes, and effortless sophistication. Martin complicates this "dream girl" by also making Stacey diabetic, a move that has been regarded as progressive by critics. Stacey's handwriting, in contrast to Kristy's and Mary Anne's, seems to have no clear predecessor. In a message exchange, Martin told me that she wanted Stacey's handwriting to be something "fanciful."

Tommasino went to work, remembering the penmanship styles of the girls she went to middle school with during the seventies. She remembered seeing this handwriting on the notebooks that students passed around in schools: "Notebooks were a big thing. We had these loose-leaf binders—kids would carry them on the bus and throughout school. They were made of denim cloth, and people were always writing on them." Of special importance was the way that someone's name appeared:

> I remember . . . how important it was to have an impressive signature. Your signature was almost like your personal logo, and so those loose-leaf covers would be filled with beautifully designed handwritten names. The really popular kids would write strongly and boldly, and the girls would add things like stars and hearts for decoration. When it came to Stacey and her personality, I'm sure I imagined someone like her from my own school days and the handwriting just followed suit.

Stacey's penmanship is an example of a girl-generated script, modeled not on copybooks and ideas from authorities but on what girls' writing actually looked like in a particular moment in time. Her lettering looked like this:

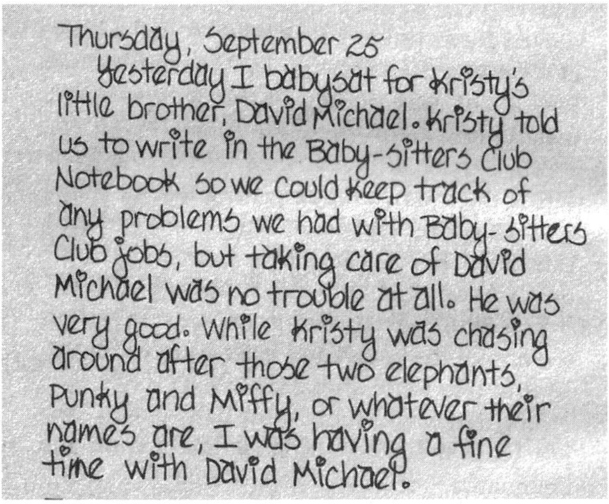

FIG. 6: STACEY'S HANDWRITING FROM BSC #1

Perhaps unsurprisingly, of the characters in the BSC, Stacey's writing seems to have inspired the most imitation. One imitator was Katie, an adult who vividly remembered her attachment to the series as an adolescent. In a post on her personal blog about this topic, Katie included an image that featured two handwriting styles: the left was Stacey's handwriting from one of the BSC books; the right was a recent to-do list. She noted her shock at how much she and Stacey had in common, from their love of Cinderella and New York City to "even our handwriting!" This image was accompanied by a few paragraphs describing the impact Stacey had on Katie's life.

> As much as the BSC had an influence on my life, Stacey McGill had a larger one. . . . I loved getting pure NYC memories of Stacey. And it's probably what led me to my obsession with the city. . . . I loved Stacey because I wanted so badly to be sophisticated as a kid, because these books came at time when I felt so awkward and not the least bit cool. I was more like a cross between Mary Anne and Mallory, honestly. Stacey gave me an escape, and she gave me some dreams to hold onto through those awkward years. And I did make it through them, in one piece. (And I did eventually make it to NYC, too!)

Katie read the BSC books actively, scooping up the best parts of Stacey to inform a new vision of herself. Her aspirational connection to Stacey ("I wanted so badly to be sophisticated") led to her imitation of Stacey, including circles over her *i*'s, a variation on Stacey's cutesy hearts.

Katie's experience is an example of what Janice Radway calls "narrative gleaning." She writes that girls rummage through culture as though it were a crowded attic of cast-offs, looking for something—anything—that suits their burgeoning sense of self, or their deepest and most inarticulate desires. In her words, "children gradually develop resources by taking up *particular* languages, objects, gestures, and habits, and those that are presented to them as they emerge always *within and through* culture. Children make and remake themselves with materials ready to hand." Readers' imitation of the scripts in the Baby-Sitters Club books is one tangible way that BSC readers engaged with the series on this level.

Radway's personal memory of narrative gleaning involved penmanship, too. She remembers mimicking the way her third grade teacher made the number seven, with a little line through the bottom of the number. Decades later, Radway was still drawing that line through her own sevens.

SCRIPTING OURSELVES

In a series that's well known for offering young girls models with whom they could identify ("I'm a Mary Anne"), the handwriting offers a tangible performance of a character, which allows readers to see them in a more intimate and realistic way. It's almost like getting to rummage through the purses of the women in *Sex in the City*, to see in actual physical detail how one character differs from another. Such intimate information is relevant not only for understanding the series, but also for understanding where we stand in relation to the series. In the BSC books, consistency is key, with a second chapter that's nearly identical across all the books and handwriting styles that stay static over decades. If I like a character, I can fashion myself after her—taking on not only her adjectives, but also the motions of her hand, the appearance of her signature.

But what readers take from texts is also unpredictable. I'm reminded of one reader, summarizing her perspective of the characters in a comment board on Jezebel's site:

@TheFormerJuneBronson: I most vividly remember that the description of the girls was word-for-word the same in every book, so that was always 2 pages or so you could skip right over. (Kristy-tomboy! Maryanne-shy! Claudia-wild fashion! Dawn-California! Mallory-wanted a pink sweatshirt with rhinestones! I can't believe I still remember all that.)

In this quickly written response, many of the characters' core details came through—yet, what's the deal with her memory of Mallory? Why does she recall, more than any other detail about her, that "Mallory wanted a pink sweatshirt with rhinestones"? It's a totally random thing to remember, but it also captures the haziness and unpredictability of reading itself. No matter how clear the signal—and no matter how consistent the handwriting—the ways we fashion ourselves in relation to the texts we encounter will always be uncertain.

If I had relied only on memory, I would have said that the babysitter I most wanted to emulate was Stacey. Yet my diary tells a different and probably truer story: there was something about Kristy that spoke to me, and there was a tangible way that I responded. I was not and am not alone. "I've experimented endlessly with different scripts," writes Florey, "straight up, right-slanting, left-slanting, print-like, florid, spare, minimalist, maximalist, round, spiky, highly legible, insouciantly scrawled. . . . What I was really looking for, of course, was myself."

The BSC and Us

ON SEEING OURSELVES REFLECTED (OR NOT)

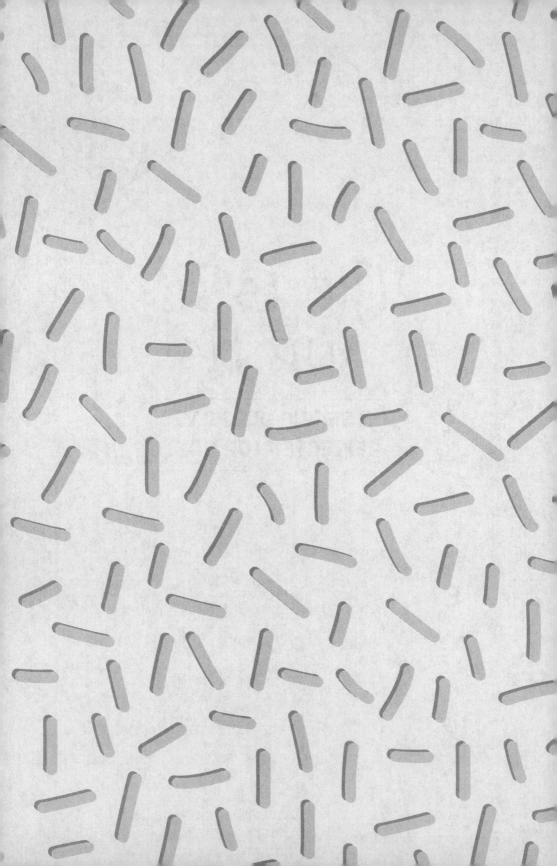

Let's Talk About Jessi

Yodassa Williams

Jessica Ramsey is a fictional young Black femme pioneer. The eldest child of the first Black family to integrate Stoneybrook, Connecticut, Jessi is the first and only African American member of the Baby-Sitters Club. While she serves as a junior officer and is not introduced to the series until book #14: *Hello, Mallory,* she holds a place as one of the most essential characters in the BSC universe. Jessi brings wit, artistic passion, and a thoughtful spirit to the series, but even further, she represents the important perspective of a Black girl entering and living within a very white world.

Jessi was a personal childhood hero for me. I discovered Ann M. Martin's series around 1994, growing up in the suburbs of Cincinnati, Ohio. I was about eight or nine, a precocious Jamaican American girl in an expansively Caucasian landscape. Similar to the Ramseys, we were the first Black family to move into our neighborhood. And similar to Jessi, I found my Blackness prompted tension in others. It truly irked me that I couldn't exist without the static. The additional surveillance in stores. The shocked reactions when I casually spoke in proper English. The taunting in school for being an "Oreo." I grew up with the feeling of being extra watched, extra judged, always under the white gaze. I had constant anxiety that I was wrong and couldn't figure how to be right.

Each night after dinner, my mom and I would watch the news. The screen would overflow with recent crimes and warnings, nearly always featuring Black faces along with assumptions of guilt. "That's all they think of us. They want us all in jail," my mother would sneer at the TV. "That's why we have to work so hard, to prove we are worth more than they think, you see?" Now, this was mid-1990s America, and my family are Black immigrants. So the concept that in America, Black people had to work twice as hard to earn half as much as white people was pressed without room for argument in my home. Yet this maxim never quite sat right inside me. Why should I have to become something else in order to receive acceptance from people who think less of me? Why should I have to perform perfection in order to belong among white people? Why isn't who I am good enough to be worthy, brown skin and all?

Around this time, Martin had already written and published seventy-five books in the Baby-Sitters Club series. My local library had every single one of these books, their pastel binders lined up like candy in the youth reading section. I loved the Nancy Drew and Goosebumps series, but my brain exploded with excitement when I saw a Black girl depicted on one of the BSC covers. And so I was sold on the Baby-Sitters Club. I devoured the first books in days, eager to meet Jessica Ramsey and discover her secrets of belonging.

Many tween books I read around that time overlooked racial issues or had no characters of color with agency to call things out. In modeling her fictional universe after our own, Martin does not allow racial tensions to be overlooked. Jessi's first scenes as a character in the Baby-Sitters Club universe are uncomfortable ones as Martin is reflecting the realities of the late 1980s and '90s suburban integration. While not directly calling it racism or bigotry, the books make clear that the town's reaction to the Ramseys is uniquely cold because they are the first Black family to move in. As a young Black reader, I was grateful these books did not soften the reaction of Stoneybrook citizens to the Ramsey family. I am grateful, too, that through Jessi and Mallory, her white friend and ally, Martin created an opportunity for readers to see racism as malicious and empathize with a girl targeted for having brown skin.

In *Hello, Mallory,* the unkind and petty reactions of various town members to the Ramseys' arrival are spotlighted and unpacked through Mallory's point of view. There are no other Black students in the sixth grade, Mallory tells us, and only six Black kids in the entire middle school. Mallory's empathetic thoughts invite readers to care about Jessi's experience in school from the start. "I wondered what being the only black student in your grade would feel like," she says. "I guessed it would feel no different from being the only anything in your grade. . . . But Jessica's coffee-colored skin was there for the world to see."

Jessi is an instant curiosity as a result of her appearance being so rare. But what disturbs Mallory (and, through their identifications with her as narrator, the reader) is that Jessi doesn't receive a standard welcome and is instead attacked in subtle and overt ways, both by those in power and by her peers. Importantly under Mallory's focused lens, we see these reactions to Jessi for what they are: senseless and cruel. When their homeroom teacher denies Jessi a chance to introduce herself, despite this being the pattern set by other new students' arrival, Mallory finds it unfair. Later in the day, when a student uses rubber bands to attack Jessi, Mallory observes with concern another teacher ignoring the abuse. And at lunch, students openly mock Jessi for existing at their school. "Can you believe that new girl?" one student says. Another adds, "She's black . . . she doesn't, you know, belong here." As the conversation continues, the girls laughing, one of them says, "I bet her real name is Mobobwee or something."

Jessi has done nothing to deserve this instant hostility and rejection. And while Mallory hears these comments and feels badly for Jessi, she struggles to reject them and speak up against her peers. Although Mallory processes with clarity that it is wrong that Stoneybrook treats Jessi as undesirable because of her skin color, she is a bit of a slow burn when it comes to truly standing up against the bullies. After she witnesses her group of mates openly dis Jessi, Mallory has a chance to join her at her lunch table. "I wanted to get up and move, but I didn't." I cannot help but think about how profound that moment could have been. Later, when Mallory finally introduces herself to Jessi, hoping that this mysterious new girl could become the best friend she has been yearning for, she finds her charming, funny, and generous in nature.

After Mallory opens up to Jessi about being rejected from the Baby-Sitters Club when she fails an unfair test, Jessi opens up in turn, sharing her experiences with racism in the town and her fears about how it will affect her dancing. This is when Mallory truly steps into her allyship and diagnoses racism as wholly pointless. "It doesn't seem fair," Mallory states. "And it's awful not to belong. . . . Maybe we're not the problem, maybe everyone else is." Though Mallory's unfair rejection from the BSC is not equivalent to the unfairness of racial injustice, her decision to empathize with and relate to Jessi invites the reader to empathize and relate as well.

I intimately recognized the pain of not belonging forced by the kind of black-and-white world that Mallory describes. But from the perspective of the inside out, as a Black girl questioning why the white world remains withholding, it was both curious and empowering to read about Stoneybrook's racism through Mallory, a white character. Until then, I had never really seen the emotional effect of racism processed in such an empathetic way from the outside. *Ah,* I thought. *Mallory gets it!* That we, as readers, meet Jessi first through Mallory feels purposeful, and in my opinion, well executed. Mallory moves past the fear and small-mindedness of others, and comes to see Jessi is the true friend she has been waiting for her whole life. It's hard not to wonder why the whole town doesn't see Jessi like Mallory does.

And Jessi's perception of the world? Crystal. Martin reveals that Jessi is completely aware of the racism going on in Stoneybrook. She sees that no one will talk to her or play with her sister, Becca. She notes the absence of neighbors stopping by with food and coupons; there's no "Welcome Wagon Lady" who invites her family to the neighborhood. She can't process how she or her family could ever belong in this town. Jessi confesses to Mallory that she doubts she will even join ballet lessons because everyone is so rejecting of her for being Black. "They'd never give me the lead, even if I were as good as Pavlova. . . . You know what would happen if they did give me the lead? . . . Everyone would be upset that a black girl got it instead of a white girl." Jessi reveals a heartbreaking fear in this passage. That no matter how excellent she becomes, she will still never be accepted in this setting. *That's exactly it,* I thought. The feeling that I was sure would haunt me my whole life. That even if I did manage to work twice as hard, or become twice as good, I would still never ever achieve belonging in a world that presents white as right.

Jessi and I also share another thing in common: ballet. It's like envisioning a past life, it feels so distant to me now, but as a young girl I was very serious about my dance lessons. From ages three to fourteen, I took ballet, tap, and hip-hop classes every single week and competed in regional and state competitions on weekends. After making the personal decision that I didn't want to shift to pointe shoes or pursue dance as a career, I left dancing and disassociated from the entire experience.

How did I know then that I couldn't pursue this passion further? Because after every big competition, our choreographer would go over our performance tapes with us. And I will never forget the one performance where my timing was off slightly from the team. Our choreographer paused and replayed that part over and over, saying, "You see how bad it looks when we're off, and for you especially, it is glaring to the judges because of how much you stand out.

We can't have that." Oh, did I mention I was the only Black girl on an all-white dance squad? Yeah. So "how much I stand out" was a Midwestern nice reference for "you have dark skin, everyone else has light skin." I started to have small panic attacks before performances, sure that my Blackness would bring the whole team down. Dancing, which once felt so freeing I could forget my body, now felt suffocated by the all too familiar static. When I quit, I felt released, but also deeply sad. What would have happened if I didn't feel I needed to fit into a white landscape? Are we just set in an impossible position, we Jessis of the world? Wanting and working to be our best, but never able to achieve belonging?

As *Hello, Mallory*'s story advances, Mallory and Jessi link up to create Kids Incorporated, their very own child-minding partnership, born from Mallory's initial rejection from the BSC. After some time, they are asked to become official BSC members. These events are monumental to Jessi as she finds her place in Stoneybrook. As a young reader, I understood that Jessi overcame the racism in Stoneybrook through her connections to others. But as an adult, I see there was more to the magic sauce than Mallory's empathy and joining the BSC that resulted in Jessi's belonging as a Black girl. Jessi's unhidden secret is this: she belonged to herself, first.

Martin makes Jessi's strength of spirit clear from her first appearance on the page. Seen through Mallory's eyes, Jessi is described as "graceful" and dignified, refusing to acknowledge her peers' puerile responses to her presence. Jessi enters Stoneybrook fresh, unknown, and very vulnerable, but it's evident that she's experienced thriving in a very different world to this new one. Personally, I would have been a bag of nerves and maybe passed out from anxiety. But Jessi remains strong, poised, and focused on her first day in what turns out to be a hostile environment. When she is hit with rubber bands by a bully but persists gracefully in class, she summons the courage of Ruby Bridges, the first Black girl to desegregate an all-white school in 1960. When she rises high above the abuse and reads peacefully at lunch time, ignoring the whispers about her and her family, she channels former First Lady Michelle Obama. Jessi does not allow her character to be defined by the assumptions of Stoneybrook. She is clear in seeing that the problem is with *them* and not *her*.

As a preteen, I definitely craved approval from others. I remember quietly studying my fellow students, trying to figure out how to manufacture social power. Is it the clothing? The way you sit? How often you speak up in class? The pain of being on the outside made me look for problems within. But

Jessi? Despite the alienation and bullying she is forced to endure, Jessi remains steadfast to herself. She does not beg for their acceptance and does not think of changing who she is for others. Jessi decides to audition for the ballet after all. She is ecstatic when she tells Mallory she's been accepted. "I got in! To the advanced class! And everyone was super nice." It's clear from her passion in the craft that she followed her heart, not her fear. The powerful Jessi lesson here is this: don't allow yourself to be defined by people who see you as less than.

In adulthood, I find myself still in awe of Jessi's ability to maintain calm in the face of so much. How did she do it? I perceive what gives Jessi the edge to thrive is that she has an already powerfully evolved presence of self. Jessi comes from a highly supportive family and community who reinforced her talents and intrinsic value at a young age. In Oakley, New Jersey, Jessi was raised with her mother, father, sister, and brother. She also lived in the same neighborhood as her grandparents, aunts, uncles, and cousin. Her best friend was her cousin Keisha, who shared her birthday. Her dance school was filled with many Black students and she played Clara in the Nutcracker. Jessi's first hometown was a world of family and intimacy that reflected her back to herself as completely worthy.

From this nurturing foundation, Jessi has developed resiliency of character. So, even under the spiritual torture of racism in Stoneybrook, Jessi's roots hold firm. She takes strength and blooms. I am grateful to feel my own story represented through Jessi. Through Jessi's introduction to the series, Martin grants readers the opportunity to empathize with a young girl living in a town that treats her as "other." In seeing her face on the cover art and reading her adventures in babysitting and ballet, I felt seen as a young Black girl living in the Midwest who just wanted to do and be excellent. Jessica Ramsey remains an unforgettable Jedi Master in the art of Black Girl Magic.

The Truth About Being a Preteen Diabetic

Jami Sailor

Even before I started to write the fifth issue of my zine, *Your Secretary*, about being diagnosed with diabetes as a tween, I knew I wanted the cover to be a take on the original cover of the Baby-Sitters Club book *The Truth About Stacey*. To me, the 1986 cover was not only iconic, but also exemplified what non-diabetic folks think is the main struggle diabetics face. We see Stacey, sunglasses perched on the top of her head above her long blonde hair and smiling face. She's looking directly at the reader with her arm around her babysitting charge, Charlotte Johannsen. The girls stand before a wall of jars filled with candy; a glass counter containing more sweets separates us from them. The cover of the 2010 reprint simply features a drawing of a thickly frosted chocolate cupcake. When I see these covers I want to scream. Okay, we get it! Diabetics aren't supposed to eat sweets. But the act of controlling one's blood sugar is much more complicated than not eating candy and cupcakes. Illustrated by Ramsey Beyer, the cover of the issue, which I titled *The Truth About Your Secretary* in homage to Stacey, featured an adult me behind the candy counter with my dog, Erasmus, standing up on his hind legs, in place of Charlotte. The zine foregrounds how diabetes had shaped my teen years and how my personal diabetic care changed as I became a young adult—a topic

83

covered by the Stacey books with more complexity and nuance than any other kids' book at the time.

Stacey McGill was one of the first fictional young diabetics whose story was available to the masses in the late 1980s and early 1990s. Anastasia "Stacey" McGill moves to Stoneybrook just before the action of the first book begins. Because Stacey has an affinity and loyalty to her hometown of New York City, she is identified as fashionable and relatively sophisticated compared to most of her Stoneybrook counterparts. Stacey is enthusiastically interested in boys and even (gasp) temporarily leaves the club for a boy. Stacey is good at math and is the treasurer of the BSC. Like me, Stacey is a type 1 (insulin-dependent) diabetic. While there were many ways in which Stacey and I were different, the story of Stacey's diagnosis was familiar to me, as was her struggle to grasp some independence from her parents with regard to her health care. The challenge of having friends who understood only up to a point; and, of course, the day-to-day effort to control blood sugar through the ups-and-downs of adolescence: these were things we, and many young diabetics, had in common.

At eleven years old I was far from sophisticated. Living in Metro Detroit, I had little concept of where NYC was on a physical or cultural map. Math class gave me headaches. I wasn't blonde and instead looked more like (coded ugly duckling) Mallory Pike. My favorite outfit was a pair of my mom's stirrup pants and a gold satin jacket with the Jordache horse on the back whose yarn mane I would charge my classmates a quarter to touch. I'd rather punch a boy than go on a date with one. While I took a class about becoming a babysitter when I turned thirteen, I did not enjoy childcare, and I distinctly remember losing a babysitting job after leaving a Rage Against the Machine cassette in the family's tape deck. I also didn't have any friends.

While the Stacey books that deal directly with her diabetes might have interested me as a kid, it wasn't until deep into adulthood that I read them. As a tween, I scoured the library and bookstores for trashy young adult horror by Christopher Pike, Diane Hoh, and R. L. Stine's Fear Street series, viewing the BSC and Francine Pascal's Sweet Valley Twins as too goody-two-shoes and too girly. But as an adult, I sought out Stacey's stories to see what my peers might have learned about diabetes from the BSC—and I was surprised to see our experiences trying to control our diabetes were similar.

Here's an overly simplified crash course to get you up to speed on type 1 diabetes if your only point of reference (like those damn BSC covers) is "diabetics shouldn't eat cake and candy." Diabetes is a chronic condition affecting the endocrine system. Type 1 diabetes, formerly known alternately as juvenile diabetes and insulin-dependent diabetes, is when the pancreas produces no insulin. Insulin is a hormone that converts sugar in the blood into energy. Type 1 diabetics manage their diabetes through a mixture of diet, insulin injections, blood glucose monitoring, and exercise. Some diabetics take insulin several times a day using syringes or prefilled pens. Others use insulin pumps. Monitoring blood sugar is important for diabetics. Diabetics work to keep their blood sugar levels from getting too low (hypoglycemia) or too high (hyperglycemia). Low blood sugar can cause a diabetic to experience loss of coordination and confused thoughts, have blurred vision and speech, and fall into a coma. Diabetics can also experience comas if their blood sugar is too high. It's very damned if you do, damned if you don't. Diabetes care is a balancing act.

In *The Truth About Stacey*, we learn that Stacey was diagnosed after passing out due to hyperglycemia (too much sugar) in her NYC school's lunchroom. Before this moment she had displayed many of the symptoms of undiagnosed diabetes, including extreme thirst, weight loss, and frequent urination. After the incident at school, Stacey spent some time in the hospital having her blood sugar regulated and learning how to take care of her diabetes through insulin injections and diet. When she returned to school, she did not share her diagnosis and was ostracized by her former best friend Laine and the rest of her friend group. After her initial diagnosis, Stacey frequently missed school because her parents made appointments with new doctors in hopes that some miracle treatment would help Stacey. Their decision to move to Stoneybrook was motivated by the belief that suburban life would make it easier for Stacey to control her diabetes.

My diagnosis may have been less dramatic, but it didn't feel that way to tween me. Like Stacey, I showed signs of diabetes before my diagnosis. I clearly remember drinking can after can of regular (non-diet) soda during the month before I was diagnosed. I also peed every fifteen minutes. I rapidly lost weight. The year was 1990 and I had somehow convinced (read: bribed with free tickets) three of my classmates to attend a New Kids on the Block concert with me. My dad bought these tickets to "share with my friends," not knowing (or more likely in denial) that I didn't have three friends to bring. As the concert approached, my parents had considered not letting me go because I'd had a severe flu two weeks before the show, but I begged and pleaded. One of my most poignant memories related to this time in my life are the symptoms of hyperglycemia that I felt throughout the concert. My dad, who was our escort, bought me several overpriced sodas at the venue concession stand. The lines I had to wait through to go to the bathroom after consuming them were excruciatingly long. I am not sure how I made it through that night guzzling down sugary soda pop, sweating, and screaming. Less than a week later I found myself, like Stacey, spending a week in the hospital having my blood sugar regulated and learning how to manage my diabetes through insulin injections and diet.

Like the McGills, my family moved the year after my diagnosis. At the time I believed that my parents finally had taken pity on me and were moving so I could start anew—someplace where my classmates hadn't known me since kindergarten and witnessed every embarrassing thing that had happened since. Finally I would escape the incessant reminders of the time I pretended to be my "identical cousin" or the time I had accepted a dare to poop alongside the creek in our backyard! But the truth of our move was related to money, a topic that hung over our heads omnipresent yet, unlike my diabetes, was never talked about. Like Stacey's parents, my mom and dad focused on my health care, sometimes ignoring other problems that might be the cause of stress in our families. Stacey's parents made huge decisions based on caring for her diabetes, decisions that seemed to mask some of their own problems.

✶ ✶ ✶

On the surface the "truth" about Stacey is that she is diabetic. But from the very first book, the members of the BSC and readers know about Stacey's diabetes. (This does not stop them, Stacey's best friend Claudia in particular, from constantly consuming high sugar snacks in front of her.) Diabetes is an invisible illness and not a diagnosis that is usually known unless it is revealed. There are diabetics who do not tell others, including their close friends and coworkers, that they are diabetic. The few times I have "known" someone has diabetes without them telling me have been because they are wearing an insulin pump or continuous glucose monitor, assistive devices that help diabetics maintain their blood glucose level.

My parents did not see secrecy as an option. During my first stay in the hospital my parents contacted the administration of my school about my diabetes. Though one of the least popular kids in my grade, I still received an outpouring of get-well cards signed by my classmates. I don't know what they were told about diabetes, but my classmates took my diagnosis in stride. One enterprising bully did create a new version of the Diarrhea Song from the movie *Parenthood* and sang "When you're sliding into first and you feel your pancreas burst. Diabetes. Diabetes." This was a welcome break from the usual harassment about my flaming red hair or the ease with which I would begin crying (and how quickly I could go from crying to violence).

The effort of taking care of my diabetes without trying to hide it is difficult enough. Discussions about whether it is appropriate to test one's blood sugar or inject insulin in front of other people are common for the diabetic community. At heart, these are discussions about disclosure. Being public about one's diabetic care exemplifies self-care and creates visibility for what can sometimes be an isolating and invisible disease. Those who argue that diabetics should go to the bathroom to take insulin or blood tests often cite people's fears of needles and blood as justification, but the implication is that diabetics should hide while caring for themselves. I fall on the side of disclosing my diabetic status and taking shots in public. I once did a demonstration in which I tested my blood sugar as part of a job interview.

While some would advise against being too open with medical information, being open about my diabetes has helped keep me safe. It might not be the first thing you find out about me when we meet, but if we spend any time together you are going to find out I am diabetic. Once Stacey stands up to her parents regarding her diabetes care, she also lands on the side of disclosure—as does Ann M. Martin. Every time Stacey is introduced, over and over in the second chapter of every BSC book, her diabetes is disclosed. This disclosure helps destigmatize diabetes care. Much like seeing someone wearing a continuous glucose monitor at their job, filling up a syringe with insulin at a restaurant, or taking their blood sugar at the park, Stacey's successes and struggles with her diabetic care throughout the BSC series create visibility and open up conversations for young adults surrounding not just diabetes but other chronic illnesses.

As a child, being diabetic was probably one of the least embarrassing or shameful things about me, and I viewed my parents telling everyone about my condition as an attempt to keep me safe and healthy. As I became a teenager, I viewed diabetes as an inconvenience. Having to test my blood sugar, an act that involved pricking my finger to get a sample of blood, slowed me down. Calculating the amount of insulin compared to the amount of food I was going to eat was math and I revolted against the act of constantly thinking about what I was consuming. It wasn't just that I wanted to eat candy and cupcakes, it was that I wanted to eat whatever I wanted without thinking about it. There was also what I later began describing as "the detritus of diabetes." Actively taking care of diabetes doesn't just take time and intention, it takes lots of medical supplies, which become medical waste. I hated having to carry around bottles of insulin, syringes, test strips, a blood glucose monitor, a lancing device to prick my fingers. Even worse was carrying around all these things once I had used them: bloody test strips, used syringes and lancets. More times than I can count a whole slew of used syringes have spilled out of a bag or purse. I've stood up and left a trail of blood-speckled test strips in my wake. The everyday stresses of living with diabetes add up for Stacey as well.

✳   ✳   ✳

Diabetics sometimes react to the stress of diabetes with noncompliance: that is, by ignoring or avoiding parts of their diabetic treatment. In *Stacey's Emergency* (BSC #43), Stacey has moved back to Stoneybrook with her mother after her parents' recent divorce. She's been falling behind in school, is struggling with exhaustion and mood swings, and feels her parents are always putting her in the middle of their fights. To cope, Stacey starts sneaking high sugar snacks like cupcakes, brownies, and chocolate bars. It's also revealed that Stacey is a brittle diabetic and her blood sugar levels are more difficult to control. One cause of brittle diabetes is stress. Uh-oh, Stacey's got plenty of it.

While visiting her father in New York, Stacey starts experiencing signs of high blood sugar—constant thirst and needing to get up to use the bathroom repeatedly during the night. At first she resists her father's suggestion to test her blood sugar, but ultimately she agrees. "Something is very wrong," Stacey tells us. "I couldn't deny it any longer." When her father can't get ahold of her endocrinologist, Stacey ends up in the hospital. It's difficult to believe that Stacey didn't know her symptoms were directly related not just to her diabetes but also to her consumption of high sugar foods. Still, she denies that something is wrong—until she can't anymore. This is a common experience for young diabetics. It was definitely my experience throughout my teen years. Noncompliance is common not only for teenagers with diabetes but for diabetics of all ages.

One of the main reasons that I preferred hanging out at my best friend Melissa's house in middle school was that her family bought Pop-Tarts and soda pop in bulk, and they didn't pay attention to what we ate. While I did have some experiences like Stacey's, where she sneaks and hides chocolate bars and brownies from her friends' and clients' houses, at Melissa's house I did not need to sneak or steal. It was a cornucopia of individually wrapped Rice Krispies Treats and Little Debbie Snack Cakes.

Like Stacey, bingeing on high sugar foods, coupled with not testing my blood sugar, resulted in me spending part of the summer between middle and high school in the hospital. During my time in the hospital having my blood sugar levels regulated, my endocrinologist suggested to my parents that my refusal to maintain my blood sugar might be an unconscious form of self-harm. My refusal to adhere to a diabetic meal plan or properly monitor my blood sugar levels were in part a denial that I had diabetes. The truth behind my doctor's prognosis would take years for me to accept. As they were for Stacey, the side effects of high blood sugar became a baseline for me. Exhaustion became the norm, as did the constant thirst and frequent urination. The Stacey books take on the immediacy of high blood sugar but do not address the long-term outcomes of teenagers who do not or cannot control their blood sugar levels. If Stacey continued to ignore the signs of high blood sugar we could have had books like *Stacey's Chronic Yeast Infection* or *Stacey's Search for a New Kidney*.

✳ ✳ ✳

When contemplating what "truth" the title is referring to, Stacey's loneliness stands out to me. Having a chronic illness can be lonely. Throughout *The Truth About Stacey*, Stacey worries about the BSC breaking up because of a rival babysitting group. She doesn't want to experience the loneliness she felt when Laine stopped being her friend. While the other BSC members know about her diabetes, their support is only surface level. They do not change their behavior or food choices. They do not check in on Stacey about her health or stress levels until she is already in the hospital. Stacey's parents are the only ones who discuss her diabetic maintenance or control with her, and only to tell her decisions they have made without consulting her. Food intake, insulin, stress, and exercise: Stacey is constantly monitoring herself. We see that sometimes she needs support from those around her.

The two covers I've seen of the popular 2006 graphic novel adaptations of *The Truth About Stacey* point to a truth that falls into the subtext of Stacey's stories. In both, the other BSC members are together smiling. On one cover they are sharing candy; on the other they appear to be talking. Stacey is set apart from them, frowning. Diabetes sets Stacey apart from the other BSC members, not merely because of what she isn't supposed to eat, but all the other things Stacey is supposed to do. Stacey has to advocate for her own treatment. She has to be aware of how her body feels. She has to face the consequences when she ignores her stress and blood sugar levels. She has to manage her diabetes alone, with no other diabetic or chronically ill teens with whom to commiserate. While the BSC books do a great job overall of conveying what it's like to live as a preteen with diabetes, what strikes me as the most painfully realistic point is Stacey's loneliness.

As a kid, I went to a summer camp for diabetic children and teenagers. This was my first time away from my parents. All the other campers and most of the counselors were diabetic like me. I got to hear about other campers' struggles with maintaining their blood sugar. At camp we talked about ways our parents supported or didn't support us in our diabetic regimens. We shared tips about our care, gossiped about doctors we liked and didn't like, and talked about what life was like being the only diabetic in our friend circles. For teenage me, diabetes camp was everything. Diabetes camp was my BSC and since we were all diabetic, no one had to be "the diabetic one." I learned how to make and keep friends, a lesson worthy of the Baby-Sitters Club. And, like Dawn's farmhouse, camp had a ghost.

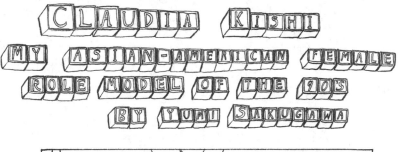

CLAUDIA KISHI
MY ASIAN-AMERICAN FEMALE
ROLE MODEL OF THE 90'S
BY YUMI SAKUGAWA

AS A JAPANESE-AMERICAN GIRL WHO GREW UP IN THE 90'S, I STILL REMEMBER THAT DURING THAT DECADE IT WAS A RARE OCCURRENCE TO SEE ASIAN-AMERICAN FEMALE FACES IN T.V. SHOWS, MOVIES, CARTOONS, BOOKS AND AS TOY FIGURES.

BETWEEN 1990 AND 1999, HERE ARE THE ASIAN-AMERICAN FEMALE FACES IN POPULAR CULTURE I REMEMBER OFF THE TOP OF MY HEAD:

MARGARET CHO IN "ALL-AMERICAN GIRL" (1994)

THE SHOW CANCELLED AFTER ONE SEASON, AND I DIDN'T WATCH ENOUGH EPISODES FOR IT TO MAKE AN IMPRESSION ON MY 9-YEAR-OLD BRAIN

TRINI KWAN/THE YELLOW RANGER IN "MIGHTY MORPHIN POWER RANGERS" (1993)

I MAY HAVE BEEN TOO BUSY CRUSHING ON TOMMY/THE GREEN RANGER/THE WHITE RANGER TO PAY ATTENTION TO THE GIRL RANGERS.

KRISTI YAMAGUCHI, OLYMPIC CHAMPION (1992)

I LOST COMPLETE INTEREST IN ICE-SKATING AFTER MY FAILED 4-MONTH EXPERIMENT IN ICE-SKATING LESSONS.

THANKFULLY, DURING MY 90'S CHILDHOOD I HAD ONE ASIAN-AMERICAN GIRL TO LOOK UP TO WHO WAS TALENTED IN ART, FASHION FORWARD, CRAZY UNIQUE, EXTREMELY CONFIDENT, AND JUST LIKE ME, A SECOND-GENERATION JAPANESE AMERICAN.

I AM SPEAKING, OF COURSE, ABOUT CLAUDIA KISHI OF THE BABY-SITTERS CLUB.

IN CASE YOU AREN'T A GIRL WHO GREW UP IN THE 90'S.......

THE BABY-SITTERS CLUB

IS A YOUNG ADULT NOVEL SERIES WRITTEN BY ANN M. MARTIN (AND HER TEAM OF GHOST WRITERS).

THE SERIES FOLLOW THE ADVENTURES OF A GROUP OF MIDDLE SCHOOL GIRLS WHO RUN A BABY-SITTING BUSINESS IN THE FICTIONAL TOWN OF STONEYBROOK, CONNECTICUT.

Kristy   Mary Anne

Claudia   Stacey

PUBLISHED BETWEEN 1986 AND 2000, THE SERIES SOLD OVER 170 MILLION COPIES. "THE BABY-SITTERS CLUB" WAS ALSO ADAPTED INTO A T.V. SHOW, A FULL-LENGTH FEATURE FILM, AND INSPIRED SEVERAL SPIN-OFF BOOK SERIES.

IN THE STORYLINE, CLAUDIA KISHI IS ONE OF THE FOUR ORIGINAL FOUNDING MEMBERS, THE SECOND WOMAN IN COMMAND AS VICE PRESIDENT, AND THE ONLY ASIAN-AMERICAN.

Dawn   Mallory   Jessi   Shannon   Abby

my life sucks

Logan

(BIG STACK OF BSC BOOKS FROM THE LOCAL LIBRARY)

JUST BABY-SITTERS CLUB BOOKS? AGAIN?

YOU CAN'T TALK ABOUT
CLAUDIA KISHI WITHOUT TALKING ABOUT HER
AMAZING SENSE OF FASHION

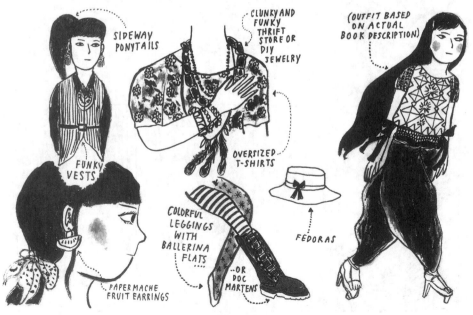

"Skin the Color of Cocoa": Colorism and How We See Jessi

Jamie Broadnax

Colorism—a particular form of racist discrimination based on skin tone—has been historically used in Black and Brown communities as a tool of division and oppression to make darker-skinned people of color feel inferior to lighter-skinned people of color. Yet colorism is not a thing of the past. We see it operating when Hollywood gravitates toward what journalist Tiffany Onyejiaka calls "a very distinct type of black girl who fits the 'Halle Berry' aesthetic: slim, light-skinned, and classically attractive in a Eurocentric sense," and when narratives from dark-skinned individuals from both the literary community and from the TV and film industry are met with apathy or indifference. Colorism remains broadly present, even and maybe especially within the Black community. At times, some reduce colorist tendencies down to having a "preference," ignoring that preferences can be steeped in prejudices.

Colorism dates back to slavery when dark-skinned slaves were forced to work out in the fields and light-skinned slaves were allowed to stay inside to work domestic duties in the home. There's also the notorious brown paper bag test, wherein privilege and opportunities were afforded to African Americans who were lighter than a brown paper bag, but not to those who were darker. These "tests" were used in social institutions such as sororities, fraternities, and churches in the early twentieth century and were performed by both whites and Blacks alike.

In the case of Ann M. Martin's Baby-Sitters Club series, the character Jessi Ramsey, the sole Black babysitter, unfortunately has not been immune to the effects of colorism. I'm going to take you on a short journey of Jessi Ramsey's skin tone changes in Baby-Sitters Club book covers throughout the years. This essay doesn't address every single book cover on which Jessi appears, but rather a handful just to gain a sense as to how her complexion was depicted. It's time to explore the dichotomy of how Jessi was described by the author compared to the way she was illustrated by various artists.

Before we dive into the issue of colorism, let's give some background on who Jessica Ramsey is. Jessi is a free spirit who has a passion for ballet dancing—call her a mini Misty Copeland if you will. Jessi's birthday is June 30 and her astrological sign is Cancer, so seeking comfort in the realms of creativity and emotions is not a stretch here. Her favorite authors are Marguerite Henry and Lynn Hall, both known for writing books about horses. I'm curious to know if Jessi's favorite authors were shaped by Martin's own biases. Although it doesn't seem impossible or even unlikely that Jessi would have interests in these authors, she grew up in a predominantly Black school, which begs the question of whether Jessi would have possibly been exposed to more diverse authors. If Martin were describing Jessi's taste in books today, I wonder if Jessi would be a fan of, for example, *The Compton Cowboys* by Walter Thompson-Hernandez, which scrutinizes the healing power of horses while also exploring the community of cowboys in the most unlikely of places—Compton, California, a predominantly African American city. I personally believe Jessi would have some interest in this book since it covers her favorite topic horses, and it is written from the lens of a Black author. But I digress.

Eleven-year-old Jessi Ramsey becomes a junior officer of the Baby-Sitters Club along with her best friend, Mallory Pike. In *Hello, Mallory*, we learn that Jessi was born in a predominantly Black neighborhood in Oakley, New Jersey, and has found herself one of just six Black students at Stoneybrook Middle School. In fact, she's the only Black student in her entire class. As you can imagine, it's a pretty jarring experience for Jessi to get acclimated to these new white surroundings. Throughout the series, Martin lightly touches on issues of prejudice. It's not until book #56: *Keep Out, Claudia!* that she explores racism as a central problem. In the story, one of Jessi's neighbors slams the door in Jessi's face, surprised to find that the sitter she's hired is Black. While I applaud Martin's efforts here to take on real issues impacting what so many marginalized people of color go through in white spaces, I can't help but think of the hypocrisy surrounding how Jessi's image is depicted on the books' cover art. Even as the BSC books teach lessons challenging racism and prejudice, their cover art conveys a colorist message, which is just as harmful. Impressionable young Black girls can ultimately be confused on how to see themselves if one moment they read a description that sounds exactly how they look, but then they see an image on a bookshelf that looks completely different.

JESSI'S REPRESENTATION IN THE BOOKS

Throughout the series, Martin has consistently described Jessi Ramsey's skin tone as "cocoa-colored." Here's Jessi describing herself in BSC #16: *Jessi's Secret Language:* "Of course if you could see me, there wouldn't be any question that I'm black. I have skin the color of cocoa—darkish cocoa, soft black hair and eyes like two pieces of coal."

And in the Baby-Sitters Club Mysteries #29: *Stacey and the Fashion Victim*, Stacey tells us: "Jessi is African-American, with cocoa-colored skin, dark eyes, and the long, muscular limbs of a trained dancer."

The author has made it pretty clear that Jessi has skin the color of cocoa, which means she is not light-skinned. At her lightest, Jessi would be medium brown-skinned. Yet, if you were to glance at the cover of *Jessi's Secret Language*, you're likely to wonder who this person on the cover is, and what did they do with Jessi Ramsey? Cocoa? Darkish cocoa? I suppose it's the kind of cocoa with milk added to it. The cover art depicts a Jessi who could likely pass, erasing her Black identity altogether. And by passing, I don't mean the early nineteenth-century *Imitation of Life* movie version, but instead wanting to look as white as her fellow white colleagues. In that same book, Jessi describes herself as "dark" when she defends her Blackness to her white girlfriends: "I . . . am not scary or awful or anything except just another eleven-year-old kid, who happens to have dark skin. (And who also happens to be a good dancer, a good joke-teller, a good reader, good at languages . . . and good with children . . .)."

A simple book cover doesn't necessarily imply that Jessi rejects her own Blackness, but it does present a colorist message. In favoring a lighter-skinned image of an African American girl, the cover encourages people to see Jessica

Ramsey as that girl, rather than the dark cocoa brown girl represented within its pages. It's a missed opportunity to give visibility to a character who could never pass for white, whose racial background is obvious to anyone who sees her. A girl who clearly looks African American from the color of her skin to the texture of her hair. Ann M. Martin made it clear in her description what Jessi looked like; the book's illustrations should reflect that.

There's little consistency in how Jessi is portrayed by the cover artists, but the lightening of Jessi's skin tone on various covers is evident. The following are just a handful of examples of a lighter-skinned Jessi:

BSC books #22: *Jessi Ramsey, Pet Sitter,* #27: *Jessi and the Superbrat,* #42: *Jessi and the Dance School Phantom,* #55: *Jessi's Gold Medal,* #61: *Jessi and the Awful Secret,* #68: *Jessi and the Bad Baby-Sitter,* #75: *Jessi's Horrible Prank,* #82: *Jessi and the Troublemaker,* and #103: *Happy Holidays, Jessi.* In these examples, Jessi's skin tone is a range of lighter tones, her hair typically tied up in a bun or ponytail. However, one thing is consistent: she's not at all that cocoa brown skin tone described by Ann M. Martin.

The artists do get Jessi's skin tone right on a few covers: for example, #36: *Jessi's Baby-Sitter* in 1990, and #48: *Jessi's Wish* in 1991 and #115: *Jessi's Big Break* in 1998. There are special edition issues that get Jessi's appearance right as well, the point being that Jessi's skin tone does occasionally shift to a darker complexion throughout the years. In these cases, Jessi's skin color matches her description in the books. We see Jessi as intended.

In August of 2019, Audible launched all 131 titles of the BSC books on their platform. The titles featured on their website (with the exception of the covers featuring actor Elle Fanning, who narrates some of the books) are all presented with the original illustrations. It's too bad that the illustrations were not updated to address colorist depictions of Jessi.

Colorism in book cover art is nothing new: depending on the illustrator, the skin tone of a fictional character can change at the drop of a hat. One of the most pointed recent examples of whitewashing was Justine Larbalestier's 2009 YA novel *Liar.* The book's protagonist, Micah, is described by the author as Black, wearing natural hair. However, the cover features a woman who clearly looks Caucasian with stringy tendrils. The widely publicized controversy sparked enough backlash to force the publisher to change the cover to depict an African American woman with natural hair.

In 2018, controversy similarly brewed around the casting of actor Amandla Stenberg for Angie Thomas's *New York Times* bestselling novel *The Hate U*

Give. In the book, author Angie Thomas describes the protagonist Starr's skin complexion as "medium-brown." The cover art clearly depicts an accurate illustration of Angie's imagined character. However, when Stenberg, who is biracial and light skinned, was cast in the leading role as Starr, some fans of the book questioned the casting.

JESSI'S REPRESENTATION IN TV AND FILM

The BSC TV and film adaptations created in the 1990s unfortunately suffered the same fate as the books with respect to colorism. It began with the 1990 HBO series starring Nicolle Rochelle as Jessi. The short-lived show lasted only one season. Rochelle, a light-skinned actor, appeared as Jessi in all thirteen episodes of the series. Her tone matched that of the lighter complexion Jessi has on the earlier book covers, which do not match the author's description of Jessi's appearance.

However, in 1995, a film version of *The Baby-Sitters Club* was released starring Zelda Harris as Jessi. Harris, a darker-skinned actor with natural hair, more closely resembles the description of Jessi in the books. In this case, the casting department got it right by making certain that Jessi's physical appearance matched the books' descriptions: "skin the color of cocoa."

In 2020, Netflix adapted the BSC books into an episodic TV series. Unlike the HBO series, which immediately brought Jessi into the BSC universe, Netflix plays out each episode in order of the books' publication. Since she doesn't appear in the first several books, Jessi is absent from the show's first season until the final two episodes, where she appears only briefly, played by Anais Lee. I could be moving into subjective territory here, but Anais Lee's skin tone isn't quite as dark as cocoa, and her hair texture is similar to that of her biracial costar Malia Baker. To be fair, Ann M. Martin never described Jessi's hair texture in the books.

Baker is playing Mary Anne Spier, who is a biracial character on the show. In the books, of course, Mary Anne is white. Netflix decided to racebend this character—as well as Dawn Schafer, who is white in the books but played by Xochitl Gomez, who is Latina, adding a bit more diversity to the historically super-white Stoneybrook. Racebending is a practice in the entertainment industry wherein a coveted role, historically given to a white actor, is played by a person of color. This gives marginalized artists and performers opportunities to play roles that otherwise would have not been available.

In an interview I conducted with Baker on BlackGirlNerds.com about playing the role of Mary Anne Spier and how book purists would feel about her playing the character, here is what she had to say:

> We need to at least try to adapt. I know from personal experience change can be really, really hard at times. But nothing is super affecting at this point. It's not this huge thing that differs from the book series. It's just that we're different races. There are some new topics involved in the series. And I feel that it's going to be really great for the next generation to be exposed to those things so that they can form their own great idea to put out into the world.

The Netflix series is a story of its own, intended to reach and resonate with a new generation of fans. The changes and liberties the creative team elected to take—racebending, bringing in storylines about trans kids, and other attempts at more inclusivity—make me see this series as more of an homage to the books than a direct adaptation. However, things are still complicated when it comes to the subject of colorism and Blackness in the BSC world. Even today, the pervasiveness of this issue is still reflected in the Netflix show.

Perhaps one day Jessica Ramsey will be seen for who she truly is and not viewed through the lens of how others wish to perceive her because it's considered "safe" or "marketable." So many YA novels succumb to colorism. However, in the case of the BSC it is even more egregious, because the many books and audiobooks and TV and film adaptations have presented opportunities to get it right and course correct yet they still, for the most part, have not. Yes, there are examples that show Jessi as the color of cocoa, but unfortunately they are infrequent and inconsistent. Until illustrators, editors, publishers, and marketers are honest about colorism, this problem will continue. Jessi's story is a cautionary tale of what happens when others choose to see someone one way, rather than to see them for who they are.

"I've Been Thinking About Families Lately"

Kristen Felicetti

I remember my excitement when I first saw the cover for The Baby-Sitters Club #33: *Claudia and the Great Search*. Claudia sits on the floor babysitting a toddler. She wears a cerulean blue sweater and sports large gold hoop earrings. Her hair's tied in a high ponytail with a matching blue scrunchie. The tagline reads: *Claudia thinks she's adopted, and no one understands!* As a nine-year-old, that's the line that hooked me. I was adopted myself. My parents treated my adoption as something positive and celebrated the day I arrived from Korea annually like a mini-birthday. Still, I felt a strange loneliness about it that I could not articulate (. . . *no one understands!*). I even knew other adoptees: there were a few of us at my elementary school, and I had attended a Korean cultural summer camp for adopted children. But the possibility that a member of the Baby-Sitters Club was adopted was on a whole other level. And not just any of the babysitters, Claudia Lynn Kishi, my favorite character, the girl who looked the most like me and shared my artistic inclinations. I devoured every book in the series with an obsessive interest, but this particular one had to be read immediately.

Claudia and the Great Search opens with Claudia's older sister "Janine the Genius" receiving an academic award. Her whole family attends the ceremony and afterward, they hold a celebratory dinner. Claudia resents how frequently Janine's accomplishments overshadow her own creative talents. This jealousy drives her to flip through a family photo album, where she reflects upon her lack of physical resemblance to her sister and parents. She's also disturbed to find few baby photos of herself compared to the numerous baby photos of Janine. She sneaks into her parents' desk, hoping to find more photos and instead discovers a locked strongbox. "All of a sudden it dawned on me," says Claudia. "I knew. I just *knew*. I was *adopted*, and my adoption papers were in there. If I were adopted, that would explain why I didn't look like anyone in my family . . . and why there were so few pictures of me."

The idea of being adopted appeals to Claudia because it provides a clear explanation for why she feels so alienated from her family. Claudia previously clashed with Janine back in #7: *Claudia and Mean Janine* and she doesn't relate to her parents either. Her investment banker father doesn't understand why she loves art, and her librarian mother wishes she read serious literature instead of mystery books. The only relative with whom she felt a true connection was her grandmother Mimi, who passed away in #26: *Claudia and the Sad Good-bye*.

Inspired by her hero Nancy Drew, Claudia goes full detective as she searches for answers regarding her adoption and the identity of her birth parents. She hunts for clues at her pediatrician's office, the bank, and the library. When she's unable to find her own birth announcement in the archives of the local newspaper, her suspicions only grow. Throughout it all, Stacey is the voice of reason, reminding Claudia that "everyone is different, and not everyone fits into her family, or his family."

When Claudia finally confronts her parents, they tell her she's not adopted. Mrs. Kishi explains that sometimes parents simply take more photos of their first child. There's less novelty the second time around and more children means less time to take photos in general. That's why there are more baby photos of Janine. The lockbox contains emergency money, not secret adoption papers. Both Claudia and Janine's births were announced in a different, out of circulation newspaper. Her mother has saved the clippings and shares them. As for not resembling either of her parents, when Mrs. Kishi shows her photos of a twelve-year-old Mimi, Claudia proudly says, "We could have been twins."

Even as a nine-year-old, I realized halfway through the book that Claudia probably wouldn't end up being adopted. The whole concept was a little far-fetched and her evidence was flimsy. But I wanted her to be adopted, because I wanted my favorite character to share another aspect of my identity. As was the case for many Asian Americans who read the Baby-Sitters Club series, Claudia Kishi was the first time I saw an Asian American character who defied tokenization and stereotypical portrayals. She might have felt like an outsider in her own family, but it was clear she was no outsider among her friends nor in the town of Stoneybrook. She was effortlessly cool, popular, and extroverted. Her wild outfits were described in envious detail by the other babysitters and portrayed fashionably on the cover illustrations. And while Kristy may have been the club's president, Claudia was its vice president and the club meetings were always held in her bedroom and on her turf. I wanted to be her but, crucially, *everyone* wanted to be her, both Asian American readers and non–Asian American readers alike.

But even if Claudia had been adopted, she still wouldn't have been the exact mirror I wanted her to be. She would have been an Asian child adopted by an Asian family, whereas I was an Asian child adopted by a white family. In elementary school, I did not have the language to properly articulate those differences. I was aware that I was Korean and my parents were not, but I would not reflect deeply or critically on the experience of being a transracial adoptee until I was an adult. As a young reader, I did see representation of a transracial adoptee in the series, but since she was a minor character (and an infant), she left less of a lasting impression than the babysitting protagonists I aspired to be. I'm referring to Emily Michelle Thomas Brewer, the two-year-old on the cover of *Claudia and the Great Search.* She was adopted from Vietnam by Kristy's mother and stepfather in #24: *Kristy and the Mother's Day Surprise.*

Emily is the catalyst for Claudia thinking she's adopted in the first place. Sometimes the babysitting subplots were unrelated adventures, but in this story the subplot actually propels the main plot and vice versa. Kristy starts a club meeting by announcing that Emily has been struggling with developmental issues, separation anxiety, and recurring nightmares. She's concerned, but a three-nights-a-week babysitting gig with another family prevents her from spending more time with her new sister. When Kristy's mom calls looking for a sitter, Claudia gets the job. At first Claudia finds working with Emily to be a challenge, but eventually she comes up with a system that teaches Emily colors and matching. Kristy's mother is so impressed she hires her to be Emily's part-time tutor. This empowers Claudia and reminds her that even if she doesn't receive the awards and grades Janine does, she is still intelligent. And while there's no direct evidence in the text, I would also like to believe that it was beneficial for Emily to be around another Asian person, that this commonality added depth to their bond. I wouldn't expect a book published in 1990 to address the racial complexities of being the only Asian member in an all-white family, though Kristy does say that "it's good for Emily to get close to people outside our family" when she mentions the emotional progress Emily has made with Claudia.

After rereading this book, I found it somewhat comical how Claudia immediately overidentifies with Emily. She neurotically wonders, "Who are my real mother and father?" and refers to the Kishis as "the people I thought were my real parents." Adoption language generally avoids this term for your biological parents since it implies that your adoptive parents are not your "real parents." I'm not bothered by Claudia's initial use of this phrase, because I wouldn't expect a thirteen-year-old to immediately know adoption terminology. Later on, she does correct her own language and says, "Deciding to take action about finding my real parents—my birth parents—was easy" and going forward speaks about her search to find her birth parents. Adoption language also continues to evolve and not every adoptee uses the birth parents / adoptive parents labels. Some might refer to their biological parents as first parents or original parents, especially if they lived with them long after their birth, or continue to have a relationship with them after their adoption. Alternatively, children adopted at an older age might not call the people who adopted them their mother/father/parents at all. As with any identity, adoptees are not a monolith.

I'm more troubled by Claudia saying, "Every day, Watson or Mrs. Brewer would say to Emily that she wasn't just adopted, she was *chosen*. And she was very, very special." While I believe that Kristy's parents have good intent here (or rather, Ann M. Martin did), telling an adoptee that they are chosen or very special is adjacent to telling them that they are lucky, or that they were "saved." Fictional and real-life adoptions are often depicted as fairy-tale narratives, a simplification that both overlooks the problems of the adoption and foster care industry (a complex subject that goes far beyond the scope of this essay) and suppresses any negative or complicated feelings adoptees might have. It frames adoption as a happy ending, and therefore, the end of the story.

Growing up, the movies and children's literature about adoptees had a similarly sentimental tone. Long before I loved the Baby-Sitters Club, I loved the movie musical *Annie*, which has the ultimate fairy tale framing—it ends with "Little Orphan Annie" being adopted by a billionaire. In *Anne of Green Gables*, another beloved childhood series, two aging siblings decide to take in an orphan boy to help run their farm. When they mistakenly receive Anne instead, they consider sending her back, but after being won over by her good-natured spirit and charm, choose to adopt her anyway. I also read less-famous titles written by well-meaning adoptive parents who wanted their kids to see themselves and their families reflected. While their intentions were good, they have their own biases, and many of these books had simplistic perspectives that did not reflect the reality of being adopted. Love conquered all. Racism was too easily resolved, or worse, intrinsic to the book itself (I had one book about a Korean child called *Chinese Eyes*). Adoptees were "miracles" or "presents" or "wishes come true."

To Ann M. Martin's credit, she did show some of the complexities of Emily's experience. Emily had an existence beyond simply being the surprise in *Kristy and the Mother's Day Surprise*. Her emotional issues in *Claudia and the Great Search* were the result of first spending two years in an orphanage and then having to adjust to a completely new country, home, language, and family. Like all the characters in the series, she never aged, so I never got to see how her adoption affected her as an older child, but as I myself got older, there would be other books instead. It has been exciting to see the recent emergence of novels, memoirs, and anthologies exploring this subject, many written by adoptees themselves. Nicole Chung writes about adoption and the search for her Korean birth family in her bestselling memoir *All You Can Ever Know*. Patrick Cottrell's *Sorry to Disrupt the Peace* and Matthew Salesses's *Disappear Doppelgänger Disappear* are two novels that feature adoptee protagonists wrestling with existential questions. In children's literature, there's Mariama J. Lockington's middle grade novel *For Black Girls Like Me* and Eric Smith's YA novel *The Girl and the Grove*. These writers are vastly different, and adoption is only one facet of their books, but they are all telling more nuanced stories than the fairy-tale version. Symbolically, I also think it's powerful to see adoptees in charge of a narrative because we've often been rewritten in the past. For example, some of us are renamed. I love my name Kristen Felicetti, but it was not my first name, which was Kim Yeon-jeong (김연정). Emily Michelle Thomas Brewer was not Emily Michelle Thomas Brewer for the first two years of her life either. Her Vietnamese name is never mentioned.

I don't think you need to be an adoptee to write a great adoptee character, though I would advise anyone to do research when writing an identity different from their own. I'm not surprised adoption intrigues writers: it's a weighty way to engage with one of the richest subjects in fiction—family and its definition. The Baby-Sitters Club explored this question boldly and unapologetically with its wide spectrum of family diversity. Consider the opening to *Kristy and the Mother's Day Surprise*. Most first chapters of Baby-Sitters Club books jump right into a scene, with a line of dialogue or action. This book breaks that formula by starting with a direct challenge to the definition of family itself:

> I've been thinking about families lately, wondering what makes one. Is a family really a mother, a father, and a kid or two? I hope not, because if that's a family, then I haven't got one. And neither do a lot of other people I know. For instance, Nannie, Mom's mother, lives all by herself. But I still think of her as a family—a one-person family. And I think of my own family as a real family . . . I guess.

I love this opening. It's got some typical Kristy brassiness, but the "I guess" tagged onto the end hints that even the series' famously bossy know-it-all feels some insecurity about her family's differences. Readers became very familiar with the makeup of every babysitter's household, thanks to the much-maligned second chapter where each character's family was summarized for the umpteenth time along with their club title, physical appearance, personality, interpersonal dynamics with other characters, hobbies, and sartorial choices. This is where you were reminded that Kristy's dad abandoned her, her mother, and her younger siblings. *Kristy's Great Idea* is the book where she creates the Baby-Sitters Club, of course, but it's also the beginning of her blended family.

Claudia's parents were immigrants, but within her friend group, it was her family that possibly had the most conventional American structure. After her grandmother's death, she lives solely with two biological parents and a single older sibling. Claudia's grief over Mimi is written in a way that respects the complexity of young readers' emotions, many of whom may also have experienced the death of a grandparent or other beloved relative. I find it especially realistic that Claudia's sadness lasts beyond the events of *Claudia and the Sad Good-bye*. If her grandmother had still been alive in *Claudia and the Great Search*, she never would have worried about being adopted. Her continued grief and newfound loneliness is what drives this quest. It's also what makes the ending—Claudia recognizing herself in a young photo of Mimi—so poignant.

She was not the only character to get this considered treatment. All the babysitters endured family changes that had lasting emotional effects. Each of the sitters' parents are shown to be loving, but they're also shown to be flawed, absent, or disappointing. Kristy's father never writes or calls, and he doesn't remember his children's birthdays. The realities of divorce are painful for Stacey and Dawn too. They're both forced to make the difficult decision to live primarily with one parent over the other.

Dawn is also frequently frustrated by her mother, who is "forgetful and absentminded" and keeps a messy house. Her mom dates a series of terrible men before marrying Mary Anne's dad, a man who has fought his own struggles with grief and depression (Mystery #5: *Mary Anne and the Secret in the Attic*). Dawn and Mary Anne are close friends and the unification of their families is a happy event, but the marriage doesn't bring an end to their problems. Becoming stepsisters is not as idyllic as they first imagined (#31: *Dawn's Wicked Stepsister*) and their entire stepfamily has troubles adjusting (#64: *Dawn's Family Feud*). Dawn remains torn between her Stoneybrook family and her life in California, where her dad lives. She makes a permanent move to California in #88: *Farewell, Dawn* and leaves the series.

Her departure was deeply felt because the Baby-Sitters Club was its own unique family. They were best friends, they were business partners, they had their own language and inside jokes, and they shared each other's triumphs and heartbreaks. They also fought, and when things were at their worst, they worried the club was going to fall apart.

Part of the appeal of the Baby-Sitters Club was the rich world Ann M. Martin created, with a cast of well over fifty recurring characters that each had their own mythos. The babysitters were its center, but their family members played a significant role. This established my own interest in finding children's literature where the adult characters were written with the same depth as the young protagonists. I still read YA and I always dislike when parents come across as flat or cartoonish. Contemporary YA sees a greater representation of queer families too, which was the one type of family not depicted in the Baby-Sitters Club even though Martin herself had a past relationship with a woman. I believe that if the series was released in today's publishing landscape, we would have seen a queer family—not to mention a visibly queer babysitter. But if you grew up in the 1980s and '90s, especially if you grew up in a small town as homogenous as Stoneybrook, the Baby-Sitters Club was a much-needed representation of unconventional families. You may not have seen your exact family reflected in the books, but you knew that you were entering a world where its traditional definition ("a mother, a father, and a kid or two") was the exception, not the rule.

As an adoptee, I'm fascinated with how families are made, or created. Both the families formed when people connect in the real world, as well as the fictional ones created from scratch for the page. I love nothing more than an epic family novel full of love and dysfunction, joy and trauma. Even in novels or stories where a character's family is never mentioned, it's always there, below the surface, providing hints at a character's motivation. Like Kristy, I'm always thinking about families, what makes one, and how they make you. Our origins hold so many of the answers to our questions about who we are. There's a wealth of material there—for writers, for artists, for anyone attempting self-reflection. It's an endless great search.

Kristy and the Secret of Ableism

Haley Moss

Reading the Baby-Sitters Club series as an elementary school student during the early 2000s, I admired the cool independence of the BSC members. I identified with both Claudia and Mary Anne; I was creative and loved junk food like Claudia, but I was also introverted and sensitive like Mary Anne. But there was one other Stoneybrook, Connecticut, resident who has stayed with me throughout the years: eight-year-old Susan Felder.

Susan is one of many diverse characters with disabilities in the series: Stacey is, of course, diabetic; Abby has asthma; Jessi babysits for a boy named Matthew who is Deaf; Claudia babysits for Shea, a young boy with dyslexia; and Claudia's own poor spelling and academic struggles lead me to believe that she may also have an unnamed learning disability or be otherwise neurodivergent. But Susan is the first character in the series who's autistic. We meet Susan in BSC #32: *Kristy and the Secret of Susan*, the only book in which she's featured. As one of too few children's books that represented autism—and in particular a female autistic character—at the time (1990), *Kristy and the Secret of Susan* is noteworthy and gets some key things right in its depictions of Susan's autism. But it also denies Susan's humanity and agency in ways that perpetuate ableist myths around autism, special education, and the autonomy of people with disabilities. Though the novel presents many opportunities for the BSC characters and their presumably neurotypical readership to learn from Susan's differences and the babysitters' at times disappointing responses to them, as a reader who shares Susan's diagnosis, I wish we had more time with Susan, especially time seeing the world from her perspective.

I was diagnosed with autism in 1997, when I was three years old and largely nonverbal. The first time I picked up *Kristy and the Secret of Susan*, I was in the third grade and had no idea we had anything in common. I didn't know at the time that I was also autistic, and that my mom had a collection of autism books hidden in her closet on a shelf behind some of her clothes. *Kristy and the Secret of Susan* happened to be one of the grade-level books on that shelf. I don't know if she hid them for reading after I was asleep or while I was at school, or because other parents who entered our home might draw negative conclusions—like when I was in preschool and other parents wouldn't let their children play with me because they falsely believed my autism was contagious. In any case, my autism was a secret to many, it seemed, including me.

When we're first introduced to Susan, the babysitters are spying on new neighbors from Australia before the club's meeting when Kristy is distracted by "a tired-looking woman leading a little girl by the hand" around the neighborhood on a walk. Susan is described as holding "her head to one side and looking ahead out of the corners of her eyes." She is taking "quick, short steps in a stiff, uncomfortable way," and she is flapping her free hand. Kristy concludes that Susan really doesn't seem like she wants to be outside, or is reluctant to be there. We're never told why, and I can only imagine based on experiences I've had or that other autistic people have had: perhaps Susan doesn't like her mother's firm grip, or the bustling of people in the neighborhood; maybe she doesn't like the way the Connecticut cold stings her skin, the sounds of nature, or the brightness of the sun.

I wasn't anything like Susan, who Martin constructs as a largely nonspeaking, gifted pianist with a calendar inside of her head that spans decades. Susan is depicted as an autistic savant: needing support for most daily tasks while excelling in a nuanced form of memory or talent. Although autistic savants are pretty rare, the savant trope is omnipresent in media depictions of autism ranging from Dustin Hoffman's *Rain Man*, who can count dropped toothpicks, to Dr. Shaun Murphy on *The Good Doctor*, whose nearly perfect memory recall and penchant for minute details help him accurately diagnose medical conditions. Unlike these characters, I've never had savant skills that I can pull out of my brain like a magic trick, though I did have a photographic memory that made memorizing lines for the school play a breeze as a kid. I was a sensitive, introverted artist and writer who became verbal after intensive speech and occupational therapy in preschool. By first grade, I'd transitioned out of repeating things I'd heard.

I learned I was autistic when I was nine, and I embraced my autism, believing I had magical powers much like Harry Potter. My parents told me I was different, but neither better nor worse than my neurotypical peers—just different, and different could be extraordinary. My nine-year-old self tossed the idea of Susan out the window, again locking her in a world of her own. We shared the spectrum but were not alike—Susan's struggles with verbal language and dressing herself are vastly different from my own social and daily living challenges—which I would later learn is to be expected. Every autistic person's experiences, traits, and talents are unique to them.

✳ ✳ ✳

To fully understand *Kristy and the Secret of Susan* in context requires a look back at the history of the disability rights movement in this country. Concurrent with the book's publication, disability rights were at the forefront of political discourse in the United States as people with disabilities were taking charge of their fates by demanding equality. The proposed Americans with Disabilities Act, a comprehensive civil rights legislation package to protect the rights of people with disabilities, was stalled in the House Committee on Public Works and Transportation. On March 12, 1990, the same month *Kristy and the Secret of Susan* was published, disability activists arrived in Washington, DC, to ascend the steps of Capitol Hill during the "Capitol Crawl": many of them abandoned their wheelchairs and mobility aids to climb and crawl up the stairs in a demonstration about accessibility. The action helped mobilize Congress into passing the Americans with Disabilities Act, which was signed into law by President George H. W. Bush on July 26, 1990.

Susan Felder, as well as all Baby-Sitters Club characters up to this point, grew up in a world where people with disabilities had protections only under the Rehabilitation Act of 1973, which extended civil rights to individuals with disabilities but was limited to federally funded programs and employment, and the Education for All Handicapped Children Act (1975), which guaranteed a free and appropriate public education to all disabled children (and which was strengthened and renamed the Individuals with Disabilities Education Act in 1990). These rights were secured by activists with complex disabilities who fought for the rights of disabled children and adults like Susan, notably in 1977 during the 504 sit-ins and the Capitol Crawl in 1990.

During the first spike in activism in the 1970s, Ann M. Martin was at Smith College, studying special education and spending her summers working with autistic children at the Eden Institute. After college, she taught fourth and fifth graders who had intellectual, learning, and developmental disabilities, including autism, and she has regularly drawn upon this background in her books. Martin's first foray into writing about autism was in 1982 with the middle-grade novel *Inside Out*, where the main character is teased about his autistic brother. Much later, in 2014, she took a stab at writing from the point of view of an autistic fifth grader in her novel *Rain Reign*.

Sandwiched between these books is *Kristy and the Secret of Susan*. In her "Dear Reader" letter for *Kristy and the Secret of Susan*, Martin shares that the book is based partly on her experiences as a therapist with autistic children during the summers she was in college. "While there was no real Susan Felder," Martin writes, "I met lots of kids like Susan and lots of families facing the same challenges Susan's parents face in the book. Autistic kids are very special, and I will always remember the kids I worked with."

Martin's positive intentions to teach young people about disability are certainly evident, and perhaps other young people identified with these characters more than I related to Susan. However, Martin largely writes in line with a medical model of disability, which understands disability as something to be treated and cured and, if not treatable or curable, as hidden from view. This model is often opposed to a social model of disability, which emphasizes the ways in which the environment and surroundings are more disabling than any condition could be.

The medical model of disability appears throughout the BSC series, where disabilities are primarily explained as secrets and scandalous truths as compared to natural variations in humanity. Stacey discloses the "secret" of her diabetes to the rest of the BSC after hiding the "truth" from her friends in New York. When Jessi babysits Matthew, the Deaf boy, their use of American Sign Language is reduced to a "secret" language. In *The Secret of Susan*, Susan's existence is hidden from nearly the entire neighborhood at first; according to Kristy, Susan is "all locked up and so secretive we don't know her." Shrouding disability in secrecy only leads to the feeling of being other, different, suggesting that the only way to be accepted is to be nondisabled or at least pass as such. Hiding it avoids difficult truths and conversations that could lead to radical acceptance and spark meaningful dialogue—a message taken to heart in the Netflix adaptation of the series, where after confronting her parents' ableist assumptions about her capabilities and divulging her "secret" to a room full of BSC clients, Stacey proudly displays a bedazzled insulin pump.

Susan's "secret" begins unfolding when Susan's mother calls the BSC to inquire about respite care three days a week while Susan is home from her "special" school for a month. Kristy isn't sure what *autistic* means, and looks up *autism* in the dictionary (she can't find *autistic*). The definition says "something about childhood schizophrenia, acting out, and withdrawal," she reports, and she rightfully declares the dictionary to be no help. When the group discusses autism for the first time, Claudia suggests, "retarded?"

Even by the standards of 1990, "retard" and "retarded" were considered offensive slurs, even if "mental retardation" was a medical term to describe intellectual disabilities. I never used the word "retard" growing up, but I knew plenty of kids who did. It always made me feel uncomfortable at best and angry at worst.

Kristy meets Susan and her mother in their home, where Susan is obviously stimming, or engaging in behaviors such as hand-wringing and flapping and clicking her tongue. I too flap my hands; for me, it's a full body joy that I cannot contain, so my body performs my feelings and takes part. It's a kind of enthusiasm I only hope that a neurotypical person can experience someday. Stims are part of our body movement and communication; unfortunately, Susan just moves throughout the story, seen but not listened to. Whereas characters like Stacey are recognized as advocating for themselves by making verbal decisions regarding their disabilities, this kind of agency is denied to Susan, despite her clear nonverbal signals, such as when she shifts her weight because she feels uncomfortable being led somewhere or picked up.

The first meeting is a missed opportunity for Kristy's big mouth, when Susan's mom wants to talk about Susan. Kristy's first instinct—to blurt out "in front of her?"—would have been a monumental show of advocacy. As many other autistic people have taught me, not speaking is not the same as having nothing to say. Susan likely understands but might not have the ability or tools to share her feelings. Kristy is in a perfect position to be a strong advocate and indulge her trademark lack of filter, but she decides against it by assuming Susan will not be listening. As a young reader, I wondered how Susan felt about the way adults and teenagers talked about her while she was around. Although Kristy later chooses to advocate for Susan, her initial silence—and its implied presumption of Susan's incompetence and lack of understanding—is familiar and disappointing for people with disabilities.

When Susan's mother explains autism to Kristy, it's depressing. According to her, Susan has savant abilities with the piano and calendar but no meaningful spoken language, and she doesn't have any attachment to her parents. If I had known I was autistic when I first read this, would I have wondered if people thought I had no emotional connection to my family too? I love my family dearly, and we have a powerful bond. Contrary to the inflated false statistics claiming an unusually high divorce rate for parents with autistic children, my parents have been happily married for over twenty-eight years and were incredibly involved in raising me. Whereas Susan's father barely appears in the book, my dad took me to school most days before work, taught me how to ride bikes and drive, and held legendary game tournaments with me. I'm not like Susan, nine-year-old me thought.

The Felder family is preparing to move Susan to a new school that better meets her needs, but Kristy hopes she can change the Felders' minds. Angered at Susan's treatment by her parents and Stoneybrook at large, Kristy pledges to help Susan make friends. "I would use the month I had with her to show the Felders that she could live and learn and make friends *at home*," she declares. "She did not have to be an outcast." Kristy is fascinated with Susan—the way her body moves, her apparent disinterest in the outside world, her ability to focus on the piano. But her goal to help Susan make friends is self-serving rather than a demonstration of advocacy. It's Kristy who wants Susan to go outside and make friends—in part because she thinks it will help Susan fit in better in the special education class at her current public school. But Susan is at her happiest when she is singing and playing piano alone. Kristy's mission leads to an eventual parade of visitors to the Felder home, including a neighborhood bully who exploits Susan by charging kids to watch her play piano and recall calendar dates from memory. In her assumption that she knows what's best for Susan, Kristy misses an opportunity to advocate for Susan and causes unnecessary problems.

Susan's mom talks about how the public-school program wasn't a good fit when Susan was younger because of her support needs. That makes sense; though I was born later, not long after the passage of the revised IDEA, I was also out of the public system after diagnosis because private schools better fit my needs for academic rigor and greater social support. Ultimately, Kristy's misguided attempts to save Susan were unsuccessful, and she was off to her new "special" school and would be hidden away from Stoneybrook once again. Perhaps Susan would have more opportunities for inclusion in 2021 than in 1990, after IDEA strengthened education rights for disabled kids. If the book were written now, set in the present, the Felders and Susan's educational team would set goals for Susan's education in an individualized education plan. Susan would have a role in determining what her goals are, too—perhaps she doesn't want to make friends the way Kristy thinks she should, and she just wants to be a musician. Maybe she'd be interested in science but has never had the opportunity to explore it. Chances are, there would now be more than one classroom for special education (which is a service, not a place) in a suburban community like Stoneybrook. Other students would be integrated with non-disabled students for some classes, such as music. Susan would likely become part of a cluster of autistic kids and be able to live at home and watch her new baby sister (named Hope, suggesting that perhaps the Felders hoped for a nondisabled child who would embody the dreams that Susan did not—but I digress) eventually grow up. That's very different than a "special" school or institution.

✻ ✻ ✻

Like that of many disabled characters in literature, Susan's main role in the book is to teach nondisabled characters a lesson; here, Susan helps Kristy and other characters recognize and challenge bullying and practice different aspects of advocacy and patience. But the lesson I most wish Susan had taught us is empathy for her. Feeling and recognizing Susan's humanity allows readers to become better allies.

Susan is a little girl who loves music, and even after all these years, I still want to enter her world. I want to know what overwhelms her heightened senses to better understand why she doesn't like people touching her, or why playing the piano brings her so much joy. I wonder whether, if she were written decades later, she'd be communicating with assistive technology. Maybe she would tell us how painful it was when someone called her a "dumbo" or "retard" in front of her or behind her back. I'll never know who Susan is, or who she could have been.

✻ ✻ ✻

While I reread *Kristy and the Secret of Susan* to write this essay, my mom did the same. She tells me she bought the book because Susan was an autistic girl, and there weren't a lot of autistic girls in literature—this is still true today; autism is more commonly diagnosed in boys, and media representation still shows a majority of male autistic characters. (Arguably though, today's most famous autistic person is a teenage girl: climate activist Greta Thunberg.) My mom remembers me reading the Baby-Sitters Club books, and she wanted me to read about Susan as a teaching tool for me to explore the autism spectrum. *Kristy and the Secret of Susan* did offer me lessons on autism, albeit not in the way my mom expected it to.

I've written my own books about my experiences on the autism spectrum, and numerous articles about how autism intersects with other aspects of my life. In my mid-twenties, I am an attorney whose interests align with disability rights as well as law and policy. I am part of Generation ADA: millennials and young people who grew up having no idea what the world was like as a more widely inaccessible place, largely unaware of our disabled predecessors' accomplishments until later on in our lives because our history textbooks didn't cover disability rights history. Despite the gains that came with the ADA and revised IDEA, these pieces of legislation are a floor, not the ceiling. Generation ADA is unpacking its own internalized ableism, taught to us by our nondisabled peers and elders, and is continuing to unlearn harmful stereotypes and actions against people with disabilities. While the ADA is far from perfect and there is still much work to be done toward a more accessible and inclusive society, it's important to reflect on how far we've come. Susan is a glimpse into the world before antidiscrimination across all aspects of American society applied to people with disabilities.

The real secret in 1990 wasn't an autistic character being hidden from her local fictional suburban community at a "special" school; a young girl who was presumed to be locked inside her own head and without a care for the world around her. The secret is the prevalence of ableism—both in fictional Stoneybrook and the real world it reflects—and that we were then, and are still, grappling with it.

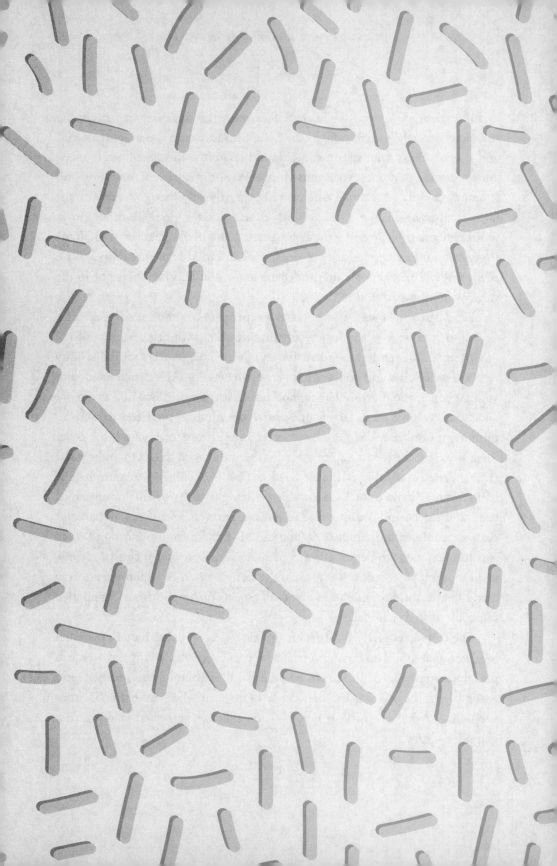

Be Bossy

ENTREPRENEURSHIP AND THE BUSINESS OF BABYSITTING

Kristy's Invisible Hand and Das Baby-Sitters Club Kapital

Myriam Gurba

My first encounter with girls as ardent capitalists happened between the covers of Ann M. Martin's Baby-Sitters Club books. The original series totaled 131 installments and from the series' first page, its entrepreneurial bent roared: "The Baby-sitters Club. I'm proud to say it was totally my idea, even though the four of us worked it out together. 'Us' is Mary Anne Spier, Claudia Kishi, Stacey McGill, and me—Kristy Thomas." The series chronicled the fictional adventures of a marginally diverse girl collective in Stoneybrook, Connecticut, as they grow and maintain a successful business. Common tween issues animated the series' capitalist story arcs. I don't remember how *Kristy's Great Idea* landed in my lap but once I devoured that debut, I needed more. Hooked, I hoarded my allowance and gophered into the couch seeking derelict change.

I brought my sweaty coins to our mall's B. Dalton Bookstore and exchanged pennies, quarters, and dimes for YA moneymaking thrills. As I acquired more books, I not only got to know the babysitters better, I felt I was making friends with them. Friends serve as mirrors, they show you who you are, and I saw aspects of myself keenly reflected by two particular BSC characters. I saw myself in Kristy. She generated ideas, stuck to her guns, and gave orders. Her stubborn tomboyishness was my stubborn tomboyishness. I also developed a special affection for Claudia. Since she was the club's token girl of color (until Jessi joined the group thirteen books later as a junior member), I saw my Chicana self reflected in her, and Claudia's presence was so important to me, so magnetic, that I doubt I would've become as emotionally invested in the series as I became had all its characters been white.

The babysitters inspired me, and Kristy's entrepreneurial vision seemed plain yet elegant; easy-to-follow too. While watching her mother grapple with childcare issues, ingenuity strikes Kristy. After finishing her homework, she sketches a business plan. She nominates her friends Mary Anne and Claudia as business partners. She decides that they'll advertise childcare services using flyers, the telephone, and the newspaper (how archaic!). The club will have set hours of operation during which clientele can call and book a sitter. To generate startup capital, each member will pay dues.

I'm writing about the club using an economic lens because I earn my paycheck doing a fearsome thing: I teach high school economics. In class, I borrow from and build upon the economic models and lessons embedded in the Baby-Sitters Club books. During lectures, I refer to instances like Kristy's entrepreneurial combination of land, labor, and capital, and one project that I assign is directly inspired by the series. I invite students to work alone or with friends to develop a business plan. Once the plan for their sole proprietorship, partnership, or other organization has been researched and developed, they present it to their classmates and me. We respond with evaluations.

My students' business plan presentations bring me joy that I was deprived of as a girl. When I tried becoming an entrepreneur, I crashed into what economists call barriers to entry. The primary barrier was bearded. I called it Dad. Dad was also part of the reason I unofficially resigned from the Girl Scouts. My best friend, a blonde tomboy, invited me to join her troop and I attended only a few meetings before cookie-selling season arrived. Like Kristy, BSC president, I'm high-key competitive. I enter contests to *win* and our troop leader incentivized us to sell, Sell, SELL, teasing us with a talc-scented trophy, a Cabbage Patch Kid doll. This prize would be awarded to the Brownie who sold the most sugar and I had major ganas to be that girl, la ganadora. Crowds the world over were rioting for Cabbage Patch Kids, the toy trend had swept California too, and rumors featuring parents who mugged children and ran off with their dolls impressed me.

"Those are good parents," I thought to myself. They were adjusting to shortages with loving violence.

Consumer tastes shifted the Cabbage Patch Kid demand curve to the right, and when I teach determinants of supply and demand, I use concrete and culturally relevant examples—like contemporary kid-centric fads—to illustrate my points. I do so in reaction to the sleep-inducing textbooks authored by assholes whose examples rely on theoretical objects, namely widgets. When widgets are used to teach determinants, not only do students never learn how to shift supply or demand, they get stuck on widgets. All their mental energy gets poured into answering the question, "*What the fuck is a widget?*"

Nobody should be tortured by this question.

Nobody should be coerced into caring about an abstraction that serves the interests of ten economists who've already got one foot in the grave.

Anyways, back to my Girl Scout debacle. When I returned home from our troop meeting armed with a catalogue and order form, I announced my intention to hit the sidewalks and travel door-to-door, cookie hustling. Before I could finish explaining my action plan, Dad interrupted me.

"That's not happening," he barked.

"Why not?!" I demanded.

"Too dangerous," he replied. The answer infuriated me but I knew there was no way around his prohibition—becoming a clandestine door-to-door salesgirl seemed impossible. It would've ended like the time I tiptoed in tap shoes.

When I discovered the technique my fellow Brownies were using to successfully peddle dozens of boxes, I grew hopeful. I suggested it to my parents. Again, Dad balked.

"Mom and I are not going to sell the cookies for you!" he snapped.

"But you won't let me go door to door selling them!" I protested. "What else am I supposed to do? All the other girls' parents are doing it! *They're* helping *their* daughters!"

"You can come with me to work one day and pin your catalogue and order form to the bulletin board," Dad offered.

Crestfallen, I agreed to his "compromise." I sold five boxes of cookies, the least in my troop. I felt like a loser. Because I was. The troop leader's daughter sold the most and the bitch received her grand prize during a small party thrown in her revenue-generating honor. When I got home from this celebration, complaining about how the venture was rigged, Dad used my disappointment as a "teachable moment."

"Myriam, you need to understand nepotism . . . " As Dad lectured me about the unjust allocation of resources to family and friends, I realized that I finally had a name for a practice I saw happening everywhere. My parents both worked for the same school district and I wondered if there wasn't something nepotistic about that. Had my father pulled strings to get my mother her job? Not wanting to start shit, I kept my questions about the matter to myself.

I still wanted to realize my babysitting ambitions, but I knew better than to follow Kristy's business model. Geographic and transportation challenges posed barriers to entry. My town, Santa Maria, was very spread out, making it tough to congregate at one person's house without soliciting rides from overburdened moms. Residential sprawl also made it tough to get to potential clients' homes.

My world differed from the fictional world of the series in other important ways. My bedroom held plenty of things: books, some dolls, a toy rifle, my sister, our bunk bed. Absent from this mess was a phone. My parents never let me have my own phone, not even once I got to high school. They thought a kid having a phone in her room was some gringo bullshit. Because my dad is Chicano, he could sometimes be gringo-y, especially in his dining habits. He, for example, occasionally tasked Mom with making meatloaf for dinner. I despised meatloaf nights and relied on ketchup to survive them. Having been born and raised in Guadalajara, Mexico, meatloaf and bedroom phones were novel to my mother. She approved of the former but not the latter, believing that if you had something to say, you should say it in front of everyone, on the living room phone.

Requests for privacy triggered suspicion and my parents granted me minimal privacy. My parents, however, were more permissive than other Latino parents. I knew some Latinas whose parents prohibited them from having bedroom doors. They ripped them right off the hinges. I also knew Latinas whose parents prohibited them from riding a bike lest they somehow lose their virginity to the thing.

Instead of belonging to a babysitters club, I became just a babysitter. Unlike my sheroes, I worked for only two clients: Mom and Dad. Unlike the club, I couldn't reject bookings. Doing so could result in punishment and the most demoralizing part of the situation was that Mom and Dad subsidized my childcare services through my allowance. I felt exploited but knew that negotiating with "management" would prove fruitless.

That they continuously thwarted my entrepreneurial dreams made me wonder what was wrong with my parents, and, by extension, me. First I wondered if they weren't so weird about my tween bootstrapping fantasies on account of us being Mexican. Then, as I got a little older, I started to wonder if they weren't being such assholes about my moneymaking schemes because I was . . . a girl. After I had that second epiphany—and this was before I'd ever heard the word *intersectionality*—I fused these concerns. I then spent time wondering what it was about my being a *Mexican girl* that provoked their restrictions.

Patriarchy rules the world and Mexico has its own flavor of this system: machismo. Machismo upholds male dominance in all spheres. Machistas rule the home and the street, and they achieve hegemony by using a wide range of tactics to enforce compliance. Physical and sexual violence are among the mechanisms waiting in the machista's toolkit.

A Chicana tomboy pedaling her bike down city streets to fill her pockets with cash would've defied the machista order of things, but my parents wouldn't state this explicitly. When I pressed them as to why they were so protective, they offered this vague justification: "Something bad might happen to you out there." In my naïveté, I thought they were insinuating kidnapping. As I entered puberty and learned about sexual assault, I realized that that was what they meant. Their concern had been for my "sexual virtue," and their concern was valid. In the United States, racially and ethnically minoritized femmes battle myriad stereotypes that oppressors use to justify the exploitation of our bodies. Brown femmes face several of these tropes including the spicy, hypersexualized Latina and the maid. Men who sexually assault us use the former trope to justify their violence. The latter is used to support the thesis that Latinas lack professional ambition and to justify our exclusion from white-collar environments.

My parents crushed my entrepreneurial dreams, in part, to shield me from exploitation and predation. This sort of exploitation and predation is very real and very dangerous. I've witnessed men brag about engaging in it. For example, at school, I once decided to sit with some faculty members who regularly congregated in my department head's classroom. All except one were white men who belonged to the history department faculty. As we ate lunch, one told a story. He explained that because his father uses a wheelchair, he requires the services of a housekeeper. The teacher said that retaining housekeepers had grown difficult. They kept quitting because his father sexually harassed his female employees, spewing lewd and lascivious language at them. Grinning, the teacher declared, "But I solved the problem!"

He waited a few moments, the way a comic does before delivering a punchline.

Another teacher urged, "How?"

Still grinning, he replied, "By hiring housekeepers who don't speak English."

I glared at him in horror, rage, and disgust. I looked at the Chicano teacher sitting across from me. He silently stared at his lunch.

I looked at all the other teachers, glaring, waiting for them to condemn what had just been said. Finally, the teacher sitting next to me said, "What? It's not like he was raping them."

Gringos like that are the reason my parents wouldn't let me go to strangers' homes to babysit.

The state of California requires me to teach that Adam Smith fathered classical economics. I'm supposed to celebrate his infamous metaphor, the invisible hand. In *The Wealth of Nations*, Smith wrote that

> [the rich] consume little more than the poor, and in spite of their natural
> selfishness and rapacity . . . they divide with the poor the produce of all
> their improvements. They are led by an invisible hand to make nearly the
> same distribution of the necessaries of life, which would have been made,
> had the earth been divided into equal portions among all its inhabitants,
> and thus without intending it, without knowing it, advance the interest
> of the society, and afford means to the multiplication of the species.

The most insidious lie in Smith's passage regards the hand's invisibility. Its color and gender are no secret. Its color is white and its gender is masculine and that's a truth students will learn, alongside Baby-Sitters Club anecdotes, if they arrive in my classroom.

Data-Sitters Club Super Special: "Business" Is to "Successful" as "Babysitter" Is to "_____"

QUINN DOMBROWSKI, ANOUK LANG, KATHERINE BOWERS, MARIA
SACHIKO CECIRE, ROOPIKA RISAM, LEE SKALLERUP BESSETTE

odel.wv.most_similar(positive=['successful', 'babysitter'], negative=['business'])
[('takecharge', 0.67197585105896),
 ('smart', 0.6682733297348022),
 ('reliable', 0.6532927751541138),
 ('athlete', 0.6501596570014954),
 ('loyal', 0.6426464915275574),
 ('outspoken', 0.64202880859375),
 ('caring', 0.6356360912322998),
 ('responsible', 0.6349359750747681),
 ('listener', 0.6343119740486145),
 ('speller', 0.633956253528595)]

It was time for another meeting of the Data-Sitters Club, precisely timed to
attempt to accommodate all six of us, from the Pacific Coast to Scotland.

"The thing that really struck me was the analogy, *business* is to *successful* as *babysitter* is to __" Maria said from her Zoom conference call square.

"*Yes!*" I blurted out, skimming our shared document with the results from Anouk's word embedding model. "Of all of them, *that's* the one that really feels like it *gets at something*."

But I'm getting ahead of myself. Hi! I'm Quinn Dombrowski—and like Kristy Thomas, I founded a club: the Data-Sitters Club. We're six academics (of one variety or another) who grew up reading the Baby-Sitters Club books, and we have come back to them as adults with more complex, nuanced questions about the language in the books. We've also got the tools to start answering them, through a combination of deep subject-area knowledge (Maria, for example, is a professor of children's literature) and experience using computational tools and methods (Anouk and I both study tools like machine learning). It's a passion project for all of us (alas, professor of BSC Studies isn't a job that exists), but it has given us a space to learn and write about computational methods, and we've been able to use the things we've written in our day jobs to deepen our understanding of foundational texts from our youth.

At this meeting, we were talking about "business language" in the Baby-Sitters Club series, and Anouk had put together what's called a word embedding model to help us understand the relationship between particular words and phrases in a corpus of the BSC books. Searching for the words most likely to complete the analogy "*business* is to *successful* as *babysitter* is to __" brought up a list of words with the highest probability of occurring in the books, including *takecharge, smart,* and *reliable* at the top. "I'd been wondering about the kind of language the books use to talk about the success of the Baby-Sitters Club as a business," mused Anouk, "and how evaluative terms of that sort might also be circulating in relation to the characters as young women more generally." For each of us, there was a particular word on the list that stood out—here are our thoughts on each of them.

QUINN

('takecharge', 0.67197585105896)
Business is to *Successful* as *Babysitter* is to *Take-charge.*

If you had told me at age ten—let alone thirteen—that at thirty-five I'd take charge of a group that would spend months digitizing, analyzing, and writing about the Baby-Sitters Club books, I'd have been incredulous. The Baby-Sitters Club books called to me at age seven from the big kids' section of the library, and I was hooked: I loved a good research project, and with help from these books, I was going to be so ready for junior high school.

But by adolescence, I had thrown the Baby-Sitters Club in the trash bin of false prophets. I couldn't really relate to any of the characters, and the one time I tried babysitting, I left the experience unimpressed—and with the realization I could make better money building websites. I doubted there was a place for someone like me in a universe as familiar as Stoneybrook. My preteen "girl power" phase centered on a different set of idols like Princess Leia, and *Sailor Moon*'s Sailor Neptune and Sailor Uranus, in downloaded episodes that left their queer relationship intact.

So why return to the BSC now, as an adult and parent who identifies as nonbinary, rather than female, and can more easily empathize with Elizabeth Thomas-Brewer than her BSC-president daughter? On one level, Stoneybrook is a convenient proxy for trying to understand some of the factors that shaped my own childhood. But more important, this series is a touchstone for many people—particularly women, who are underrepresented among scholars using computational methods. Using this series as a starting point might make those methods more accessible—especially if we complement our analysis with a detailed walk-through of how we did it, so other scholars can try it themselves.

ANOUK

('reliable', 0.6532927751541138)
Business is to *Successful* as *Babysitter* is to *Reliable.*

Reading the BSC novels in the 1980s in suburban Sydney, Australia, my remembered impressions are first, the exotic sheen of American consumerism that shimmered in the background of each story (barrettes! fashionable clothing! endless varieties of unfamiliar candy!), and second, the thrilling frisson of participating vicariously in the social dramas of a group of girls with far more glamorous lives than my own. Three-odd decades later, my collection of scholarly interests—digital humanities, twentieth-century literature, print culture, reception study—have equipped me to use computational tools to discern patterns in the language of the BSC books that may not be particularly noticeable while reading them but that become visible at scale.

One such approach is word embedding models: mathematical represen-tations of the relationships between words (known as word vectors) in a col-lection of texts. Algebraic operations can be performed on word vectors to explore how their meanings are related, for example, by looking at analogies between a group of words found in a set of texts. When asked "*king* is to *queen* as *man* is to ___?" a human being has no problem answering "woman," but it's more remarkable for an algorithm, trained on a word embedding model, to make that leap. And, sure enough, a word embedding model applied to the Baby-Sitters Club series, working from the way each term is positioned in relation to other terms across millions and millions of words, will deliver the answer of *woman*. But the next words in the list are more intriguing: *witch, chewbacca, exotic, artist, stunning, redhaired, owner, person, model.* These offer some additional associations with woman-ness to ponder: identity-related terms like *witch* and *artist*, but also descriptors that reference physical appearance like *exotic, stunning,* and *model. Chewbacca,* meanwhile, refers to the Perkinses' dog, and with only twenty-eight appearances in the dataset, it's a good reminder that with a smallish dataset, less frequent words will deliver less reliable results. And while "reliability" in the series tends to mean timely, experienced, and responsible—the backs of each of the books describe the club as "seven reliable babysitters," after all—within the hard sciences it translates to things like specific statistical tests and the ability to replicate one's results. For the DSC reliability means, in addition, grounding our computational findings in our disciplinary knowledge—for instance, DSC member Lee's familiarity with the linguistic differences between the way French is spoken in France and in Quebec, Roopsi's expertise with critical race theory, and Quinn's knowledge of a vast array of technologies and their uses and limitations when wrangling humanities data.

Word vectors sometimes produce obvious answers. Take for instance the vector for *dawn*—i.e., the words that appear the most commonly in closest proximity to, and hence are the most strongly associated with, this name—and subtract the vector for *stacey*, and you get a list of words that are specific to Dawn's family and household: *jeff, tigger, sharon, sweetheart, schafer, stepmother, richard, carol.* But word vectors also have the capacity to bring to light associa-tions that may not register for a human reader, but that when reinforced many times form a cloud of associated meanings—what scholars in linguistics call a semantic prosody. Start with *jessi* and subtract *mallory*, and you get a much less factual and much more evaluative list: *very, pretty, little, lot, casual, stretching, cool, nice.* Jessi minus Mallory, it would seem, is pretty and cool. This appears to conform to the books' casual cruelty in their depictions of Mallory, until you consider that the narratives that spend the most time describing Jessi *using the word Jessi* (i.e., that aren't in Jessi's own first-person voice) are Mallory's, and Mallory is effusive in her praise for her best friend in a way that the other narrators are not. It's an apt illustration of the way that, when analyzing books with quantitative techniques, what you find might be skewed by all kinds of factors. Through data analysis, we can delve into, for instance, the ideological messages that the books deliver to young readers about the qualities associated with success. Of course, the world delivers its own messages about books like The Baby-Sitters Club. . . .

ROOPSI

('listener', 0.6343119740486145)
Business is to *Successful* as *Babysitter* is to *Listener*.

I've never been a good listener. Much like Kristy, I have natural tendencies to jump in, interrupt, and always talk, though I've learned to keep it in check. As a child, I devoured the Baby-Sitters Club books, waiting impatiently for the Scholastic book order form each month or badgering my parents to take me to a bookstore. I kept reading the books long past the age of appropriateness, curious to know how the babysitters turned out, and began seeing the books in a new light. Who on earth would allow eleven- and twelve-year-olds, who seemed so grown up when I was seven, to watch their children? How was entrepreneurial girl power actually an extended lesson in the joys of capitalism? Why did the series go for colorblind racism in its insistence that it didn't matter to the other club members that Claudia was Japanese and Jessi was Black? That is, I've learned to listen to the books in a new way, with the perspective of an adult.

The role of race in the Baby-Sitters Club books is a topic that has preoccupied me for years. I wonder, for example, how word choices in the original series reflect perceptions of race in white dominant culture in the United States in the 1980s and '90s. Does how race is represented change over the course of the series, well into the 2000s, as public discourse on race changed? How do articulations of race, like the exoticization of Claudia's "almond-shaped eyes" or the insistence that it does not matter to other club members that Jessi is

Black, translate to other languages in cultures with different racial frameworks? As the resident skeptic of computational textual analysis, I wonder if counting words or looking at which words appear in proximity help us answer these questions. I'm not sure, and I worry about the ways in which our desire to find these answers may influence our interpretation of the patterns that computational textual analysis reveals.

These concerns point to the practice of listening as one that is critical to computational textual analysis: to avoid jumping to conclusions about these patterns and instead to listen to what they are saying, cross-referencing them with what the books in the series are saying. Equally as critical is listening to each other—to the perspectives and expertise that each of us brings to how we interpret the results: when Quinn points out the challenges of text encoding, when Anouk shares an article demonstrating the use of word proximities, when Maria says we're mistaking a common practice in children's literature for a significant finding. Listening, as a form of collaboration, is a feminist practice at the heart of the Data-Sitters Club's work and will perhaps help us better understand the power the Baby-Sitters Club has had on the imaginations of so many young people in the 1980s and 1990s—and how, in the 2020s, they're continuing to influence a new generation. After all, it's when the babysitters stop listening to each other, in BSC #100: *Kristy's Worst Idea*, that the club just falls apart.

MARIA

('caring', 0.6356360912322998)
Business is to *Successful* as *Babysitter* is to *Caring*.

When I was growing up, I imagined my future would look something like this: I'd wear suits and towering heels to an important job, and work in a tall, glassy building. At night I'd go home to my chic skyscraper apartment with a great city view. And somehow I'd also get married and start having children in my twenties, too—the plan was to be financially successful, independent, and powerful, but also loving, beloved, and feminine, all at the same time.

Business is to *successful*, in the BSC books, as *babysitter* is to *caring*—among other things. You can be *take-charge* and *outspoken* at the same time as *reliable* and a *listener*; self-determination and softness can go hand in hand. Dawn's ability to out-parent the beautiful but disorganized single mom in *Dawn and the Impossible Three* with her patience, compassion, and ingenious babysitter tricks is just one example of how the BSC members' work is not only a source of empowerment and income, but also a sign of these American girls' gendered virtues.

Of all the terms in the vector analysis above, the word *caring* jumped out at me because of how well it captures my own struggles to figure out what success means to me, as well as the sometimes contradictory values associated with my career as a professor and scholar of children's literature. While interviewing for the Rhodes Scholarship in 2005, I remember being asked repeatedly how studying children's literature could possibly help "fight the world's fight." Eventually I lost my temper and lashed back against the bias implicit in the idea that something associated with childhood, women's work, the humanities, and care is necessarily trivial—when in fact these are often the bedrocks on which lives and societies are built. To my amazement, the committee selected me. And, as I've come to learn, the strange hierarchies of success in elite spaces both within and outside of academia turned out to be a lot more complicated than the glittering high-rise pictures of my youthful imagination.

Studying a partially ghostwritten adolescent girls' series like the Baby-Sitters Club may seem to some like a fun nostalgia trip at best and a waste of time at worst. But analyzing children's and young adult literature can lay bare the structures that silently shape our everyday interactions and most sacred beliefs. In giving our attention to texts that meant so much to so many readers as they charted their various ways toward adulthood, we recognize that these books, these structures, and these readers are as important to our world as financial models, canonical literature, and scientific breakthroughs. My vision of professional success is still always evolving, but I love that where I am now allows me to work on subjects that I care about while maintaining intellectual and financial independence. And in the Data-Sitters Club, as with the best collaborative projects, I have my own gang of coworker-friends to learn from, laugh with, and bounce ideas off of in the process.

KATIA

('loyal', 0.6426464915275574)
Business is to *Successful* as *Babysitter* is to *Loyal*.

In the 1980s and early '90s, I was an American kid growing up in Germany because of my dad's job, and the Baby-Sitters Club was an important cultural link with the United States, a place I knew we would be moving "home" to one day, but where I'd spent little time. The BSC gave me some insight into not only the parts of American girlhood my own experience lacked, but also a familiar world that I could rely on, even when I moved schools, left friends behind, or felt culturally betwixt-and-between. I was a loyal reader, although the books were recognizably formulaic, and some of the plots could get a little unbelievable (shipwrecked, really? and how many gangs of thieves, haunted houses, and threatening phone calls can one group of girls encounter in a year?).

The books are designed to generate loyal readers. The formula at the beginning is carefully scripted so there's no need to read in order. Plot elements repeat throughout the series, and often echo those of classic children's series about girls growing up, learning, and developing friendships by Louisa May Alcott, L. M. Montgomery, and Maud Hart Lovelace, to name a few. Mystery is one of the most striking genres in the series, a clear debt to Carolyn Keene's Nancy Drew books. Even before the BSC Mystery series was launched in 1991, one in five of the BSC novels follows a plot where the girls work together to collect clues, investigate, and solve a mystery. Whether Martin and the BSC ghostwriters took their inspiration from these earlier books or not, it's notable that all are series. While Martin's BSC was originally planned as a series of four, the BSC books—like each of these other series—grew in number as loyal readers clamored for more adventures. BSC #12: *Claudia and the New Girl* is even dedicated "to the loyal readers of the Baby-Sitters Club books."

"Loyal" in the BSC universe doesn't usually refer to readers, however. Running a corpus search for the phrase "loyal BSC" brings up two hits: "loyal BSC clients" and "loyal BSC friends." These demonstrate the key values associated with loyalty in the books: the loyalty required of clients in order to build a successful business and the loyalty expected in friendships as close as those of the BSC members. What's funny about the BSC series is it generates loyalty in its readers precisely by combining these two categories: a successful business model (the BSC book formula) and a close relationship (the emotional attachment readers felt for the various BSC members). As a tween reader, I was also drawn to the series for precisely these two reasons.

When my family finally did move to the United States, I was in seventh grade and still reading BSC books, although I was then as old as Kristy was when she founded the club. In my new English class, we had a "free reading" period once a week. One day, done with all the class reading and happily immersed in a BSC book, I was surprised when my teacher book-shamed me in front of the class. She explained that the issue wasn't that I was reading for fun, but that the BSC books were "too young" and "not challenging enough" for me. This was the first time I was cognizant of what Claudia always complains about: that some books (for her, Nancy Drew mysteries) are more lowbrow and less valued than others.

The question of the social value of literature is central to my research now that I am a Russian literature professor. My work at first seems far afield from the BSC, although both Dostoevsky and Tolstoy appear briefly in BSC books. (Watson's copy of *Crime and Punishment* accidentally ends up in the Rodowskys' yard sale in #44, and #66 begins with the famous first line of *Anna Karenina*, "Happy families are all alike.") My research focuses on the cultural impact of gothic fiction—the popular, "trashy" stuff that everyone was reading in nineteenth-century Russia—on the long, philosophical novels that established nineteenth-century Russian writers like Dostoevsky and Tolstoy as great. Rereading the Baby-Sitters Club books now, I keep thinking about the cultural impact of the series, and how we might measure it. I wonder about all the loyal BSC readers, what they're doing now, and how the series informs their lives and work today.

LEE

['smart', 0.6682733297348022)
Business is to *Successful* as *Babysitter* is to *Smart*.

I, too, read the BSC books from afar, but not *as* far—just north of the border in Montreal, Quebec. I loved to read, and as a *smart kid*, was supposedly above book series, especially book series like the Baby-Sitters Club, in the same way Janine and Claudia's parents didn't approve of Claudia's love of the Nancy Drew series. I wasn't a genius like Janine, and while I was good at school and excelled at math like Stacey, I recognized myself most in Claudia's messy, disorganized room, although I envied her style smarts and social intelligence. I could be naive like Mary Anne but had none of her patience and active listening skills. Like Kristy, I was brash and competitive, but it also meant that I was a great team leader (I swam competitively) and ended up eventually becoming a good coach, too. As I learned as a young reader, there were so many different ways to be smart in these books, and while one BSC member over another didn't perfectly match my brand of smarts (which turned out to be ADHD) there were so many different and complementary ways to be a smart girl.

Outside of Judy Blume, there were few other places I could turn to read about strong female friendships where everyone got to shine in their own way, displaying their own "smartness" and strength, whatever that happened to be. But, still, the series wasn't deemed *serious* enough for a smart kid like me.

Fast-forward a few more years to graduate school. I was studying the most *serious* of disciplines, at least in the humanities: *comparative literature*. I was told that if I was *smart*, I would give up writing on the nascent internet. That I would choose the authors and works that I studied and wrote about and published wisely. Writing on the internet was fundamentally unserious and unworthy of my time, and would be looked down upon by those who may one day look to hire me as a (most serious) professor. I stopped for some time, but I eventually started writing online again. And if it weren't for that, I wouldn't have ever been included in the Data-Sitters Club, given the opportunity to (mostly) seriously write about the books I had long abandoned but never stopped loving.

My daughter now reads the BSC graphic novel adaptation and watches the new Netflix series. She took up the books long before I became a part of the Data-Sitters Club, and while she rolls her eyes at me when I describe the work I'm doing on the books (look, what thirteen-year-old is excited by the sociocultural and linguistic differences between French translations of the same book?), I still feel a sense of responsibility to her, and to my younger self, to show that you can be smart about books that have long been disregarded.

It is smart to write about the books you care about on the internet. It is smart to get a girl-gang together and talk about these books as a group. It is smart to follow your passion, your interests, even if people are telling you not to. It is all smart, it is all worthy, it is all deserving of being taken seriously. She deserves to be taken seriously, in all her facets.

We deserved it, too, and now we're (finally) asserting it.

I Am My Own Mr. Mom: Gender, Caregiving, and Labor in the BSC

Caolan Madden

The Baby-Sitters Club is the child of a deadbeat dad.

I mean, not really. We all know the club was Kristy's Great Idea, that it rose fully formed from the brain of Kristy Thomas one night when her mother had to make a million phone calls to find childcare for six-year-old David Michael. But one reason Mrs. Thomas had to rely on such an elaborate system of afterschool sitters to begin with was because Mr. Thomas ran out on the family when David Michael was an infant, forcing Mrs. Thomas to work full-time to support her four children—a situation that she feels guilty about but that has shaped Kristy into the brilliant caregiver and entrepreneur we know and love. Patrick Thomas is Kristy's distant, absent, deadbeat father, but he's also the mother of invention.

Given these origins, we shouldn't be surprised that the BSC series focuses on the details and logistics of childcare, that it takes childcare seriously as labor, and that it is explicit about the many configurations of families that care for the babysitters themselves and the children they sit for: while there are no visibly queer families in the BSC universe, there are divorced moms, widowed dads, stepparents, adoptive parents, grandparents, aunts. As a daughter of a single mom and a dad who "ran off" like Mr. Thomas—as a "Divorced Kid," in BSC parlance—I'm particularly attuned to the series' rich variety of absent and inadequate dads, and to the suggestion that we don't really need these dads anyway, that at best their absences are the catalyst for new, creative forms of caregiving. And as the mother of two young daughters, I'm beginning to recognize the influence the BSC has had on my thinking about gender, parenting, and labor.

✻   ✻   ✻

My own father left in 1987, when I was six years old, right around the time I started reading the Baby-Sitters Club books. My little brother was two. I remember an explosive family fight, my father yelling about a lost library book. A few days later we learned that he'd gotten on a train to Chicago and was staying at his mother's house in Bloomington, Illinois, a thousand miles from where we lived in Providence, Rhode Island.

I wish I could remember if this happened before or after I first read *Kristy's Great Idea*. In 1987 I wouldn't have considered myself a Divorced Kid. My parents were just living apart; they didn't get a formal divorce until I was ten. So I don't know if I would have recognized myself in Kristy, or my mom in Mrs. Thomas, or my dad in Mr. Thomas. Now that I'm a parent, I'm shocked that my father could stand to leave us. But back then I didn't blame him for leaving, for never paying my mom child support, for—eventually—marrying someone else. My dad didn't have any money. He was an artist and a prairie wanderer; the New England narrowness of Providence was killing him, he said. When he married my stepmother, I was glad someone was taking care of him—he needed care, I felt, more than I did.

✻   ✻   ✻

Just as the BSC books encourage you to identify with one or more of the club members—I'm a Mary Anne/Claudia hybrid—it also offers a range of dad archetypes. Here's an incomplete list; tag your dad (mine is a Deadbeat with, uh, Claudia rising):

The Deadbeat Dad: Mr. Thomas, who can't handle the responsibility of parenthood and takes off for the opposite coast, doesn't call or write, and doesn't pay child support. Fuck this dad.

The Disneyland Daddy: Dawn Schafer's dad, who also lives thousands of miles from his children but who, as Dawn explains, "feels *really* guilty" and tries to assuage his guilt by overindulging his kids: "A Disneyland Daddy doesn't feel like your father anymore. But I guess he's better than no father at all."

The Workaholic: Stacey McGill's dad, who provides for the family but is never home, and who after his divorce from Stacey's mom lives a short train ride away in glamorous NYC but is always missing important family events due to work.

The Strict Micromanager: Mary Anne Spier's dad, who bravely raises Mary Anne on his own after her mother dies, but who refuses to let her grow up, insisting she wear "babyish" clothes and observe strict curfews. (It's worth noting that, in keeping with our cultural expectations of mothers and fathers, the only dad we encounter as a primary caregiver has that role because his wife has died.)

The Bland Married Dad: Ann M. Martin seems to agree with Tolstoy that happy families are all alike, or at least that happy first husbands are all alike. Claudia and Mal and Jessi all have unremarkable dads who don't cause any trouble. (But also! Only three of seven core club members live with both biological parents! Wow!)

The Lovable Millionaire Stepfather: Kristy's stepfather, Watson Brewer—or, as he's affectionately described in BSC book #81, "Mr. Mom."

☀ ☀ ☀

It's appropriate, given the BSC series' embrace of blended families, that the best dad in the books is a stepfather. If Patrick Thomas is defined by absence, Watson is his opposite: nurturing, reliable, financially stable (a millionaire, to be precise!), perennially *present*, all qualities that are foregrounded in the title and plot of *Kristy and Mr. Mom*, in which a heart attack leads Watson to scale back his work as a health insurance CEO to stay home with his enormous family. (Between *Kristy's Great Idea* and *Kristy and Mr. Mom*, Mrs. Thomas and Watson get married and the Thomas family moves from their modest middle-class neighborhood to Watson's ritzy "mansion," soon to be joined by adopted toddler daughter Emily Michelle, Kristy's grandmother Nannie, and, every other month, Kristy's stepsiblings Karen and Andrew.) I never read *Kristy and Mr. Mom* as a child—by the time it was published in 1995 I was in high school and wasn't really keeping up with the BSC series, except for the occasional bathtime comfort-read. But in its treatment of gendered assumptions about work, caregiving, and domestic labor, the book is a reminder of how important the presence or absence of dads and the caretaking that they do or make possible is to the economy of the BSC universe—and to ours.

As an adult, I was struck by the title's goofy, outdated reference to the 1983 Michael Keaton film, and by the similarities between the book's cover illustration and the movie poster: both Watson and Keaton are depicted wearing red-and-white aprons, the universally agreed-upon symbol of Mr. Momhood. The movie *Mr. Mom*, like *Cocktail* and to a lesser extent *Baby Boom*, is a product of Reagan-era economic anxiety and reactionary gender politics, part of a fantasy 1980s cinematic universe in which men are ejected from the workplace to accommodate ball-busting, shoulder-padded businesswomen, so that they have no choice but to take on the feminized roles of caretaker or sex object. The phrase "Mr. Mom" gets at the heart of these anxieties: it's jokey, alliterative, an oxymoron because *of course* a man can't be a mom, *of course* it's impossible for a dad to be a nurturing parent. It marks domestic and affective labor as low-status, feminine work, and the men who perform that labor as comically feminized and pathetic. At the same time, the phrase can elevate the status of domestic labor—a man is doing it, after all. In stories that make use of the "Mr. Mom" trope—the movie, but also countless folktales and sitcom episodes—men often come to appreciate that housekeeping and childcare are real work, while their wives often excel in the workforce due to the management skills they've developed as housewives and mothers; at the end of these stories, mothers and fathers return to their traditional roles, but with a new understanding and respect both for domestic labor and for the women who perform it.

As we might expect from a series so committed to nontraditional families, *Kristy and Mr. Mom* revises some of these tropes. (In a note to the reader at the end of the book, Ann M. Martin describes her own parents' egalitarian approach to household chores: "my father didn't work at home, but he and my mother divided the household responsibilities pretty equally.") When Kristy jokingly refers to Watson as "Mr. Mom," he embraces the nickname; and initially, at least, he does a great job taking care of the family. "In a short time," Kristy tells us, "Watson had changed from Mr. Hot Shot Executive, driving a snappy red sports car and making deals on his car phone, to plain old Mr. Mom." Plain old Mr. Mom! The revolution already happened, and we didn't even notice.

Watson's choice doesn't seem to have any effect on his wife's identity as a mother or as a career woman—Elizabeth Thomas-Brewer may have started working out of necessity, but she kept her job after marrying a millionaire—but it does threaten Nannie, who abruptly moves out when she feels she's not needed. At the end of the book, Watson doesn't go back to the office full-time, but he does realize he's not cut out for full-time caretaking; the chaotic household, drowning in toddler vomit and buried in Watson's work faxes, has to be rescued first by supermom Mrs. Thomas, then by Nannie's return as a long-term caregiver for the family.

Unlike Nannie, Kristy doesn't seem threatened by Watson's new role—despite her disgust for Watson earlier in the series, she loves him now, touchingly describing him as "my father" to the 911 operator when he has his heart attack. But it does seem like Watson-as-Mr.-Mom is taking up a space that Kristy has filled for years. The syntax of the novel's title both unites her and places her in opposition to "Mr. Mom." A self-described "tomboy" and budding jock who has kind of come around to the value of mascara, Kristy is no stranger to the complex network of gender roles that Watson is just starting to juggle. As a skilled nurturer (she's the president of the *Baby-Sitters* Club) and a brilliant, aggressive entrepreneur (she's the *president* of the Baby-Sitters Club), she has already done away with any contradictions between the roles of high-powered executive and tender shaper of young minds and hearts. She commands total respect (*Mr.*) and enduring love (*Mom*). Is Kristy the *true* "Mr. Mom" in this story? Must Watson return to his sterile computer terminal in order to make way for Kristy to forge a new world for us all?

✳ ✳ ✳

The phrase "Mr. Mom" and the complex gender relationships it invokes is going to mean something very different to a pregnant trans guy, or to a trans mother bracing herself for being misgendered one more time, or to queer parents navigating assumptions about gender roles in their relationship, than it means to me, a cis woman who grew up underfathered and who found ways of thinking about caregiving in these books. I was never a tomboy; I don't really feel like a "Mr. Mom" myself. But I can imagine finding a model for parenthood outside a strict gender binary, not in Kristy's guilt-ridden working mom or her deadbeat dad, but in Kristy herself. The ideas about gender, work, play, and childcare invoked by "Mr. Mom" are fundamental to Kristy's character and to the BSC universe in general. Kristy is a Mr. Mom because she has had to compensate for her absent dad. Kristy is also a Mr. Mom because she is a Girl Boss and—like every member of the BSC—a competent and loving caregiver. The BSC helps me imagine a kind of parenting that is work but also joyous and fun, that allows for other pleasures and interests, that is simultaneously compassionate, creative, authoritative, cooperative.

One reason the club members are such great babysitters is because they form close bonds with the kids they sit for and pay attention to their charges in a way the kids' parents often don't, helping to solve family problems that the parents of Stoneybrook didn't even know were there. The babysitters can help their charges with these issues because they're dealing with similar ones in their own lives—a fact that is demonstrated in every novel by the entanglement of the main plot, which often focuses on a problem in the narrator's personal life, with a babysitting subplot that addresses similar issues. Like their charges, many of the club members struggle with communicating their needs and desires, with differentiating from their parents and siblings, with building their identities. Claudia's struggles in school make her an effective, empathetic tutor for Shea Rodowsky, who has dyslexia; Stacey, a diabetic, notices that Dana Cheplin's insulin dosage needs adjusting; Mallory's own longing for a more grown-up look helps her see that the Arnold twins need separate identities. And Kristy and Dawn develop special bonds with Divorced Kids, especially those with toxic or absent dads: Buddy Barrett, whose dad briefly kidnaps him to teach his mom a lesson; Jake Kuhn, whose dad moves away when his parents divorce; Karen and Andrew, who resent a custody arrangement that keeps them away from Watson after his illness. The babysitters talk through their charges' dilemmas and their own at club meetings and sleepovers; these experiences make the girls better babysitters, better caregivers and friends. So do the other aspects of their lives: friendships, relationships with grandparents and aunts, schoolwork, creative work, athletics, fashion, books. Dadlessness isn't depicted as a self-replicating trauma; it's one of many opportunities for empathy, for openness to new family arrangements, to new forms of caregiving and love.

✳ ✳ ✳

The babysitting subplot in *Kristy and Mr. Mom* is about two moms who try to get away with paying one babysitter to do the work of two. The book is about balancing the labor of caregiving and the labor of paid work, and while the economic value of caregiving is sidestepped in the main plot, it's emphasized in Mrs. Marshall's desperate ploy to carve out a few hours for her and her friend to make it to an afternoon jazzercize class. If you're a parent or you've worked in childcare, you've met plenty of Mrs. Marshalls: middle-class or upper-middle-class women, almost certainly white, exhausted by the nonstop intensity of motherhood, by the cost of childcare. Well-meaning, often politically progressive women who talk about the need for universal childcare, but whose solidarity with working-class women only goes as far as their own vacation and kitchen renovation budgets, their own headspace, the unrelenting mental load, their need for just a minute to *think*. Women who use this exhaustion to justify paying their nannies below a living wage—or, in this case, to justify springing five young children on Dawn, to act shocked and refuse to pay when Mallory calls Jessi for backup. It's hard to advocate for yourself when you're faced with a Mrs. Marshall, but finally Stacey and Claudia insist that she pay for two sitters, and when she refuses they walk right out the door, leaving Mrs. Marshall gaping in the doorway behind them, all dressed up in her jazzercise gear with nowhere to go.

Notably, we never see Mr. Marshall at all.

✳ ✳ ✳

What did those BSC dads teach me: deadbeat Patrick Thomas, Disneyland Daddy Mr. Schafer, strict grieving Mr. Spier, workaholic Mr. McGill, invisible Mr. Marshall? They and their daughters must have taught me that it was OK to be a Divorced Kid. But more important, I think they taught me that sometimes kids are wiser than their parents, and that the parent archetypes we were presented with—with all the gendered expectations that accompanied them—aren't the only options. What if being a mom doesn't have to look the way you expect? What if you don't need a dad to be a whole person?

And what if you can be a whole person and still be a parent? Like Ann M. Martin, and under the influence of the BSC, I babysat a *lot* as a teenager. When I finally became a parent myself, more than twenty years after I first started babysitting, I think I brought BSC caregiving values to the job. With a partner so present and loving and dorky and smart that he puts Watson Brewer to shame, and funny, wise mom friends who passed on tips about baby-led weaning and raising socially conscious kids as we sprawled on blankets in the park, my early motherhood felt like sharing a sitting job—or a sleepover, or a pizza party—with my best friends. I hoped that I was ready to listen to my children, to see them for who they really are, to roughhouse with them, to give them the tenderness we associate with mothers, the energy we associate with fathers. I looked forward to a rich life full of caregiving and ambition and joy, where my husband and I could both be a kind of Mr. Mom, shaping an egalitarian marriage in which we both could parent and jazzercise and create.

✲ ✲ ✲

In the early years of my parents' marriage, I think they hoped for that, too. Like Martin's parents, they shared household chores, and their domestic arrangements defied gendered expectations about caregiving and labor. My mother was a college theater professor, and during our infant and toddler years, my dad was Mr. Mom, taking care of us while my mother taught, carving woodcuts while I drew with crayons, earning money painting houses during my mother's summer break. But more and more, my dad looked for ways to escape: he smoked pot with some woman my mom hated, he went out dancing, he tripped on acid while he was giving us a bath, he went on monthlong hitchhiking trips, he left, he left, he left.

I don't think my dad left because being Mr. Mom is emasculating. I don't think those '80s movies got it right. I think the BSC books come closer: dads leave because they can. Because moms stay.

Even as a single parent, my mother managed to make work/life balance seem easy, although it must have been so hard. She rarely hired babysitters; she seems to have scheduled most of her teaching during our school hours. So I grew up with this idea that you can work and yet be totally present for your children, that caregiving isn't so hard after all.

Like Kristy, though, I'm my own dad in more ways than one. I dream of escaping: maybe just an hour of jazzercise. Maybe hopping a train in the middle of the day, not telling anyone where I'm going. Of course I feel that way even more now, when circumstances have made me a full-time caregiver.

✲ ✲ ✲

I began this essay planning to write about absent dads, about how Kristy-as-Mr.-Mom has taught me a way to parent, to nurture, that subverts or sidesteps the expectations we have for and the disappointments we feel about both moms and dads. I was going to say, we are all Mr. Mom! But as I struggled to write this essay on Mother's Day 2020 during a global pandemic, carving out a couple of hours to write as my sleep-deprived husband played with our six-year-old and our two-year-old, I realized that this is also an essay about parenting and work, about childcare, about labor. This is a time when the invisibility of domestic labor is becoming more visible to some people, if not to others. I minimize the file in which I'm writing this essay to read a Twitter thread about how impossible it's going to be to reopen the economy without daycares, to read countless articles about how mothers are bearing the brunt of educating and caring for children now that schools have closed. When I began my life as a parent, I wanted lots of time with my kids and also time for other kinds of work and play. A Kristy-level balance. But until this country starts to recognize childcare as labor, to help families shoulder the burden of an existing economic crisis exacerbated by a pandemic, that balance is impossible. There is no way to do this work of childcare and this other work at the same time.

At the end of *Kristy and Mr. Mom* Kristy realizes that it's her job as president to clarify the BSC's policies to Mrs. Marshall, who apologizes: "I forgot how professional you are." This, of course, is a common error: because we require paid caregivers to demonstrate that they love their jobs and their charges, we forget how professional they are. We forget that caregiving is work. But the babysitters never forget.

Great Ideas

THE WORLD BEYOND STONEYBROOK

THE JADED QUITTERS CLUB

DAWN'S MISGUIDED POWER MOVE

◄► SARCASTIC

SIO GALLAGHER

Could the Baby-Sitters Club Have Been More Gay?

Frankie Thomas

This is an allegory, but it's also true: I grew up in Chelsea, the Manhattan neighborhood that was, at the time, the center of gay life in New York. We moved there in 1989, when I was two. I was one of very few children in the neighborhood. There was a park right across the street from my building, but only grown men hung out in it, and I wasn't allowed to play in it. I was enchanted by the rainbow flags that hung from windows in the summertime, but I couldn't get any adult to tell me what they were for. ("Brotherhood," my preschool teacher told me and refused to answer follow-up questions.) In elementary school we had an art teacher who was openly living with AIDS, and every Christmas he had us decorate paper gift bags to donate to a meal service for AIDS patients. When he died, in 1996, I was nine years old and had still never heard the term *gay*. I was in middle school when I first began to encounter it, but only from classmates, and only as an insult. I was thirteen when I was finally deemed old enough to be told who in our family was openly gay. (My late grandfather, for one. Long story.) I told my ten-year-old brother and got in trouble for upsetting him; he was too young, I was chided, to handle such things.

Such was the cultural cognitive dissonance around homosexuality in the 1990s. To say it was a transitional period does not begin to capture the weirdness of growing up internalizing the idea that gay people were deserving of rights, worthy of social acceptance, and outrageously inappropriate to discuss in front of children. This paradox is crystalized in the 1993 *Seinfeld* episode that gave us the catchphrase "Not that there's anything wrong with that!" That episode won a GLAAD award. So did the first season of *Friends*, in which every utterance of the word *lesbian* was met with uproarious canned laughter, as if the word itself were raunchy and daring—and it was, in 1995.

Gay people were, of course, nonexistent in children's entertainment. The Scholastic industrial complex would sooner have published a bomb-building manual than allow an openly gay book character in the 1990s. But the paradigm shifted so rapidly in the mid-2000s that even I am occasionally tempted to judge the books of my childhood by the standards of subsequent decades— hence my long-held, largely irrational grudge against Ann M. Martin.

Martin was the creator, original author, and public face of the Baby-Sitters Club. Although the vast majority of the series was ghostwritten, her name and face and cutesy bio ("She likes ice cream, the beach, and *I Love Lucy*, and she hates to cook") appeared on each book; she was as familiar as an aunt. When the news came out in 2016 that she was a lesbian, I was surprised by the uncomplicated rejoicing among my queer-woman cohort, and then surprised by the force of my own resentment. My knee-jerk reaction, I'm not proud to say, was: *So what? What did she ever do for us?*

To which the obvious rejoinder would be: *She gave us Kristy Thomas, you idiot!* When queer women look back fondly on the Baby-Sitters Club, it's usually with a focus on Kristy, the club's founder and president. Even Martin herself revealed in a 2014 interview that Kristy was her favorite—no surprise there. The books incessantly reminded us, in those exposition-laden early chapters, that Kristy was a "tomboy"; that she wore a "uniform" of jeans, sneakers, and a baseball cap; that she loved sports, especially baseball, and coached a children's softball team; that she loathed dresses and makeup, didn't "need" a bra, and—the books were oddly fixated on this detail—*didn't even have pierced ears*. Kristy, in short, was a lesbian-coded character if there ever was one.

But the coding went only so far. On a textual level, the series was constantly insisting on the babysitters' heterosexuality—their interest in boys, their attractiveness to boys, their availability to boys—and Kristy was no exception. Kristy's recurring love interest was Bart Taylor, the handsome boy next door who coached a rival children's softball team. "I have a crush on Bart," Kristy informs the reader on the first page of *Kristy's Mystery Admirer* (BSC #38), a book that ends with him kissing her at the school dance. In *Snowbound* (Super Special #7), Bart is stranded overnight at Kristy's, and Kristy, in a panic, sets her alarm for 5:30 AM to give herself a makeover. She shaves her legs, blow-dries and curls her hair, puts on mascara and blush. Much is made of how unusual this is for Kristy, but Bart's approval makes it all worth it:

> Bart whispered to me, "You look beautiful, Kristy."
> I relaxed. "Thanks," I said.
> Okay. I had made it. Bart had spent the night at my house. . . . He was sitting next to me, telling me I looked beautiful.
> If Bart and I could weather that, we could weather anything.

Snowbound, too, ends with Bart taking Kristy to the school dance. School dances were held in seemingly every other book. A young reader could easily get the impression that life itself was a school dance, and that you couldn't show up to it without an opposite-sex date.

☆ ☆ ☆

Still, the series did seem aware on some level that Kristy was not available to boys in the same way that her fellow babysitters were. Her romance with Bart came to a permanent end in the unpronounceably titled *Kristy + Bart = ?* (#95), in which Kristy finds herself recoiling from Bart's kisses. At the book's emotional climax, Kristy telephones Mary Anne—the only BSC member with a "steady boyfriend," and therefore the BSC's resident authority on relationships—and tearfully confesses that being with Bart "sometimes makes me feel weird and I'm not sure I'm ready for what he wants me to be."

It's an intense scene; I imagine a generation of queer girls tensing up with recognition as they read it. This was a precious opportunity for the series to reach out to those readers, to reassure them in age-appropriate language that there would always be a place for them at the school dance—or, indeed, that the world was bigger than a school dance.

Here, instead, is what follows:

> "It doesn't sound like you're ready for Bart to be your boyfriend," Mary Anne said.

"But I'm thirteen!"

Mary Anne was silent for a moment. "Kristy, how old were you when you first learned to walk?"

"Nine months," I replied. . . .

"I was fifteen months old," Mary Anne said. ". . . Don't you see, Kristy? Claudia and I weren't ready to walk when you were. But eventually we learned, and now who cares? . . . People don't do everything at the same rate. . . . If you're not ready, you're not ready, Kristy."

It's taken for granted, in this scene and in the rest of the book, that Kristy will "eventually" pair up with a boy. It's universal and inescapable, like death. If the prospect makes Kristy "feel weird," this can only mean that she's "not ready" for the inevitable. In fact, the book ends on the implication that Kristy may be ready sooner rather than later. She's crushed to learn that Bart took another girl to—yes, really—the school dance, and the book's wistful final lines tease the possibility of Kristy and Bart getting back together:

But I have to admit, when I see [my brother] Charlie and [his girlfriend] Sarah together, I get this funny feeling in my stomach. I don't really understand it, but it doesn't matter. After a while, it goes away. And so do my thoughts of Bart. More or less.

(Could the "funny feeling" at the sight of Sarah be read another way? It could, I suppose, but there's little else in the text to support it. Sarah barely registers as a character.)

I realize it's not quite fair of me to blame Ann M. Martin for *Kristy + Bart = ?*, which was published in 1996, long after the ghostwriter takeover. (A note at the front of the book—"The author gratefully acknowledges Peter Lerangis for his help in preparing this manuscript"—tacitly credits Lerangis as ghost author.) But *Kristy + Bart = ?*, like all late-period BSC books, contained a bonus "Dear Reader" letter attributed to Martin herself, complete with a handwritten signature. For all I know, this too was ghostwritten, but either way it's a rather remarkable document.

Dear Reader,

Kristy + Bart = ? is about a confusing time in Kristy's life, a time when she's faced with decisions she's not ready to make. A lot of kids have written to me to say that they feel pressured to have a boyfriend, or to be in a relationship they don't feel ready for. I wanted to address this issue in a BSC book, and felt that Kristy was the most likely character to find herself in this situation. Eventually, Kristy is mature enough to realize that people are ready for different things at different times. And just because her friends have boyfriends doesn't mean that she's ready for such a relationship right now.

The word "ready" appears in nearly *every single sentence* here, to the point that it threatens to lose all meaning through repetition. Knowing what we now know about Martin, it's hard not to read into it a certain bitterness, to hear her grinding her teeth as she recites corporate-approved platitudes carefully stripped of any suggestion of queerness. One wonders if she originally pushed for different wording. Perhaps not; perhaps she assumed there was no use even trying.

Poor Ann M. Martin! It wasn't her fault, and it surely gave her no pleasure, that her fictional universe was a vast heterosexual hellscape. How, in the 1990s, could she and her ghostwriters possibly have gotten away with disturbing that universe?

Except they almost did. There was a time, shortly after the publication of *Kristy + Bart = ?*, when they came breathtakingly close.

In 1997, a new Baby-Sitters Club spin-off called California Diaries began to appear on supermarket shelves. The crossover character was Dawn Schafer, the occasion for the spin-off her relocation from Connecticut to California. Despite Dawn's presence in the new series, its cover art signaled forcefully that it would *not* contain babysitting. Rejecting the original series' kiddie aesthetic of letter blocks and pastels, the California Diaries had matte covers with soft-focus photographs of gorgeous, unsmiling teens. They were plunging into pool water, or sprawling on disheveled bedsheets, or just gazing sadly into the distance. Sometimes, at first glance, they even appeared to be naked. In a word, they were *sexy*—a quality heretofore utterly alien to the BSC universe. The California Diaries clearly communicated, without having to say it explicitly, that they were for *mature* readers, those who had grown far too cool for the Baby-Sitters Club. I was ten years old, and I was instantly hooked.

I can only assume that Scholastic didn't think it through, because the spin-off's fundamental flaw was obvious from the start: with the original Baby-Sitters Club series still ongoing, the California Diaries could not violate the *Ground-*

hog Day time line of the BSC universe, whose characters were not permitted to age past eighth grade. The California Diaries got around this, sort of, with the belabored premise that Dawn and her California friends were transferred from their overcrowded middle school to a high school *building*, which placed them in tantalizing proximity to high schoolers. With the main characters permanently stunted at age thirteen, though, the dramatic potential was severely limited. Alcohol was consumed, but never by the first-person narrator, who could only look on disapprovingly until the drinking was punished. Anorexia was contracted and cured within a single book. There was no problem that could not be solved by confiding in a trusted adult (except when Sunny Winslow's mom died of cancer, but that wasn't sexy). No one even kissed with tongue.

And amid all this there was Ducky McCrae, the only boy and only bona fide high schooler (a sophomore) in the core cast. He hung out with Dawn and her fellow eighth-graders because his peers bullied him. You might expect this arrangement to generate some romantic tension, but Ducky's relationship with the girls was purely platonic. He went shopping with them. He listened sympathetically to their chaste dating dilemmas and had none of his own.

It's difficult to describe Ducky without sounding like I'm speaking in coy euphemisms, flapping my wrist suggestively, as if trying to talk over the heads of children. He was *sensitive*, if you know what I mean. He *enjoyed fashion and Broadway musicals*, if you know what I mean. He was *just one of the girls*, if you know what I mean. Not that there's anything wrong with that!

✳ ✳ ✳

Have you ever played Taboo? It's a card-based party game in the tradition of charades. You draw a card with a secret word on it (say, *mustard*), and you must convey this word to the group without uttering it or any of the related forbidden words on the card (*yellow, condiment, spread, Dijon, hot dog*). "It's a . . . flavor agent . . . used on grilled meats . . . and a weaponized gas in World War I," you sputter until someone shouts "Mustard!" or time runs out.

Reading the California Diaries is like an endless game of Taboo in which the secret word is always *gay* and time always runs out. At the climax of *Ducky: Diary One* (#5), Ducky is taunted by a male classmate: "You can't change, can you? . . . I give you all these chances to be a NORMAL GUY, and what do you do? Act like a WIMP. Maybe that's the way you ARE, huh? Maybe there's a REASON you can't meet girls! Maybe I'm wasting my breath and all these guys are RIGHT about you—" The bully is quickly cut off before he can specify what, exactly, "all these guys" are speculating.

The series liked to use *wimp* as a stand-in for the unsayable word. In *Dawn: Diary Three* (#11), Ducky is the target of it once again: "'You know what? You are a wimp,' Sunny said to Ducky. '. . . No wonder your friends are a bunch of thirteen-year-old girls. Guys think you're a dweeb, and girls your own age don't even look twice at you.'"

Dawn, the narrator, is shocked and aghast at Sunny's G-rated words. "Ducky cast his eyes to the floor," Dawn narrates gravely. "For a moment, no one said a word." Dawn observes "the stricken look on Ducky's face" and imagines that "he felt the way I would feel . . . if he had just insulted me in the most hurtful way he could think of." This reaction makes no sense—none of this makes any sense—unless you mentally swap out *wimp* and *dweeb* for, well, you know— (*Ding*. Time's up.)

It takes Ducky two entire books to forgive Sunny for the cruelty of her outburst. (I mean, she called him the W-slur!) By *Ducky: Diary Three* (#15), he is reconciled with Sunny but troubled by his lack of attraction to her:

I'm not very good at guy things. And I just don't get it. It's like all the other guys have this book of rules that someone forgot to give me.

Or maybe I got the book, but some of the pages were left out.

Or maybe I got a different book? Is there more than one book of how to be a guy?

…What am I?

Am I a failed guy?

Suddenly, in the next paragraph, he seems to realize something he can't quite articulate:

Wait a minute: Just because I'm not IN LOVE with Sunny doesn't make me a failure. And there are plenty of guys who cook (aka RICH AND FAMOUS CHEFS) and like cool clothes (ROCK STARS, MOVIE GUYS).

Still, if I understood this whole guy thing, would I feel so freaked out about Sunny?

I work in a bookstore. Where on the shelves is the book on how to be a GUY???

Ducky: Diary Three was published in 2000, by which point I was thirteen and hyper-attuned to all things Ducky McCrae. Reading about him felt like trying to hear my favorite song on a just-out-of-range radio station, waiting anxiously for the static to clear. I was beginning to suspect that the unspeakable G-word might apply to me, and I kept careful track of books that dared to deploy it. In the entire Animorphs series it appeared exactly twice. (Spin-off book Megamorphs #4, Tobias: "Was it really true that [this cultlike organization] didn't care if you were young or old, male, female, black, white, Asian, Christian, Jew, Muslim, Buddhist, atheist, straight, gay, rich, or poor?" And Animorphs #23: *The Pretender*, Tobias again: "Hard to imagine humans welcoming [Hork-Bajir aliens] into the local Boy Scout troop when they couldn't even manage to tolerate some gay kid.") A minimal gesture, but it rocked my world. It's a major reason I remember Animorphs so fondly, and a major reason I soured on Ann M. Martin. If nerdy old Animorphs could say the word, was it too much to hope that the sexy California Diaries would go there?

It was. Ducky was never allowed to figure out why he wasn't attracted to girls, why he felt so different from the other guys. *Ducky: Diary Three* is the final book in the series. The above-quoted "What am I?" reverie ends, unresolved, with Ducky at his bookstore job, staring curiously at a collection of poetry:

> It's a mix. Whitman. Adrienne Rich. And Baudelaire.
> Maybe I'll have to check them out sometime.

"Come on! *Whitman!*" I imagine the ghostwriters shouting in a last desperate attempt to win this unwinnable game of Taboo. "Fucking *Adrienne Rich!*" But that clue was too esoteric even for me. Who was it intended for? Who was any of it intended for? If this thwarted coming-out narrative was meant as a coded reassurance for readers like me, it failed: for my thirteen-year-old self, Ducky McCrae never inspired hope or courage or anything but closeted despair.

On the other hand, he's never left me. I remember Kristy Thomas as a frustrating character in a book series I read a lifetime ago, but I remember Ducky McCrae as if he were a real guy I used to know. Every now and then, I even catch myself wondering what became of him—did he ever come out? Is he happier now? No, of course not; he's trapped forever, along with the rest of the Baby-Sitters Club, in the hetero hellscape of the Scholastic industrial complex.

Or perhaps I'm only projecting. Perhaps some part of me is still holding *Ducky: Diary Three* in my hands, studying the page where Ducky is studying the poetry book in his own hands, the two of us a recursive image of kid readers in the '90s, searching for something that can't speak its name.

Jessi on the Margins: Black Characters Then and Now

Chanté Griffin

I remember the day my boxed set of the Baby-Sitters Club books arrived. It was my sixth grade culmination and I was adorned in my Sunday best: a flower dress my mother had sewn that was covered with pink and lavender flowers; cream stockings; and black patent leather heels. (They were my first pair of heels, and you couldn't tell me that those one-inch block heels didn't make me look grown and gorgeous!) After the ceremony and the obligatory photos with my familial entourage, my teacher, a blonde white woman with short hair, came running toward my family, arms flapping to get my attention: "These just arrived in the mail!"

Reading the books that summer felt like as much of a treat as the cherry-flavored popsicles my little sister and I licked in the California sunshine. In my mind, Kristy, Mary Anne, Stacey, and Claudia were my BFFs, even without the matching heart necklaces to prove it. When Mallory and Jessi joined the club, I embraced them too. But something didn't sit right with me about Jessi, even though we both had moved to neighborhoods and schools where we were suddenly one of the few Black kids; and even though we both were experiencing racism for the first time at those schools.

As an eleven-year-old, I couldn't articulate what I now recognize as an adult: that the series' depiction of Jessi's racial identity lacked the kind of cultural sophistication I needed as a young reader, particularly as a young reader who was Black. In some ways, Jessi's inclusion in the series was ahead of its time given the lack of diversity in children's and young adult literature. In other ways, it was also painfully reflective of that time.

It's challenging to offer a critique about a writer whose books you loved as a kid, really difficult to highlight what she got wrong when you know that she tried hard to get it right. I'm tempted to skip over certain words like little girls skip over certain squares in hopscotch—just to spare her feelings. Although I wish that race would've been handled differently in the BSC series, I appreciate that it was addressed. For example, my heart leapt when Jessi received the role of Swanilda despite her concern that the town's racism might prevent it. As a former commercial model, I know what it's like for casting notices to say "sorry, no Black girls," or "light-skinned Black women only." I know what it's like to read those notices, to feel pain, and to grieve that I won't be selected. So when Jessi won the coveted role, my tear ducts filled with pride and relief. Even while rereading the book as an adult.

My angst with Jessi's character, though, started with her introduction in BSC #14: *Hello, Mallory.* Although Mallory initially describes Jessi as "beautiful," noting that "She was long-legged and thin, and even sitting down she appeared graceful," Mallory also adds: "Also, she was black."

"Wow," Mallory tells us, noting how few Black students there are in her school. "This was pretty interesting."

While my eleven-year-old self knew only that she didn't like that Jessi's presence was "interesting," my adult-self realizes that I wanted to meet Jessi first, and any ensuing racism later.

Throughout *Hello, Mallory,* it becomes painfully obvious that to some of the residents of Stoneybrook, Blackness was the black elephant in the room that they didn't know how to address directly, but that sometimes loomed as a source of discomfort. This was true even for Mallory and her more progressive family, who welcomed Jessi in ways their neighbors didn't. Mallory and Jessi's discussion about the racism Jessi was experiencing in town particularly stood out:

"I don't belong in this school, or even this town. Neither does my family."
"You mean because you're, um . . ."
"You can say it," Jessi told me. "Because we're black."

This conversation was difficult for me to read as a preteen *and* as an adult. While I understand that the point of this scene was to bond Jessi and Mallory and to discuss a critical issue, I wanted it to play out differently. As written, it suggested to me that being Black was a taboo topic that Mallory couldn't address directly. I'm saddened that eleven-year-old Jessi had to coach her future BFF on how to talk about race. I'm saddened, too, that when she met Mallory's mom for the first time, Jessi had to endure her surprised (*wow, I didn't expect a Black person to walk in*) look. While Jessi would go on to enter that home innumerable times without incident, that introduction remained etched into my eleven-year-old mind.

When Jessi introduces herself at the start of each book she narrates, she notes that she is "black" or "African American." For example, in BSC #16: *Jessi's Secret Language*, after she introduces her mom, dad, little sister, and brother, she tells us: "My family is black. I know it sounds funny to announce it like that. If we were white, I wouldn't have to, because you would probably assume we were white. But when you're a minority, things are different." Yes, it *did* sound funny to my eleven-year-old self, as I never thought that my Blackness was worth stating, not even to my sixth-grade pen pal, who had never met me because she lived in another state. Every time I read Jessi's self-descriptions, I felt uncharacteristically self-conscious about my race. Jessi's incessant labeling of herself as Black, coupled with her explanations about why she needed to, left my preadolescent self feeling unsettled and pushed to the margins.

Looking back I realize that Jessi's identity was steeped in race in ways the white characters' identities weren't. Back then, however, I didn't have the words to describe the discomfort I was experiencing or questions to challenge Ann M. Martin's logic: *Were protagonists assumed to be white? If so, were they presumed to be white only by white readers or by all readers? Was Martin making Jessi accommodate the white gaze?* In her 2016 article "The Pervasive Whiteness of Children's Literature: Collective Harms and Consumer Obligations," Brynn F. Welch writes that "the pervasive whiteness" of children's literature feeds the idea that "white is the norm or default while other races are variations from that norm." An example she cites is how skin color gets described in many children's books: "White skin is the default and as such requires no special attention. Deviations from this default, however, require comment or explanation." This explains why I felt uncomfortable every time Jessi said "I'm black," "We're black," and "You should know that we're black." All of those statements clearly—even if unintentionally—positioned

Jessi as outside of the norm. (Claudia's descriptions mirrored this pattern, too.) Kristy, Mary Anne, Stacey, Dawn, and Mallory were never similarly burdened with describing themselves as white. They lived fictional lives unburdened by race.

Welch observes that "race often defines characters of color." It's this aspect of Jessi's construction that my eleven-year-old self intuitively disliked. Because her introductory story into the series and resultant self-descriptions conspicuously centered her race while unintentionally positioning her on the margins, being Black, then, became a plot point she could never escape, despite her varied babysitting adventures.

Neither could Jessi escape the stain of racism that can subtly vilify its victims more than its perpetuators. For instance, in BSC #55: *Jessi's Gold Medal*, she tells us: "People have gotten used to us (doesn't that sound weird?)." Yes, Jessi, it does! Here, Blackness gets positioned as the thing that needs to be gotten "used to." As if *it* were somehow problematic, instead of people's attitudes. As if being Black and the dirty racism against Blacks are imperceptibly intertwined. As a result, Jessi's Blackness is either something to be whispered about, ignored, or overcome, and being Black is simultaneously an unmentionable stain and an always-mentioned stain that parenthetically sullies Jessi's intelligence, discipline, and babysitting badassery.

Looking back, I recognize that I wanted Jessi's stories to be "culturally conscious," a term author Rudine Sims defines in her book *Shadow and Substance*. Sims explains that culturally conscious stories integrate a character's universal experiences with her race and culture. In the BSC, this happens only too rarely. For example, to me the best part of BSC #103: *Happy Holidays, Jessi* isn't the exploration of Kwanzaa but rather the matter-of-fact *pecan pie* mention. When reading about the Ramseys, I wanted to witness more details like that, details that celebrated Black life and culture in daily life. I wanted Jessi's race and culture to be seamlessly integrated into her life and babysitting adventures, and not just used as story plots. We could have seen Jessi endure a marathon-braiding session with her mom in preparation for her synchronized swimming classes. Or watched her travel to another city to have a Black hairstylist braid her hair if her mom didn't know how (because obviously nobody in Stoneybrook would know how to braid extensions). Either would have rung as authentic and affirming for me and other readers like me. Seeing Jessi's cultural context—my cultural context—would've helped me feel known, seen, and celebrated while reading the series.

What the eleven-year-old me wanted, too, was not just for African American culture to be celebrated in the BSC, but for Blackness to be *centered*: for Black skin to be as unassuming as white skin, to make no accommodations for the white gaze. The late Nobel Prize winner Toni Morrison mastered this: introducing readers to Black female protagonists who were not necessarily physically described as Black yet exuded a cultural consciousness that showed readers they were. While perhaps it's unfair to compare kids literature to fiction crafted by one of the most celebrated writers of our time, I mention Ms. Morrison because she refused to write Black women the way they had been written about in an industry that centered whiteness. She broke the broken mold, and created a new one.

I recognize that Ms. Martin too broke the mold when she wrote teen and preteen girls as ambitious, talented, multifaceted businesswomen. Yet she missed an opportunity to challenge norms about how Black characters were written in YA and children's literature. When Jessi is first introduced to readers, Martin's description could have included a description of Jessi's brown skin, without the racial tag, and she could have described the skin of white characters so that all characters received equal treatment under the pen. Similarly, Jessi's beautiful description of her father's laugh in *Jessi's Gold Medal*, which she described as "deep and booming," and "sort of like James Earl Jones, the famous actor," could've stood alone, without adding that he was Black.

The painful irony is that, even as Martin tried to dismantle the pervasive whiteness of children's literature by including Jessi in her series (not to mention the ever-chic Claudia Kishi), in book after book after book, Jessi bore the brunt of accommodating that whiteness, even in her own character's POV. In book after book after book, I too was made to bear the brunt of the pervasive whiteness of children's literature: each supposition to Jessi's "difference" was unmistakably a supposition to my own.

Looking at Jessi's character now, it's clear that she was a glimmer of what was to come in YA and children's literature: young, gifted, and Black characters who fully reflect their racial and cultural heritage without being unduly defined by it. Jessi came before Black female protagonists like Jade (*Piecing Me Together*, 2017), Starr (*The Hate U Give*, 2017), and Natasha (*The Sun Is Also a Star*, 2016), all written by Black women writers. But these protagonists would emerge only after the publishing industry was called out for its lack of diversity.

At the 2014 BookCon, an event sponsored by BookExpo America, the lineup of children's authors featured thirty white authors and one cat. There were zero writers of color. *Zero.* Backlash quickly ensued, and the #WeNeed-DiverseBooks movement emerged, pushing for diversity in children's books. A study published by the Cooperative Children's Book Center highlighted the disparity. Analyzing the 3,200 books their library received in 2013, the study found that only 93 (2.9 percent) of those books were about Black characters, 69 (2.2 percent) were about Asian Pacific Americans or Asian Pacific Islanders, 57 (1.8 percent) were about Latinos, and 34 (1 percent) were about American Indians. The remaining 2,947 books (92.1 percent) featured either white characters or animals. *Let that sink in.*

More than thirty years after Jessi's babysitting debut, the need to advocate for more diverse stories, including nuanced stories about Black women and girls (especially those written by Black women), remains.

Thanks to activism on Twitter and beyond, it's becoming increasingly difficult for the publishing, TV, and film industries to avoid telling a multitude of stories starring a diverse cast of characters. The emergence of the seemingly perennial #OscarsSoWhite hashtag, coupled with the #ownvoices hashtag—which supports kid lit about diverse characters written by authors from that same marginalized group—has brought increased attention to the need for diversity on the page and on the screen. As a result, more talented, underrepresented writers are flooding readers' pages and screens. Jamaican American author Nicola Yoon's *The Sun Is Also a Star*, a love story about a Jamaican-born girl and a Korean American boy falling in love as she seeks to avoid deportation, was so popular that it was adapted into a feature film, as was Angie Thomas's *The Hate U Give*, which explores police shootings of unarmed Black men.

Of course there have always been talented Black women writers penning tales worthy of the page-to-screen honor, just like Martin's series; but for centuries, closed doors have often excluded them from high-profile publishing opportunities. This lack of inclusion and celebration led to the creation of the Coretta Scott King Book Awards in 1969. Its website states that it honors "outstanding African American authors and illustrators of books for children and young adults that demonstrate an appreciation of African American culture and universal human values." It's important to note that the Coretta Scott King Book Awards celebrated Black writers and Black stories—*before* Twitter hashtags demanded diversity in children's literature and *before* the Newbery Medal Selection Committee gave its top prize to its first Black author in 1975.

As efforts to diversify children's literature have gained momentum, particularly over the last five years, more Black authors have received their just due, including honors from the Newbery Medal Selection Committee, which typically lead to increased sales and national recognition for its acclaimed authors. Recently, 2020 was a stellar year for Black storytelling as *The Undefeated* by author Kwame Alexander and illustrator Kadir Nelson and *Genesis Begins Again* by author Alicia D. Williams became 2020 Newbery Honor Books. That same year, the Newbery Medal went to Jerry Craft's graphic novel *New Kid*, which follows the life of seventh grader Jordan Banks as he navigates life on the margins at a prestigious private school.

One of my personal favorites is Renée Watson's *Piecing Me Together*, a 2018 Newbery Honor Book and recipient of a Coretta Scott King Book Award, which portrays Jade, a high-school-aged collage artist navigating her identity as an artist and new student at a prep school across town. Watson shows how Black culture, plus racism and sexism, permeated every part of Jade's life: from where she ate, to the artists she studied. But, unlike Jessi, her Blackness didn't loom ominously over her. It was simply a foundational truth from which her life and art bloomed. Jade bravely pieced together an identity that fused together the best and worst that life brought.

Books like *Piecing Me Together* and *New Kid* are giving young Black readers the gift of seeing themselves alive in print as beautiful, complicated, thriving beings. Yet I understand that all kids need diverse books, not just Black kids. "Because of the long shadow of racial segregation," Welch writes in "The Pervasive Whiteness of Children's Literature," "many Americans will learn about people of other races from second-hand representations. Consequently, the second-hand representations are powerful, especially for young children, because these early representations can shape lasting impressions."

As a writing and literature coach, I teach my students not to just consume a diversity of good books, but also to critically unpack the literature they consume by asking: *Do I identify with this? Why or why not? Whose perspective is centered in this book? What works? What could be different? How?* I hope my students will know that their lives are worth being reflected back to them, that their stories are worth being told: stories about their Blackness, stories unrelated to their Blackness, and stories that reflect their cultural heritage. Ultimately I want them to find protagonists that they can hold in their hearts for a lifetime, just like I hold Kristy, Mary Anne, Stacey, Claudia, Dawn, Mallory, Jessi, and Jade in mine.

MAKING "THE CLAUDIA KISHI CLUB"

SUE DING

As a kid, I read voraciously. I lived vicariously through books, running away to the Metropolitan Museum of Art or befriending dragons or churning butter on the frontier. I encountered all kinds of people in these stories—good and evil, old and young, magical and mundane—but rarely came across characters of color. The books I read focused on white families in suburbia, white kids on adventures, white knights in fantasy worlds.

This seemed normal to me at the time—as an Asian American kid growing up in an extremely white town in Upstate New York, I didn't encounter a lot of people who looked like me. But subconsciously, I craved representation. I was so desperate to be seen that I latched onto Spinelli from the animated TV show *Recess*, with her straight black hair—a badass Asian tomboy! More than a decade later, I realized her name was . . . Spinelli . . . and internet research confirms she was 100 percent Italian American (to be fair, many people seem to have been confused about this).

When I did encounter an Asian character, they usually didn't get to be the protagonist or save the day, and they definitely didn't get to have a love interest. Often they were sidekicks, or worse, stereotypes: unattractive and robotic nerds, nefarious Chinatown gangsters, exotic geishas, and mystical elders who spoke like Yoda. Invisibility felt preferable to racial caricature—the cringe of bad "Asian" accents, squinty eyes, and buck teeth, "me love you long time."

In the rare books I read that centered the experiences of non-white characters (usually by writers of color), protagonists often seemed defined by their oppression. They were impoverished laborers, marginalized immigrants, victims of racism. Later, I appreciated the importance of these stories of struggle and resistance. But at the time, the characters in these books felt fundamentally other: foreign and often historical, endlessly self-sacrificing in the face of tragic circumstances.

I couldn't look around my town and imagine being friends with these characters, and I didn't see myself reflected in them. Their stories didn't make me feel empowered—if anything, they made me feel like more of an outsider. I longed for more exciting and glamorous role models, but above all else, I wanted to read about characters whose lives and concerns echoed my own (I idolized Kristi Yamaguchi and Michelle Kwan, but as someone who dreaded gym class, I could never really relate to their commitment to athletic achievement). Where were the characters of color who worried about math tests, hung out at the mall, and just wanted a date to the Spring Fling dance?

I finally found what I was looking for at the Scholastic Book Fair, that most hallowed of school events. I still remember the colorful cartoon displays, glittering merch, and endless shelves of glossy paperbacks. I had no particular interest in babysitting, but as I reverently browsed through the books, something led me to pick up *The Baby-Sitters Club #2: Claudia and the Phantom Phone Calls*.

The cover illustration left Claudia's ethnicity somewhat ambiguous, but within the first few pages of the book, written in first person, Claudia explains that her last name is Kishi and her family is Japanese American. She also describes her love of mystery books and junk food, her huge crush on Trevor Sandbourne, her passion for art, and her aversion to homework.

In just a few pages, Claudia emerged as a fully fleshed-out character: someone who brought enthusiasm and creativity to everything she pursued, who cared about her family but struggled with their expectations, and who was charting her own idiosyncratic path through life. In the first of many, many iconic Claudia outfit descriptions in the series, she writes:

> Traditional clothes look boring and are boring to put on. So I never wear them. I like bright colors and big patterns and funny touches, such as earrings made from feathers. Maybe this is because I'm an artist. . . . Today, for instance, I'm wearing purple pants that stop just below my knees and

are held up with suspenders, white tights with clocks on them, a purple-plaid shirt with a matching hat, my high-top sneakers, and lobster earrings. Clothes like these are my trademark.

At a time when most kids—certainly me—were just trying to fit in, to not say or wear or do anything that would be made fun of, Claudia's impervious confidence was awe-inspiring. She was unafraid to be her unique and wacky self, and if someone at school laughed at her tie-dyed leggings, purposely mismatched socks, or enormous papier-mâché jewelry, who cared?

Claudia was an instantly iconic character (and no doubt responsible for countless readers' questionable DIY outfits over the decades). Lots of young readers aspired to her self-assurance and her bold style and related to her academic struggles or her insecurity about her overachieving older sister. For many Asian Americans, though, Claudia was a revelation.

Claudia was not only a rare Asian American protagonist, but she also defied stereotypical portrayals of Asian and non-white characters. She was popular, confident, and fashionable. She wasn't a sidekick or a token person of color with a Very Important Message about diversity. And unlike many depictions of Asians as perpetual foreigners stuck in the past, Claudia was unmistakably a modern American teenager. While her Japanese heritage was an important part of her character, she wasn't defined only by her race. She felt like a fully realized human being, and a protagonist of her own story.

Claudia was a role model that I was desperately looking for: a cross between a hip older sister and a high priestess. The fact that she was an aspiring artist further ensured my devotion. I had always loved art and was constantly badgering my parents for more art supplies. I dreamed of becoming a painter who also had a highly successful fashion line (and maybe a crafting side hustle). But in art class and in the museums we visited, most of the art I saw was created by white men: Michelangelo, Jackson Pollock, van Gogh, and the rest of the Western art canon (with an occasional cursory mention of Frida Kahlo and Georgia O'Keeffe).

Reading about Claudia was an important early affirmation that I too could be an artist. Even though she was a fictional character, and only in middle school, her art was never treated as an unimportant or lesser pursuit. Several storylines dealt with her ambitious projects, her development as an artist, and her struggles to balance her artwork with the rest of her life. Like the Kishis, my parents appreciated art but felt it was more important to prioritize pragmatic subjects like math and science. Claudia's commitment to her art helped inspire me to stick to my convictions about pursuing a creative path—first as an art student, and then as a documentary filmmaker.

It was groundbreaking to have a protagonist like Claudia in a series as mainstream and hugely successful as the Baby-Sitters Club. She was one of the only Asian American characters in popular media when the books debuted in 1986, and has retained a cult following beyond Asian American fans. While I outgrew the BSC books by middle school, as an adult I noticed the series—and particularly Claudia—popping up all over the blogosphere and then the growing universe of social media. I was delighted to discover Kim Hutt Mayhew's blog *What Claudia Wore*, obsessively and snarkily documenting every single Claudia outfit across the series. There was also a steady stream of which-character-are-you quizzes, fan art, and BSC nostalgia accounts on platforms from Livejournal to Instagram. Millennials had come of age, and we were paying homage to the media that shaped our childhoods.

Many fans waxed lyrical about Claudia, but I noticed a recurring theme: Asian American women naming Claudia as the first Asian American character they encountered, and the first character they saw themselves reflected in. I realized that there was a whole community of Asian American women who had grown up with Claudia—an entire Claudia generation. And she had been an especially important role model for young creators of color, many of whom were now producing stories of their own: groundbreaking work that centered a diverse array of experiences and voices.

I had been thinking of creating a documentary about Claudia for a while, but it finally clicked when I realized that these inspiring creators, as modern-day Claudia Kishis, were the perfect voices to speak to her lasting influence. I started reaching out to writers and artists who had spoken about Claudia's impact on them, or who had created new work around the character. I had an amazing time interviewing them about their favorite Claudia moments, the ups and downs of representation in the BSC, and their own creative projects. And I dubbed these creators—and the nascent film—*The Claudia Kishi Club*.

All of the interviewees brought different personal perspectives to Claudia while also sharing some similar experiences. For many, the sheer novelty of Claudia's existence still stood out as a thrilling discovery. Gale Galligan, creator of several recent BSC graphic novels, remembered reading her first Claudia book: "I had to stop and flip back to the description and go, 'Wait

wait wait, she's not white!'" Encountering an Asian lead character—especially one as stereotype-smashing and flamboyant as Claudia—was an unfamiliar and exciting experience.

Author Sarah Kuhn pointed out that Claudia's popularity, both in the books and within the fandom, was also unprecedented. Claudia was arguably the most aspirational member of the BSC (sit down, Stacey fans), even for non-Asians. Sarah pointed out, "For an Asian American or any woman of color character to be the cool one is so unusual." More often, Asian American fans have to content themselves with a less central, less desirable character as their representative (frequently the nerdy sidekick or responsible best friend).

Gale recalled that the few Asian American narratives she encountered growing up didn't reflect her Thai heritage, or her experience as someone of mixed race. Most Asian American media that experienced any mainstream success—from *Mulan* to the *Joy Luck Club*—focused on East Asian stories, and either historical or first-generation immigrant characters. Gale noted, "Seeing someone like Claudia who was kind of forging her own path definitely helped me feel more connected to my own identity. Just knowing that there's not one way to be an Asian person. Like I can just be me and that's fine."

Claudia also served as an important creative role model for many of her fans. Artist Yumi Sakugawa commented, "Reading about her at such a formative age just gave me this very tangible anchor of a Japanese American woman who was making art, even if she was fictional. I didn't even know that option existed." In addition to navigating this dearth of Asian American women artists in mainstream media, several interviewees found themselves at odds with parents who were less than supportive of their creative goals. Sarah's mother "always wanted [her] to have a job that had health insurance" (same). And despite author C. B. Lee's award-winning books, her parents "still see writing as a hobby"—calling to mind Claudia's own struggles to get her parents to take her art seriously.

The Kishi family resonated with many of the creators I interviewed. They recognized their own families in the Kishis' multigenerational household (a family model rarely represented in popular media), in which Claudia's grandmother Mimi played an important role. Naia Cucukov, executive producer for the Netflix BSC series, related to Claudia's close relationship with her grandmother—like Mimi, Naia's grandmother lived with her family. "Mimi was kind of just the OG cool grandma. She was empathetic and caring, and she understood what all of the girls were going through."

Meanwhile, Claudia's genius older sister Janine was a total nerd stereotype—obsessed with homework and computers, no social skills—but their often fraught sister dynamic rang true. C.B. connected powerfully with Claudia's feelings of inadequacy: "Janine is the kind of daughter that I felt like my mom would have wanted, and I was definitely not. And I would constantly have this specter of the perfect daughter kind of hanging over me." (At the same time, many of the interviewees confessed that, with their straight As in school, they had some Janine qualities too—and I was even a spelling bee competitor. Claudia would never!)

Of course, while Claudia was both relatable and groundbreaking, she wasn't perfect. Our cultural discourse around race and representation has progressed since the book series ended, and looking back, it's clear the books sometimes reproduced problematic racial tropes. Claudia was often described as "exotic-looking," with "almond-shaped eyes"—a descriptor that confused me every time. Almonds were roughly eye-shaped, so didn't everyone have almond-shaped eyes? Besides failing to convey any real information about the character's appearance, the phrase stuck out because I never saw food comparisons used to describe white characters' features.

The books also glossed over the realities of life as a person of color in America, largely confining issues of racism and discrimination to two books that serve as "very special episodes" within the series—one for Claudia and one for Jessi, the sole Black member of the club. In both books, the girls encounter overtly racist new arrivals to town (a babysitting client and a neighbor, respectively), whose bigotry is presented as a total outlier in the community. Together with the rest of the club, the girls "solve" the problem and it recedes from view for the rest of the series.

Phil Yu, creator of the *Angry Asian Man* website, contended that the BSC's treatment (or rather, avoidance) of racial issues was highly unrealistic—that discrimination, ignorance, and microaggressions would be much more frequent occurrences in a place like WASPy Stoneybrook, Connecticut. Based on my own experience growing up in a predominantly white town, I have to agree. For the *Claudia Kishi Club* documentary, Phil read selections from *Keep Out, Claudia!*, in which a new client will only hire white babysitters. Claudia is shaken, saying, "I'd never thought of myself as different until I met Mrs. Lowell."

Exasperated, Phil declared, "Congratulations, Claudia! You just learned a few things about good old-fashioned racism." The book is written as if Claudia is discovering the concept of racism for the very first time—but as Phil pointed out, no person of color growing up in a white town could be so blissfully oblivious. Imagining more realistic storylines, Phil created a series of parody BSC covers with updated titles like *Claudia and the Model Minority Myth* and *Claudia Kishi, Only Asian at This Damn School*.

While discussions of race were lacking in the series, the artists and writers featured in my film generally appreciated Ann M. Martin's efforts toward diversity. The series still stands out as ahead of its time in many ways, from storylines around disability and single parenthood to acing the Bechdel test. I like to think that its lasting popularity is partly attributable to this ethos of inclusivity. Representation has a very real impact on our lives—the images and narratives we see in popular media teach us which voices are valued in society, and help define what we think is possible for ourselves.

Since the books were first published, the landscape for more inclusive storytelling has improved considerably. While dramatic disparities in media production and representation persist, more and more creators of color are telling their own stories, as well as achieving mainstream success. When I think about Asian American characters, I can no longer list them on one hand—and the creators I interviewed for *The Claudia Kishi Club* are all doing their part to add to this growing universe.

C.B. and Sarah are taking on the historically white, male world of genre fiction: C.B.'s Sidekick Squad YA series follows the adventures of queer POC superheroes, and Sarah's Heroine Complex series and *Shadow of the Batgirl* graphic novel center badass Asian American women characters. Yumi manifests a fantastical, intersectional, and radical vision of Asian American identity in her recent project *Fashion Forecasts*. Phil has spent nearly two decades promoting Asian American stories and creators, while also—as per his *Angry Asian Man* moniker—calling out racism and whitewashing in popular culture. And Gale and Naia, with their work on the new BSC graphic novels and Netflix show, are creating more inclusive iterations of the BSC adapted for modern times and a new generation of fans. As for myself, I'm grateful for the opportunity to experience and uplift this profusion of Asian American stories and voices.

Making a film can be incredibly lonely—I spent weeks at a time cloistered in my apartment, sluggishly writing grants and frantically filming stop-motion sequences. But one of the most rewarding aspects of making a film is in the collaborative creativity and the people you share the experience with. I had inspiring conversations with creators who embody Claudia's artistry and boldness. I met a new generation of Claudias in the Linda Lindas, a tween girl rock band who wrote and performed the end credits song for the film. And I loved hearing from countless fans who reached out to share their own Claudia stories. After all, the Claudia Kishi Club extends far past the group in the film. It encompasses not only all Claudia fans, but also everyone who has ever craved seeing themselves represented, who has felt empowered by a meaningful character, and who has declared themselves worthy of having, and telling, their own story.

From Girl Friends to Monster Sitters: How the BSC Spawned a Whole Moral Universe

Gabrielle Moss

Like many unpopular children, I spent most of my childhood dreaming about the future. And like many children who spend a lot of time dreaming about the future, almost all of my future predictions turned out to be wrong. Despite my fervent second grade hopes, I don't have a robot butler, we're still waiting for our flying cars, and for whatever reason, I never ended up getting married to Jason Priestley (I'm going to chalk that one up to scheduling issues). However, I did get one prediction right: the Baby-Sitters Club actually did stay popular forever.

Honestly, at the time, the odds seemed better for the Jason Priestley thing. Trends come and go in general, but in children's book publishing, they come and go especially hard. One day, every single YA book is about a postapocalyptic future where only *one* chosen girl has the power to save everything! The next day, every book is a charming, realistic romance novel, and that chosen girl is dragging her crossbow straight to the discount bin. It's the way of YA,

a literary culture that has, since its inception in the 1940s, been strongly gov-
erned by trends—from the wholesome froth of what YA scholars refer to as the
"malt shop" books of the 1950s and '60s, to the social issues–focused "problem
novels" of the '70s, all the way to the apocalypto-fic of the 2010s and beyond.

But decades after its debut, the Baby-Sitters Club has done more than
simply stay popular—though it *has* stayed incredibly popular, racking up
over $180 million in sales on more than two hundred print volumes, two TV
shows, one movie, and a line of vaguely American Girl–esque dolls.

But for a whole generation of readers, the Baby-Sitters Club is something
more than nostalgia. It's a series that expanded our understanding of life and
ourselves. I mean, I don't have to explain that to you—you're the one who
decided to spend time reading this book, instead of cleaning your gutters,
learning French, or checking on what your kid is eating under the couch (it's
just a cracker that fell there! It's fine! It's FINE! Keep reading).

The BSC earned this lasting legacy, in part, by making inclusive values
and progressive beliefs part of the series' core—values like honoring diverse
voices and experiences, promoting empathy, and suggesting that girls make
great leaders. These values were far from standard in young adult lit in 1986,
when *Kristy's Great Idea* first popped up on the scene. But today, they form the
backbone of modern YA.*

Of course, this change can hardly be credited to Ann M. Martin alone—
countless YA writers, including many writers of color and writers with marginalized identities who never had a crack at the kind of mainstream mega-success
the Baby-Sitters Club enjoyed, created today's diverse and inclusive YA culture
together.

But the fact that the BSC was the first major YA series to stress the importance of diverse identities, the first to examine classism, racism, and chronic
health issues (as well as the first to say that running your own business and
emotionally supporting your friends were activities at *least* as important as trying to get some random dude named Bruce's attention) has become a key part
of a legacy now analyzed by publications as fancy as the *New Yorke*r ("The Fem-

---

* Technically, the Baby-Sitters Club is categorized as middle grade fiction, for slightly younger readers
  than YA. But among actual readers, these delineations are rarely observed, with young readers moving
  freely between middle grade and YA fare. The Sweet Valley High and BSC books shared readers, and
  BSC's influence can be felt in children's books for all age groups, from grade schoolers to teens. So, for
  the purposes of this essay, I am considering BSC part of YA culture. If you don't like it, go sit on a Kid
  Kit.

inist Legacy of the Baby-Sitter's Club," 2016) and the *Atlantic* ("The Legacy of 'The Baby-Sitters Club,'" 2012).

But I think in order to truly understand the BSC's legacy and how it made such an impact, we have to examine the knockoffs. You remember the Baby-Sitters Club knockoffs, right? Series like Susan Saunders's Sleepover Friends (1987–1991), Nicole Grey's Girl Friends (1993–94), and even Susan Smith's Samantha Slade (1987–88) that popped up in the wake of the BSC, cashing in with readers who had a sudden and insatiable hunger for books about girls . . . doing stuff. Most of these books were written hastily, with no greater goal than selling copies to a few confused parents or kids who had exhausted their supply of actual BSC books. But they turned one series' messages into a trend, making them omnipresent within tween literature. These churned-out BSC knockoffs gave the original series' ideas about female friendship and inclusivity heft and widespread critical mass in the culture. And when something becomes a trend—goes from being singular to mass—it makes an impact. It's like the difference between just the Beatles, and the entire British Invasion. The sheer mass of imitators helps reinforce the original's message, giving it greater reach. If every single book you pick up in the Waldenbooks kids section presents at least some of the values of the Baby-Sitters Club, those values spread more widely. They don't just become the vision of a single series; they become the standard.

What I'm saying is: if you have appreciation for the impact the BSC made in our culture, a teeny, tiny part of you should also be thanking *Samantha Slade: Monster Sitter*.

Okay, okay, fine, I'm asking you to take a lot on faith here. But let's think about the YA world that the BSC first crash-landed in. YA has existed as a formal category since 1944, when New York Public Library children's librarian Margaret Scoggin first used the term in her *Library Journal* column to delineate the difference between books for children and books for tweens and teens. Most historians would peg the genre's beginnings to 1942, when Maureen Daly's *Seventeenth Summer*, the book widely regarded as the "first" YA title, was published. In the decades since, the genre was subject to a few major waves of trends—in the '50s and early '60s, "malt shop" books, like Anne Emery's *Dinny Gordon* novels, chronicled the pre-feminist adventures of middle-class suburban girls who just kind of hung around, thinking about dances and various tartan skirts they wanted to buy; in the '70s, "problem novels" that dealt frankly with social issues including sex, drugs, and discrimination, like S. E. Hinton's *The Outsiders* and Judy Blume's *Forever*, were everywhere.

By the '80s, that trend had passed, replaced by a move away from social awareness. If the '70s belonged to Judy Blume and her ilk, the early '80s belonged to a series of light romance novels called Wildfire. While the YA books of the past had courted parents or teachers, attempting to assure them of its literary value or moral instruction, YA books in the '80s started being marketed directly to young readers, through cheap paperbacks available all over the mall. These books made no promise of literary or moral value—they just promised fun you could afford on your allowance.

The books of the early '80s YA romance boom weren't always regressive, though they sometimes were. But they were rarely preoccupied with questions about the larger world, and what roles women might play in it. They were far from inclusive, on any level—heroines were white, thin, straight, and, more often than not, wealthy (or, at the very least, wealthy enough to be hanging around the mall instead of getting an after-school job). And while these protagonists may have been class president or played on the tennis team, they had one real interest: dating. Blame Reagan, blame executives who wanted to cash in on the romance novels that always sold well in teen book clubs, blame teens who just wanted to lose themselves in something fluffy—but by the early '80s, social issues books had been swept aside, replaced within YA bookshelves by various romance series that focused on white female protagonists chasing the ultimate goal: the love of boys who generally possessed all the charisma of a well-ironed pair of Dockers.

And at the peak of this mountain stood Francine Pascal's Sweet Valley High, which, for a time, was the world's most popular YA series. Launched in 1983, the soap operatic tales of Jessica and Elizabeth Wakefield, two wealthy, white teenagers who engaged in constant borderline-sociopathic hijinks, became the first YA to hit the *New York Times* bestseller list, in 1985. The Wakefield twins obsessed over their bodies (which, the series constantly reminded us, were each a "perfect size 6"), seemed to have no real healthy relationships with other women, and though they ostensibly had interests and career goals, had a terminal inability to think past prom. But, most of all, the Wakefields thought about dating. Of course, plenty of smart, thoughtful YA books examine the perils and pleasures of romance (not least of all the BSC, in *Boy-Crazy Stacey*, etc.). But for the Wakefields, dating was somehow both all-consuming and totally trivial. The series' first book, *Double Love*, introduces the sisters by showing them fighting over local hunk Todd Wilkins. A trip to the UK (SVH #132: *Once Upon a Time*) is mostly an opportunity to find new

British boyfriends. In *Brokenhearted* (#58), a volume about Elizabeth trying to juggle paramours Jeff and Todd, Jessica gets sidetracked by the prospect of even more potential dates: "Jessica walked away from Aaron and Ken, flashing them both a big smile. They were both very attractive—she had dated each of them a number of times. In fact, not too long ago she had contemplated falling in love with Ken for lack of anything better to do."

Though Sweet Valley obviously rose out of the preexisting romance trend, they shaped the YA moment that followed in their image. Over-the-top drama became the order of the day in YA, with knock-off series like Rosemary Joyce's Dream Girls (1986), about beauty queen rivals, and Kristi Andrews's All That Glitters (1987), about teens on an actual soap opera, taking the baton.

✳ ✳ ✳

Though it may feel like the Baby-Sitters Club appeared out of nowhere to teach a generation all about friendship and novelty earrings, the series was actually birthed out of a preexisting YA trend, too—though one that wasn't totally in the spotlight at that exact moment. Former Scholastic editor Jean Feiwel dreamt up the BSC after realizing that books about babysitting—like Francine Pascal's *My First Love and Other Disasters* in 1979 and Martha Tolles's *Katie's Baby-Sitting Job* in 1985—always sold fairly well. She commissioned Ann M. Martin to write a miniseries of four books about four friends who were babysitters, one volume focused on each sitter.

The first book in the series, *Kristy's Great Idea*, was published in August 1986 with a print run of thirty thousand copies. However, as the months went on, it became clear that the Baby-Sitters Club was on track to vastly surpass all of the books it had been intended to imitate. By the time the sixth book, *Kristy's Big Day*, was released in July 1987, Scholastic had boosted each new volume's initial print run to 100,000 copies each.

Mainstream media coverage at the time seemed fairly flummoxed as to why exactly the Baby-Sitters Club was so successful. N. R. Kleinfield's 1989 *New York Times* article, "Inside the Baby-Sitters Club," doesn't point out that the books might have resonated because they made leadership look fun, told female readers it was great to have interests and a unique personality, or reflected a wide variety of tween experiences—from Jessi's life as a Black ballerina in a majority-white town, to Stacey's struggles with diabetes—that to that point had been largely shut out of YA. It doesn't posit that Martin's simultaneous focus on friendship and babysitting suggested that you could both feel supported and take tentative steps toward independence at the same time—an idea that thrilled tween readers.

And Kleinfield certainly doesn't suggest that readers might have been drawn to the books because Martin set out to craft strong, independent characters—as Martin told the *New Yorker* in 2016, "I didn't want to present one-dimensional girls who only cared about boys and makeup and what to wear to the next dance." Instead, the article credits the books' success solely to the popularity of "books about groups of girls" and being "uncommonly well written for a paperback children's series."

But the knockoff series understood. Crafting a good knockoff is all about understanding exactly what it is about the original that draws its audience—almost distilling it to its essence. For Sweet Valley High knockoffs, that meant zeroing in on high drama. And for Baby-Sitters Club knockoffs, that meant focusing on supportive female friendships.

Okay, the *New York Times* article was right about one thing—most of the knockoffs were not "uncommonly well written." Sleepover Friends, which debuted in 1987, often read a bit dry as it unspooled stories of a group of girls who met each week for sleepover parties ("The Sleepover Friends had decided early in the week what to wear to the party. We'd all agreed on pants with the cuffs rolled up, two shirts, and colored sneaks. Kate walked in the front door wearing a long printed sweater, pink leggings, and gray high tops. 'Whoa!' said Stephanie.")

The same could be said of any of the knockoffs—like Samantha Slade, a series that only lasted for four volumes after debuting in 1987, combining the babysitting trend with tween horror fiction by depicting the life of a girl who provided childcare for a family of *Munsters*-type monsters.

L. E. Blair's Girl Talk, which debuted in 1990, was the third incarnation of a preexisting media property—the brand had released a board game aimed at tween girls in 1988 (the one with the "zit stickers," remember?) and a short-lived TV show hosted by a wee baby Sarah Michelle Gellar in 1989. But in the books, a group of junior high school friends worked together to do things like plan school dances and play sports, while pulling directly from BSC archetypes ("Randy Zak has just moved to Acorn Falls from New York City, and is she ever cool!"), with little finesse.

Cherie Bennett's Sunset Island, possibly the longest-running of the BSC knockoffs, debuted in 1991 and ran through 1997, following the adventures of a bunch of girls working as nannies (which is TOTALLY different than babysitting, okay?) for the summer in the resort town of Sunset Island, where they learn lessons about the importance of being themselves, and also slightly less important lessons about winning the local Battle of the Bands. Nicole Grey's 1993 series Girl Friends, the only BSC knockoff to take the series' inclusivity seriously, followed a group of racially and financially diverse high school friends who meet at a rally against gun violence and go on to have adventures both serious (absentee parents, boyfriends with substance abuse issues) and frivolous (writing an advice column in the school paper, planning school dances). Kris Lowe's short-lived 1998 series Girls R.U.L.E. depicted a BSC-esque group of friends who wanted to be junior park rangers but ran into sexist barriers at every turn.

As someone who has reread each of these books in adulthood, I would recommend that you do not reread these books in adulthood; you can really see the seams (and the fact that the author probably had about a week and a half to crank them out). But even when these books are sloppy and rushed, you can see that the dynamics had changed from those early '80s YA novels. The emphasis isn't on rushing around, trying to catch some dude's eye; it's about trying to protect and nurture your relationships with other women, or feel independent by making your own money, or change the world because you feel like you really have a place in it. It's about passing the Bechdel Test every damn day. The values that the BSC had projected were suddenly trendy.

Without these knockoff books, the BSC could have remained a more singular voice, screaming for agency in a sea of books about fighting over prom dates. But with BSC values expanding out of the series and becoming the definitive values of a large chunk of YA literature, a sea change occurred. Once a generation of readers saw that YA books were starting to become interested in representing real girls' experiences, there was no going back. Yes, a lot of these books were hastily written cash grabs, created with nothing approaching the level of thought and care Martin put into crafting the Stoneybrook Seven. And yet, it is impossible to ignore that as the '90s marched on, it became harder and harder to find a YA heroine only preoccupied with her love life. BSC made being a bold, thoughtful, responsible girl normal; but if it hadn't become a trend, spreading to other corners, allowing us to hear similar messages in different voices and from different perspectives, the impact of the babysitters might not be as strong as it is today. So Samantha Slade and the rest: we salute you! We just might not want to reread you any time soon.

No Ship Too Small: A Deep-Dive into Baby-Sitters Club Fan Fiction

Logan Hughes

The difference between being a fan and fandom is other people. You can be a fan by yourself. Fandom requires community.

I've been a fan since my childhood days of consuming Baby-Sitters Club books by the fistful, but I didn't enter fandom until my mid-twenties. I'd moved far away from my college friends to strike out on a new life in a new country, and I was lonely. Fan fiction was a reliable source of online friendship and supportive writing buddies. My favorite subgenre was gay romance, known as slash fiction because of the relationship-based tagging convention: "Kirk/Spock." It was a subculture that celebrated the strangest parts of me: my nerdiness, my queerness, my baby-trans interest in seeing the world from a male point of view—what *Toast* writer Danny M. Lavery calls the "slashfic-to-gay-trans pipeline."

It didn't occur to me to combine my love of slash fic with my love of the Baby-Sitters Club, although I was the kind of adult fan who owned stacks of the books and reread them at the most stressful times of my life. To me, slash was something you did to reclaim toxically masculine sci-fi and procedural shows and transmute them into kinder, gentler, queer romance stories. The beautiful violent man on TV becomes the beautiful vulnerable man who questions his feelings and expresses his love for another beautiful man, perhaps this one a scientist. The Baby-Sitters Club didn't seem to call out for that kind of treatment. Then I signed up for Yuletide.

Yuletide is a massive rare-fandom fanfic exchange that takes place every year around Christmastime. Fanfic writers describe the story they wish existed and the fandoms they're willing to write, and story requests are matched to offers via an increasingly high-tech web form. I began participating in 2009, the same year the festival moved from the blogging platform Livejournal to the fan-run website Archive of Our Own (AO3). I had never read any other BSC fan fiction and had no idea what would be requested. Were BSC readers kids and teens, or adults who'd read the books when they came out, like me? Would my recipient want a kid-friendly babysitting storyline, a gossipy teen story about who likes who, or maybe femslash (lesbian romance), where two of the sitters got together?

My 2010 recipient was an AO3 user known as mizzmarvel who typically wrote m/m slash about comic books. I never in a million years would have predicted her request: m/m slash about a future relationship between teenage Byron Pike (one of Mallory's younger brothers) and Jeff Schafer (sole younger brother to Dawn). It's hard to overstate how delighted this request made me. It had not occurred to me that I could write my favorite genre for the Baby-Sitters Club, a series with almost no men. I never would have come up with the idea, but when I began to imagine their futures, I could see the possibilities. Byron is sensitive and misunderstood; Jeff is a cool surfer dude with emotional problems. Ideas were already forming in my mind.

As soon as I sat down to write, my story poured onto the page effortlessly. The Pike triplets are now fifteen and run the BSC. Byron and Jeff's slow-burn summer romance unfolds against a backdrop of BSC business drama. By the end of the month, I'd finished an epic, fifteen-chapter, BSC-book-length story that remains one of the fan works I am most proud of.

✻ ✻ ✻

Ten years later, my recipient, mizzmarvel, and I are still friends. (As is conventional in fandom, I'll refer to fanfic writers by their usernames.) Unlike me, she was active in BSC Livejournal communities in their heyday in the early 2000s.

When I recently asked her what it was like, she waxed nostalgic. "Suddenly there were communities for niche BSC interests—one all for femslash! Ones where you just follow someone's BSC Sims storylines! Interactive RPGs!" she wrote to me over email. "We could bond over what seemed like universal fan experiences, like wondering how you pronounce 'Myriah,' misreading 'Byron' as 'Bryon,' and having a dream where you stumble on a new BSC book you've never heard of before."

Fans fled Livejournal in the late 2000s when its new parent company began purging accounts it deemed unacceptable, including erotica and even nonsexual LGBT content. Creators responded by banding together and building Archive of Our Own as a safe haven for fan fiction, especially slash. Many BSC stories and writers have since found their way there. Here's a glimpse into the vibrant world of BSC fic on AO3.

THE PASSAGE OF TIME, NOSTALGIA, AND REUNION ARE COMMON THEMES.

If I had to sum up the general mood of BSC fic in one word, I'd say "wistful." Almost all the stories age the characters, usually to late high school or early adulthood. Reunion stories are common. Surrounded by old friends, older versions of the protagonists remember old joys and sorrows, take second chances, and resolve unfinished business. In this way, the stories serve as a metaphor for writers' experiences as we dip back into favorite books from childhood.

Nostalgia is often an explicit theme. In "Something Old, Something New" by an AO3 user called emilyfrost (Yuletide 2013), the now-adult ex-sitters throw Mary Anne a surprise wedding shower in Claudia Kishi's bedroom:

"Sh!" Claudia hissed. "I heard the door downstairs—Dad's going to bring her up in a moment."

We all sat still at that—and I swear that Mallory was holding her breath. Then the door swung open and Mary Anne stood there, staring in wonder. "You guys . . ."

"You're just in time, Mary Anne," Kristy said ominously from her chair. Habitually, we all looked at the radio clock which stood on Claud's old night stand, just ticking over to 5:30 PM. Kristy cleared her throat. "I hereby call this meeting of the Baby-Sitter's Club to order!" she declared, and Mary Anne burst into tears.

Modernizing the characters can be a creative translation project: what would Claudia wear now? Does Dawn love avocado toast, or is she keto? And what would a babysitting service look like now? In "(Not) Like Uber But For Baby-Sitting" (Yuletide 2015), user cbomb envisions a *Vox* article in which early-twenties sitters describe their juggernaut app:

> I meet the founders of the monumentally successful app, BSC, at the home of Kristy Thomas' family in Stoneybrook, Connecticut. This is no Silicon Valley coworking space. There's no exposed brick, no polished concrete, no succulents and no astroturf.

Fans are writing the epilogues that we want to see. We're also purposely creating satisfying emotional experiences for each other. Gifting is huge, whether for Yuletide or just because. When you write for someone else, you want to make sure they get a gift they will treasure.

EVERYONE IS (ARGUABLY) QUEER.

Epilogues and reunions aren't the only reason to age the characters; it's also done to facilitate romance. Romance and erotica are highly popular fanfic genres in all fandoms. Few BSC fics are sexually explicit, but many center romantic relationships (known as "ships" in the fanfic community).

About one-fifth of the BSC fic on AO3 is f/f slash (lesbian romance). This proportion is quite a bit higher than the typical fandom; less than 10 percent of the stories on AO3 as a whole are tagged f/f. (Conversely, m/m slash is much less common in BSC than on the archive as a whole; less than 10 percent of BSC stories are m/m, compared to almost half of AO3.) What's remarkable isn't just the amount of f/f slash, but its extreme variety. In most fandoms, there are one or two favorite ships: Harry Potter and Draco Malfoy; Crowley and Aziraphale; Captain America and the Winter Soldier. The BSC fandom has come to no such consensus.

Pairs of best friends are obvious choices, and there are plenty of stories about Kristy getting together with Mary Anne, or Claudia with Stacey. But

there are also stories that pair more tenuously connected sitters, like Kristy/
Dawn, Mallory/Mary Anne, or just about any other combination you can
imagine. User Amberina's "Shit Just Moves On, I Guess" (2017), a Stacey/
Dawn story, comments on the club's many permutations:

> "Claudia and I were not just friends in high school."
>
> Dawn didn't giggle. She didn't even look particularly surprised. She
> just listened.
>
> "And when I decided to go to Caltech, we broke up." Stacey swallowed
> hard. "Claudia wasn't very happy with my decision." There, it was out.
>
> Dawn seemed to be thinking hard. After a while, "Mary-Anne and I
> weren't just stepsisters."
>
> That did surprise Stacey, but she tried hard to remain calm and mature
> about the matter. "I didn't know that."
>
> . . .
>
> They poked at their salads, a silence settling over them until Stacey broke
> it, musing, "God, the BSC is gay."

Non-sitters are also fair game. "The Kristy Thomas Guide to High School
Romance" by kbs_was_here (2005) is an enemies-to-lovers story featuring
club nemesis Cokie Mason.

> I knew I was being mean, but I didn't care. Who did she think she was,
> anyway? Just because a girl's popular and gets manicures and looks good
> in just about anything and always smells really, really good doesn't mean
> she knows jack about getting things done.

Future fic also opens up the possibility of pairing sitters with their charges.
In marginalia's "And I let her steer" (2004), Stacey runs into a college-age
Charlotte Johanssen.

> In the end, after Stacey had slyly picked up the check and they had both
> ensured they each had the other's email address and sworn to use them,
> Charlotte held Stacey tight and whispered low, "I think that's half the
> reason I came to school in New York, to look for you."
>
> Stacey's head spun, dizzy on the afternoon and the words and scent of
> Charlotte's hair. Charlotte was tall now, and it made all the difference in

the world when she pulled back from the embrace and leaned down to kiss Stacey . . .

"Because," as she said after, "I knew you wouldn't dare."

BSC writers delight in the creative challenge of making plausible cases for a variety of different relationships, a game played in community with other writers. Writers will choose a pairing to write based on a prompt from a fan-run challenge or exchange, a theme week on a group blog, or an informal conversation with other fans. It's common to write another writer's favorite pairing as a gift. Compared to other fandoms I have known, BSC writers seem less driven to write by their own passion for a textual character or relationship, and more by the writers' relationships to one another.

QUEER REPRESENTATION IS WIDESPREAD EVEN OUTSIDE OF SLASH FIC.

Writers just want the sitters to be queer. Issues such as queer identity and coming out are not solely the domain of slash fic. They're also frequent topics of gen ("general" stories with no particular pairing). For example, user bookplayer's California Diaries–inspired "Coward. Closet. Pride." (2011) explores Kristy's self-identification as gay through journal entries:

> So then I stared at the paper a little while longer, and then I had to pick up my pen and just form the letters, like a little kid practicing how to write.
>
> Seeing it written makes it better. I can write it again.
> I'm gay.
> I wrote that like normal. I guess I'd better get used to it. I'm Kristy, I'm fifteen years old. I like softball. I'm gay.

Other LGBTQ identities are also explored. "Accordingly Adorned" by Piscaria (Yuletide 2010) envisions Claudia as a trans boy:

> The night before he meets Stacey McGill for lunch at the Hard Rock Cafe, he stays up until midnight assembling just the right outfit. It had to be perfect. Nothing, he thought, had ever driven him further in his quest for sartorial perfection than Stacey. They used to delight in being equally fabulous, albeit in different ways.

In "At the Shallow End" (QueerFest 2014), kandrona imagines a bisexual Janine Kishi to respond to the prompt, "Any fandom, any character, a bisexual character explains mathematically why being bi doesn't double one's chances of a date."

> "Even if I do accept that I can 'pick from both guys and girls,' ignoring the possibility of a partner whose gender is neither male nor female—and certainly the number is low enough that I can treat said possibility as insignificant statistically if not in practice—it still does not follow mathematically that my pool of potential partners is double that of a heterosexual. Let us assume that I can select from any eligible heterosexual or bisexual male, or homosexual or bisexual female. From there—"
> "Oh god." Claudia buried her face in her hands.

What do we make of the high proportion of queer identity and coming out stories? It may be that slash writers are so accustomed to incorporating lesbian and gay identity issues that it carries over into gen. And, while I don't know much about the real-life identities of most other BSC writers, I suspect that many, like me, are queer themselves. I know I'm not the only queer adult for whom "tomboy" Kristy Thomas was the closest thing to representation in the rather conservative landscape of 1990s children's publishing. Even though there are no canonically LGBT characters, the Baby-Sitters Club has somehow always felt like a queer text to me, even before I really understood what that meant. Learning in 2016 that Ann M. Martin was queer, too, felt revelatory. As Heather Hogan wrote in *Autostraddle*:

> I feel shocked that Ann M. Martin is gay. In a wonderful way! My bisexual sister and I spent half our lives devouring these books in our tiny little town in rural Georgia, and even though neither of us had language or an outlet for our feelings at that age, we were being babysat by the ultimate babysitter and now it's apparent that she was also our queer guardian angel! She protected our imaginations!

As a queer writer for whom writing slash was part of a long-term process of coming to terms with my trans identity, the positive representations of queer folks in slash fandom generally and in BSC specifically have definitely helped me to feel welcome and valued. Lesbian stories recognized and normalized the types of relationships I was really having at the BSC members' age, while stories about gay teen boys provided an outlet to explore the male coming-of-age that I felt simultaneously drawn to and shut out from. I can now see ways in which my own and others' fics can be idealized or unrealistic, but I continue to be moved by fans' genuine effort to vividly empathize and relate to people with different identities. As a person who has inhabited a number of different gender and sexual orientation labels over the years, I can attest to the importance of this space for personal exploration.

TERTIARY CHARACTERS ARE LIVING FULL LIVES OFF-SCREEN.

Among BSC stories on AO3, straight romance is about as common as f/f slash. While some stories feature canon pairings, like Mary Anne/Logan and Stacey/Sam, others cast a wider net. Claudia's nerdy sister Janine and Kristy's jock brother Charlie are paired in some forty stories, making them the second most popular pairing in the fandom, despite appearing in no scenes together in canon. In a 2010 comment on the babysittersclub livejournal, kakeochi_umai explains that this pairing started as a community joke:

> The Janine/Charlie pairing has been a running gag in [livejournal community] bsc_snark . . . I think it started when we were talking about how Charlie always drives Kristy to Claudia's place and then drives her back half an hour later. It seemed like a waste of gas for him to make two trips in such quick succession, so we wondered if he'd found something to occupy his time during the meeting.

Baseballchica03 dramatizes this idea in "The Charlie Thomas Hypothesis" (2008):

> "Um," Charlie cleared his throat. "I was wondering if you wanted to come with me."
> "Are you suggesting a date?"
> "Well, yes, I guess. We've been sneaking around during their babysitter meetings for weeks. I thought it might be nice to actually go out and do something together."
> Janine averted her eyes from his gaze. "I don't usually follow athletics."

"Come on," he prodded. "Baseball is all physics and geometry. I know you'll love it."

Charlie/Janine stories often involve similar themes: the jock/nerd odd couple, the *Breakfast Club*–like realization that people are more than their reputations, anxiety about college and the future. Although some of these ideas are drawn from the text, it's clear that these works intentionally reference and engage with each other. The culture of fanfic is highly collaborative, and writers build upon each other's work: essentially, writing fanfic for fanfic.

This brings us to the most popular pairing in the fandom.

BYRON PIKE AND JEFF SCHAFER ARE STAR-CROSSED LOVERS.

I didn't know it when I first received mizzmarvel's Yuletide request, but Byron/Jeff was then, and remains now, the number-one most popular pairing in the BSC fandom on AO3. (Granted, they still make up less than 10 percent of the BSC stories in the archive, since the fandom encompasses such a wide variety of pairings.) Like Charlie and Janine, Byron and Jeff are not a pairing that arose naturally from the text, but one that was willed into existence—in this case, by mizzmarvel.

Specifically looking for m/m slash in the BSC fandom, she was frustrated to find only one Logan/Bart story. "With so few strong male characters of a similar age, it was difficult to even come with a plausible slash pairing, let alone one that would flow naturally and be of any interest to anyone," she explained in a 2005 post on the Livejournal community ship_manifesto. Her solution was to set the stories five or more years in the future, when the sitting charges are the new teens.

Both characters experience struggles that could easily translate to future characterizations as young queer men with relatable anxieties. Gentle Byron struggles with feelings of alienation from his identical triplet brothers. Jeff gets into schoolyard fights until he is allowed to move back to live with his father in California. In the first ever Byron/Jeff fic, "Blue" (2003), mizzmarvel reinterprets his anger as internalized homophobia: *Travel back in time a few months and tell me I'd be doing this. Go ahead. I dare you. I'd laugh. No, scratch that. I'd punch you right in the face, then laugh. I mean, the idea's just too ridiculous. I'm a guy. I like girls. Duh.*

Byron and Jeff's relationship comes with built-in conflicts. Pressure to fit in with the triplets heightens Byron's fear of coming out to his family. In "Pen Pals" by Piscaria (Yuletide 2010), Byron purposely comes out to Jeff first because distance lowers the stakes.

> Silence on the other end. Then Jeff asks, "Do you really think your brothers would freak out?"
>
> "I know they would," Byron says miserably. "You should hear them. They're always going on about how gay everything is."
>
> "But you guys were, like, the Three Musketeers!" Jeff protests.
>
> "That was a long time ago," Byron says. "We're not kids anymore, Jeff."

Distance is the major conflict that all Byron/Jeff fics must handle some way or another, as both characters have strong ties on opposite coasts. Jeff's connection to California is almost mystical, as in Lauren's "Sunlight in Your Skin" (Yuletide 2009):

> "Have you ever really thought Stoneybrook was home?" [Byron] pushed the letters to one side and propped his head on his arm, looking at me.
>
> I reached out and ran one finger down his side. My tan was faded enough that I was nearly as pale as him. "Sometimes."
>
> He caught my hand and studied it, tracing the lines on my palm and then turning it over to kiss the back. "Your skin's so warm. It's like you trap the sunlight and keep it inside you."

Mizzmarvel may have "discovered" the Byron/Jeff relationship, but dozens of other writers have taken on the mantle. At first they seem like a surprising pairing, but their storylines, both in canon and fic, have many of the traits that appeal to m/m writers: the conflict between sensitivity and toxic masculinity, angst, star-crossed love. The ideas raised by this pairing also speak to the themes of BSC fic generally: reunion, nostalgia, and reuniting with childhood friends to find them changed, yet comfortably familiar.

THE FUTURE IS BRIGHT.

It's the new generation that makes mizzmarvel hopeful about the future of the fandom. "I'm excited to see how things evolve with the Netflix series—I think we're going to be seeing kids enter the online fannish space in a big way for the first time," she wrote me. "I hope it's a happy place for them." By shifting attention from the main sitter characters to their charges, writers can also symbolically pass the torch from one generation to the next. Kristy and the others learn to see their former charges as leaders, and we can imagine an ever-evolving BSC landscape extending beyond the horizon.

Acknowledgments

Thank you first and foremost to Ann M. Martin for creating the Baby-Sitters Club series, which has inspired so much joy, thought, and celebration for us and so many others. Heartfelt thanks, admiration, and shoebox Mallomars to all of our contributors for their BSC wisdom and insights; we are so honored to share this club with you all. So much gratitude to Kara Rota and the amazing team at Chicago Review Press for giving this book a home, and to our agent, Rach Crawford, for her incredible care and encouragement, and for believing in this project from the start.

Marisa thanks Becca Klaver, Caolan Madden, Seth Landman, and Matt L. Roar for their support and feedback on various stages of this project, and her mom, Holly Jardine, for taking her to the library every week and keeping her BSC collection well-stocked.

Megan thanks Max Zev, Jillian McManemin, and Jeanne Thornton for feedback and support; the various book clubs who have provided some form of BSC-style friendship over the years; Mary and Tom Milks for supporting their kid's constant, occasionally rude reading habits; and whoever it was who posted to Queer Exchange looking to offload three bags of vintage BSC books just as this project was getting off the ground.

Notes

I Want to Be a Claudia but I Know I'm a Stacey ★ *Marisa Crawford*
An earlier version of this essay was first published on *Weird Sister*.

Scripts of Girlhood ★ *Kelly Blewett*
Author's Note: Thanks to Abby King Kaiser, who used to beautifully illustrate the notes she passed to friends in middle school, for creating the samples of Spencerian and Palmer handwriting styles used in this essay.
footnote page 63: Margot R. Becker, *Ann M. Martin: The Story of the Author of the Baby-sitters Club.* New York: Scholastic, 1993.
"I wanted the handwriting included": Facebook message to author, December 20, 2015.
"The editors gave us a description": Kelly Blewett, "An Interview with Hollie Tommasino," *Los Angeles Review of Books*, August 18, 2018.
The handwriting narrowed: Sara K. Day, *Girls Reading* (U of Mississippi Press, 2013).
"As a little girl": Blewett, "Interview with Hollie Tommasino."
One 1855 article: Tamara Plakins Thornton, *Handwriting in America: A Cultural History* (New Haven, CT: Yale UP, 1996).
Tommasino recalled using rapidograph pens: Blewett, "Interview with Hollie Tommasino."
"I wrote my 'a's and 'e's": HL [Anonymous Poster], "Re: In Which We Copy Down their Handwriting by Elena Schilder," ed. Will Hubbard, *This Recording* (SquareSpace, August 8, 2012), Accessed April 29, 2015.

"Mary Anne is my best friend": Ann Martin, *Kristy's Great Idea,* BSC #1 (New York: Scholastic, 1986).

"Even though Kristy": Ann M. Martin, *Claudia and the Phantom Phone Calls,* BSC #2 (New York: Scholastic, 1986).

critic Joseph Noshpitz: Joseph Noshpitz, "Nancy Drew and the Baby-Sitters Club," *The Journey of Child Development: Selected Papers of Joseph Noshpitz,* ed. Bruce Sklarew and Myra Sklarew (UK: Routlege, 2011), 145–65.

she perceived Mary Anne's writing: Elena Schilder, "In Which We Copy Down Their Handwriting by Elena Schilder," *This Recording,* ed. Will Hubbard (SquareSpace, August 8, 2012), Accessed April 29, 2015.

"before the Civil War": Kitty Burns Florey, *Script and Scribble: The Rise and Fall of Handwriting* (Hoboken, NJ: Melville House Publishing, 2009), 69.

"conformity and ordinariness": Thornton, *Handwriting in America.*

"As president of the Baby-sitters Club": Ann Martin, *The Truth About Stacey,* BSC #3 (New York: Scholastic, 1986).

"What [Palmer] described": Thornton, *Handwriting in America,* 67.

"real, live, usable": Thornton, *Handwriting in America,* 67–68.

"hardly changed over a hundred years": Joe Coffey, "Cedar Rapids Man Created Palmer Method of Handwriting Taught to Millions," *Gazette,* August 20, 2019; Web, October 12, 2020.

"the tight, controlled, cheerful cursive of a young athlete": Schilder, "In Which We Copy Down."

"Stacey is glamorous": Martin, *Claudia and the Phantom Phone Calls,* 5–6.

something "fanciful": Facebook message to author, December 20, 2015.

"Notebooks were a big thing": Blewett, "Interview with Hollie Tommasino."

In a post on her personal blog: Katie, "babysitter's club week!" *Read What You Know* (Wordpress, November 11, 2009), Accessed April 30, 2015.

"children gradually develop resources": Janice Radway, "Girls Reading, and Narrative Gleaning: Crafting Repertoires for Self-Fashioning Within Everyday Life," *Narrative Impact: Social and Cognitive Foundations* (LEA Press, 2002), 176–208.

"@TheFormerJuneBronson": SwirlGirl [Anonymous Poster]. "Re: Scholastic's Great Idea: Updating *The Baby-Sitter's Club* by Margaret Hartmann." *Jezebel.* G/O Media Inc. Web. December 31, 2009.

"I've experimented endlessly": Florey, *Script and Scribble.*

Let's Talk About Jessi ★ *Yodassa Williams*

Text quotes in this chapter are from Ann M. Martin, *Hello, Mallory*, BSC #14 (New York: Scholastic, 1988).

"Skin the Color of Cocoa" ★ *Jamie Broadnax*

a very distinct type of black girl: Tiffany Onyejiaka, "Hollywood's Colorism Problem Can't Be Ignored Any Longer," *Teen Vogue*, August 22, 2017.

Of course if you could see me: Ann M. Martin, *Jessi's Secret Language*, BSC #16 (New York: Scholastic, 1988).

Jessi is African-American: Ann M. Martin, *Stacey and the Fashion Victim*, BSCM #29 (New York: Scholastic, 1997).

I . . . am not scary: Martin, *Jessi's Secret Language*.

We need to at least try to adapt: "Malia Baker Says 'The Baby-Sitters Club' Will Be Great for the Next Generation," Black Girl Nerds, July 1, 2020, https://blackgirlnerds.com/malia-baker-says-the-baby-sitters-club-will-be -great-for-the-next-generation.

"I've Been Thinking About Families Lately" ★ *Kristen Felicetti*

Text quotes in this chapter are from Ann M. Martin, *Claudia and the Great Search* #33 (New York: Scholastic, 1990) and Ann M. Martin, *Kristy and the Mother's Day Surprise* #24 (New York: Scholastic, 1989).

Kristy and the Secret of Ableism ★ *Haley Moss*

Text quotes in this chapter are from Ann M. Martin, *Kristy and the Secret of Susan* #32 (New York: Scholastic, 1990).

Could the Baby-Sitters Club Have Been More Gay? ★ *Frankie Thomas*

An earlier version of this essay was first published in *The Paris Review*.

Even Martin herself revealed: Jen Doll, "Writing About Autism and Remembering 'The Baby-Sitters Club': A Q&A with Ann M. Martin," Elle, October 7, 2014, https://www.elle.com/culture/books/interviews /a15526/ann-m-martin-baby-sitters-club-interview/.

Jessi on the Margins ★ *Chanté Griffin*

white is the norm or default: Brynn F. Welch, "The Pervasive Whiteness of Children's Literature: Collective Harms and Consumer Obligations,"

Social Theory and Practice 42, no. 2, (Special Issue: Dominating Speech, April 2016), 367–388.

Analyzing the 3,200 books their library received: Cooperative Children's Book Center, "Children's Books by and about People of Color Published in the United States," Annual Statistics, http://ccbc.education.wisc.edu/books /pcstats.asp (accessed June 4, 2015).

"Because of the long shadow": Welch, "The Pervasive Whiteness."

From Girl Friends to Monster Sitters ★ *Gabrielle Moss*

YA has existed as a formal category: Anne Rouyer, "How did YA Become YA?," New York Public Library Blog, April 20, 2015, https://www.nypl.org /blog/2015/04/20/how-did-ya-become-ya.

She commissioned Ann M. Martin: Sally Lodge, "The Baby-sitters Club to Reconvene," *Publishers Weekly*, January 7, 2010, https://www .publishersweekly.com/pw/by-topic/childrens/childrens-book-news /article/41524-the-baby-sitters-club-to-reconvene.html.

By the time the sixth book: Lodge, "The Baby-sitters Club to Reconvene."

"I didn't want to present one-dimensional girls": Brooke Hauser, "The Feminist Legacy of the Baby-Sitters Club," *New Yorker*, December 9, 2016, https://www.newyorker.com/books/page-turner/the-feminist-legacy -of-the-baby-sitters-club.

"books about groups of girls": N. R. Kleinfeld, "Inside the Baby-Sitters Club," *New York Times*, April 30, 1989, https://www.nytimes.com/1989/04/30 /books/paperbacks-children-s-books-inside-the-baby-sitters-club.html.

No Ship Too Small ★ *Logan Hughes*

"'Sh!' Claudia hissed": emilyfrost, "Something Old, Something New," Archive of Our Own, 2013, https://archiveofourown.org/works/1089674.

"I meet the founders": cbomb, "(Not) Like Uber But for Baby-Sitting," Archive of Our Own, 2015, https://archiveofourown.org /works/5413388.

"Claudia and I were not just friends": Amberina, "Shit Just Moves On, I Guess," Archive of Our Own, 2017, https://archiveofourown.org /works/9801554.

"I knew I was being mean": kbs_was_here, "The Kristy Thomas Guide to High School Romance," Archive of Our Own, 2005, https://archiveofourown .org/works/1515131.

"In the end, after Stacey": marginalia, "And I let her steer," Archive of Our Own, 2004, https://archiveofourown.org/works/10346175.

"So then I stared at the paper": bookplayer, "Coward. Closet. Pride.," Archive of Our Own, 2011, https://archiveofourown.org/works/306166.

"The night before he meets Stacey": Piscaria, "Accordingly Adorned," Archive of Our Own, 2010, https://archiveofourown.org/works/143650.

"Even if I do accept that I can": kandrona, "At the Shallow End," Archive of Our Own, 2014, https://archiveofourown.org/works/1436869.

"I feel shocked": Heather Hogan, "Baby-Sitters Club Creator Ann M. Martin is Queer, How Did I Not Know This," *Autostraddle*, September 6, 2016, https://www.autostraddle.com/baby-sitters-club-creator-ann-m-martin -is-queer-how-did-i-not-know-this-350912.

"The Janine/Charlie pairing has been": kakeochi_umai, Comment on LiveJournal, 2010, https://babysittersclub.livejournal.com/1018049 .html.

"'Um,' Charlie cleared his throat": baseballchicao03, "The Charlie Thomas Hypothesis," Archive of Our Own, 2008, https://archiveofourown.org /works/603159.

"With so few strong male characters": mizzmarvel, ship_manifesto LiveJournal comment, 2005, https://ship-manifesto.dreamwidth.org/157754.html.

"Travel back in time": mizzmarvel, "Blue," Archive of Our Own, 2003, https://archiveofourown.org/works/2372675/chapters/5240120.

"Silence on the other end": Piscaria, "Pen Pals," Archive of Our Own, 2010, https://archiveofourown.org/works/142929.

"Have you ever really thought": Lauren, "Sunlight in Your Skin," Archive of Our Own, 2009, https://archiveofourown.org/works/37321.

CONTRIBUTORS

Kristen Arnett is the *New York Times* bestselling author of the debut novel *Mostly Dead Things* (Tin House, 2019), which was listed as one of the *NYT* top books of 2019 and was a finalist for the Lambda Literary Award in fiction. Her next two books (*With Teeth: A Novel* and an untitled collection of short stories) will be published by Riverhead Books.

Kelly Blewett is an assistant professor of English at Indiana University East, where she directs the undergraduate writing program and teaches writing and pedagogy courses. Her scholarship explores writing pedagogy, reading, editorial practices, and feedback. She's still an avid reader who journals about what she's reading.

Jamie Broadnax is the CEO and founder of the online publication Black Girl Nerds. Broadnax graduated with a master's degree in film from Regent University and a bachelor of science in broadcast journalism at Norfolk State. She's covered some of the greatest entertainers, from cultural tastemaker Ta-Nehisi Coates to billionaire media mogul Oprah Winfrey. Outside of BGN, Broadnax has written for *Variety*, the *Hollywood Reporter*, the *New York Post*, *Huffington Post*, *Vox*, *Vulture*, *IGN*, *Essence Magazine*, the *Lily* (*Washington Post*), and *SYFY*.

The Data-Sitters Club (Quinn Dombrowski, Anouk Lang, Katherine Bowers, Maria Sachiko Cecire, Roopika Risam, and Lee Skallerup Bessette) is a group of six academics who grew up reading the Baby-Sitters Club and now apply their subject-area and technical expertise to answering grown-up questions about the series.

Sue Ding is a documentary filmmaker based in Los Angeles. She directs and produces nonfiction films—including the short documentary *The Claudia Kishi Club*—for platforms including the *New York Times*, Netflix, and PBS. She also creates and curates interactive, immersive, and multiplatform projects. Her work explores the intersection of identity, storytelling, and visual culture.

Jennifer Epperson is a proud Texan who splits her time between Houston and New York. She has written personal essays and reporting pieces for *Texas Monthly*, *Dame*, *Elle.com*, *Outline*, *Man Repeller*, and *Lenny Letter*. She also writes sketch comedy for I Feel Funny and Magnet Theater in New York.

Kristen Felicetti was born in Korea and raised in Rochester, New York. She is the founding editor in chief of the *Bushwick Review*. She currently lives in Brooklyn, where she is working on a YA novel.

Siobhán Gallagher is a Canadian illustrator living in Ridgewood, New York. Her work involves observational humor, personal confessions, and feminist storytelling. She is a frequent contributor to the *New Yorker* and author of *In a Daze Work: A Pick-Your-Path Journey Through the Daily Grind*. Her work has been featured in the *New York Times*, *Huffington Post*, and *Us Weekly*.

Chanté Griffin is a Los Angeles–based writer whose work centers racial justice. Her articles, essays, and interviews have been published by *The Root*, the *Washington Post*, *Ebony*, and others. In her free time, she enjoys raking up late fees at her local library and pretending she's really active on The Twitter: @yougochante.

Myriam Gurba is a writer and artist. She is the author of the true-crime memoir *Mean*, a *New York Times* editors' choice. Her essays and criticism have appeared in the *Paris Review*, *TIME.com*, and *4Columns*. She has shown art in galleries, museums, and community centers. She lives in Long Beach, California, with herself.

Logan Hughes is a software developer, birdwatcher, and fanfic enthusiast. He is the author of *Sixth Grade Detective*, a middle grades interactive novel from Choice of Games. He lives in Boston with his partner and a growing collection of succulents.

Caolan Madden's writing on gender, popular culture, and poetics can be found in various journals and anthologies, including *Triple Canopy*, *Victorian Literature and Culture*, *Victorian Studies*, *Weird Sister*, and the forthcoming *Electric Gurlesque*. She is the author of the poetry chapbook *VAST NECRO-HOL* (Hyacinth Girl Press, 2018).

Kim Hutt Mayhew is the creator of *What Claudia Wore*, a blog dedicated to the Baby-Sitters Club's iconic outfit descriptions. *What Claudia Wore* enjoyed an enthusiastic audience of millennials and was covered by publications such as *Jezebel* and *Nylon*. Her current nostalgia project, *Cover Critiques*, revisits the book covers of classic eighties and nineties series. You can find her online at kiminimalism.com.

Gabrielle Moss is the author of *Paperback Crush: The Totally Radical History of '80s and '90s Teen Fiction* and has written for the *New Yorker*, *Buzzfeed*, GQ.com, *Slate*, and other places. She is finally mature enough to admit that she is, and always has been, a Mallory. Keep up with her flights of violent whimsy at www.gabriellemoss.net and twitter.com/gaby_moss.

Haley Moss is an attorney, author, artist, and activist who went viral as Florida's first documented openly autistic attorney. She is especially passionate about neurodiversity, the law, and inclusion of people with disabilities in society and the workplace. You can find Haley at haleymoss.net or @haleymossart on social media.

Jami Sailor is a librarian living and working in the Arizona desert. They have been making zines, small-circulation self-published magazines, for almost as long as they've been diabetic. Jami's favorite beverage is lemonade, which yes, sometimes makes their blood sugar high.

Yumi Sakugawa is a second-generation Japanese Okinawan American interdisciplinary artist and the author of several books including *I Think I Am in*

Friend-Love with You, Your Illustrated Guide to Becoming One with the Universe, and *The Little Book of Life Hacks.* She currently lives in Los Angeles.

Jack Shepherd is the better half of the Baby-Sitters Club Club, a podcast in which two hopeless goofballs grapple unsuccessfully with the intimidating immensity of Ann M. Martin's oeuvre. Currently, he lives in Austin, Texas, with his cat, Sarah, his other cat, and a human child.

Buzz Slutzky is a nonbinary/trans/queer and Jewish interdisciplinary artist, filmmaker, educator and performer based in Brooklyn, New York. Their visual art practice works at the intersections of history, politics, humor, self-identity, and queerness. They teach at SUNY Purchase and the Leslie Lohman Museum of Art.

Frankie Thomas is the "YA of Yore" columnist for the *Paris Review*. They are the author of the novella *The Showrunner*, and they once appeared on *PBS NewsHour* to geek out about Latin. They hold an MFA in fiction from the Iowa Writers' Workshop and live in New York City.

Jeanne Thornton is the author of *The Dream of Doctor Bantam* and *The Black Emerald*, as well as the forthcoming *Summer Fun*. She is the editor, with Tara Madison Avery, of *We're Still Here: An All-Trans Comics Anthology*, and she lives in Brooklyn. More information and work is available at http://fictioncircus .com/Jeanne.

Yodassa Williams is a Jamaican American storyteller. An alumna of the VONA/Voices Writing program and host of the podcast *The Black Girl Magic Files*, Yodassa launched Writers Emerging, a wilderness retreat for BIPOC writers, in 2019. Her debut YA Fantasy, *The Goddess Twins*, is a "Black Girl Magic" adventure published to wide praise in May 2020. Find her online at yodawill.com.

EDITORS

Marisa Crawford's writing on pop culture, art and feminism has appeared in *Harper's BAZAAR*, *The Nation*, *Hyperallergic*, *VICE*, and elsewhere. She is the author of two collections of poetry, *Reversible* and *The Haunted House*, both from Switchback Books. Marisa is the founder of *Weird Sister*, a website and organization that explores the intersections of feminism, literature, and pop culture. Once on the school bus in fourth grade, someone told Marisa that she dressed like Claudia Kishi, and it may have been her life's proudest moment.

Megan Milks is the author of *Margaret and the Mystery of the Missing Body* and *Slug and Other Stories*, forthcoming from Feminist Press. They are a Lammy finalist and the recipient of the 2019 Lotos Foundation Prize in Fiction. Megan's stories have been published in three anthologies and many journals including *Fence*, *LIT*, *PANK*, and *Western Humanities Review*; and they are the editor of *The &NOW Awards 3: The Best Innovative Writing, 2011–2013*; and coeditor of *Asexualities: Feminist and Queer Perspectives*. Megan's BSC identifications combine a queer kinship with bossy tomboy Kristy Thomas and a readerly affinity with shy, bookish Mary Anne Spier.